REGNUM EDINBURGH CENTENARY SERIES

Life-Widening Mission

Global Perspectives from the Anglican Communion

REGNUM EDINBURGH CENTENARY SERIES

The Centenary of the World Missionary Conference of 1910, held in Edinburgh, was a suggestive moment for many people seeking direction for Christian mission in the twenty-first century. Several different constituencies within world Christianity held significant events around 2010. From 2005, an international group worked collaboratively to develop an intercontinental and multi-denominational project, known as Edinburgh 2010, and based at New College, University of Edinburgh. This initiative brought together representatives of twenty different global Christian bodies, representing all major Christian denominations and confessions, and many different strands of mission and church life, to mark the Centenary.

Essential to the work of the Edinburgh 1910 Conference, and of abiding value, were the findings of the eight think-tanks or 'commissions'. These inspired the idea of a new round of collaborative reflection on Christian mission – but now focused on nine themes identified as being key to mission in the twenty-first century. The study process was polycentric, open-ended, and as inclusive as possible of the different genders, regions of the world, and theological and confessional perspectives in today's church. It was overseen by the Study Process Monitoring Group: Miss Maria Aranzazu Aguado (Spain, The Vatican), Dr Daryl Balia (South Africa, Edinburgh 2010), Mrs Rosemary Dowsett (UK, World Evangelical Alliance), Dr Knud Jørgensen (Norway, Areopagos), Rev. John Kafwanka (Zambia, Anglican Communion), Rev. Dr Jooseop Keum (Korea, World Council of Churches), Dr Wonsuk Ma (Korea, Oxford Centre for Mission Studies), Rev. Dr Kenneth R. Ross (UK, Church of Scotland), Dr Petros Vassiliadis (Greece, Aristotle University of Thessalonikki), and coordinated by Dr Kirsteen Kim (UK, Edinburgh 2010).

These publications reflect the ethos of Edinburgh 2010 and will make a significant contribution to ongoing studies in mission. It should be clear that material published in this series will inevitably reflect a diverse range of views and positions. These will not necessarily represent those of the series' editors or of the Edinburgh 2010 General Council, but in publishing them the leadership of Edinburgh 2010 hopes to encourage conversation between Christians and collaboration in mission. All the series' volumes are commended for study and reflection in both church and academy.

Series Editors

REGNUM EDINBURGH CENTENARY SERIES

Life-Widening Mission

Global Perspectives from the Anglican Communion

Edited by Cathy Ross

First published 2012 by Regnum Books International

Regnum is an imprint of the Oxford Centre for Mission Studies
St. Philip and St. James Church
Woodstock Road
Oxford OX2 6HR, UK
www.ocms.ac.uk/regnum

09 08 07 06 05 04 03 7 6 5 4 3 2 1

British Library Cataloguing in Publication Data
A catalogue record for this book is available from the British Library

ISBN: 978-1-506476-62-9

Cover photo by kind permission of Oddmund Køhn
Typeset by Words by Design

The publication of this title is made possible through the generous financial assistance of The Commission on Theological Education of Evangelisches Missionswerk in Deutschland (EMW, Dr. Verena Grüter), Hamburg, Germany

Distributed by 1517 Media in the US and Canada

CONTENTS

Foreword
The Archbishop of Canterbury vii

Preface
Cathy Ross x

INTRODUCTION

The Story of this Book
Janice Price 3

THE FIVE MARKS OF MISSION

The First Mark of Mission: To Proclaim the Good News of the Kingdom of God
Kwok Keung Chan 13

The Second Mark of Mission: To Teach, Baptise and Nurture New Believers
Andrew Thompson 31

The Third Mark of Mission: To Respond to Human Need by Loving Service
Vicentia Kgabe 47

The Fourth Mark of Mission: To Seek to Transform Unjust Structures of Society
Irene Ayallo 57

The Fifth Mark of Mission: To Strive to Safeguard the Integrity of Creation and Sustain and Renew the Life of the Earth
Kapya John Kaoma 75

OTHER THEMES

Gender: Representation and Presence at Edinburgh 2010
Caitlin Beck 95

A Visual Gospel: Imagery as Mission
Luiz Coelho 113

CONCLUSION

Receiving a New Day of Mission
Mark McDonald 137

Appendix:
The Five Marks of Mission and the Anglican Communion
John Kafwanka 143

Bibliography 153

List of Contributors 161

FOREWORD
The Archbishop of Canterbury, The Most Revd Dr Rowan Williams

It is clear from the essays collected here that the experience of the 2010 World Mission Conference in Edinburgh was both affirming and frustrating for those taking part – affirming because of its recognition of how the centre of gravity has moved in global Christianity; frustrating because of the relative slowness of so many global Christian bodies to catch up with this and to embody it in the way they do business and in the way they represent themselves. This remarkably gifted and creative Anglican delegation at least had some claim to embody the ethnic, gender and age balance of the Communion. But what they write here gives us no cause for complacency, and these reflections will – or should – provide plenty of food for thought in the various councils of the Communion in the coming years.

Rather than attempt a response to each of the papers here – though they all deserve detailed and grateful study – I shall try to pick out a few general themes that seem to be surfacing. The first of these is both simple and very wide-ranging. We have unprecedented opportunities and channels for communicating with each other in the twenty-first century, but we have not yet worked out how to *meet* each other honestly and effectively. So many of our global bodies (Anglican and other) are set in ways that represent a post-war North Atlantic style – driven by carefully calibrated procedures, resolutions, working groups, 'platform' positions. They are about negotiation, about the painstaking work that has to be done in order to find a common language and a common policy.

I don't believe this is a waste of time. But it increasingly feels sterile; and it hands effective power to those who know how to use the procedures. When – as in the 2008 Lambeth Conference and some subsequent meetings – we try to find other ways of doing things, we often hear the accusation of avoiding decisions on the real issues and of falling between two or more stools, producing talking shops that don't do enough either to foster honest relationships or to resource better discussion. This may not be fair (I would say that, of course!), but it is a real set of perceptions. We have not yet found how to meet at this level. And there are plenty of people (not only Europeans or Americans) who do not specially want to see new ways of meeting develop because that would open the door to new questions about power. The challenge that is expressed in some of what follows is to show what *friendship* might mean in the Body of Christ; the way we have normally done things doesn't shape itself easily to such terms, yet the category of friendship, in the Bible and in the spiritual tradition, from the Quakers to St Teresa of Avila, is so potent and distinctively gospel related that we can hardly write it off.

And this focuses the issue of the language we use when we meet, including the language of worship. The questions of gender sensitivity are among the obvious ones here, and they are well treated in this book; but they are only the most acute of a number of questions about how we each genuinely seek to give room to voices that are not ours. Much has been said about the danger of importing liturgical forms from the Middle Ages or Reformation Europe into other cultures. But that danger is not much lessened by replacing those either with synthetic 'globalized' modern music and devotional rhetoric (American fundamentalism reproduced in African or Asian dress) or with ready-made emancipationist language representing what we in the North or West like to think of as 'progressive' faith.

A point made poignantly here is that the simple binary split between liberals and conservatives is hugely unhelpful in understanding the various shapes of global Christian faith and practice today. Christians under 25 do not on the whole begin with this kind of map – certainly not in the 'developing' world. A language and an ethos of worship that genuinely goes beyond all of these anxieties and half-solutions in what is really the field of cultural politics needs hard work and much honesty and real imagination. It is why the new communities like Taize and Iona have contributed so much that has the flavour of authenticity, even given the difficulties even their practice can generate. It is why there is no substitute for really fostering the composition of new material in the actual local languages of our world, despite the problems of translation.

Which reminds us of the paradox that Christianity is both the carrier of a truly universal vision and the enemy of 'globalization' as a strategy that smoothes over differences. These essays all in their different ways make a real and vital contribution to what we think about the nature of the *Church*. All that we might want to say about the 'Marks of Mission' has to be focused on what we mean by 'Church'. And here above all we need a renewed and radical biblical theology of the Christian community. The biblical church is not an association of human individuals with common interests; it is not a carefully controlled organization with a complex layered hierarchy; it is not a global corporation; it is not a hidden network of affinity between sensitive souls. It is a sign of the future. It is the active presence of Christ coming through in our acts and relationships. It is where God longs to see the human race moving, in loving friendship with Jesus, a friendship so deep that we can speak of sharing his life and his prayer. In any and every setting, it offers an alternative way of inhabiting the world (and this includes, though we have so often forgotten this, inhabiting a world of material things and processes that demand our respect not our exploitation). It offers a pattern of life lived always in the expectation that the neighbour and the stranger alike will have a gift from God for you. And so it is a community that seeks to treasure the differences between cultures and people, so that this gift may be as rich as it can be; a community that learns to live in the world without the saltwater passion of greed; a community that is defined above all by its gratitude for being invited into love (by its *eucharistia*, in word and act and sacrament). And it is absolutely right and essential to say, as is said more than once in these pages, that there is no alternative to holistic mission once you have seen the point about what the Church is. What is going on in the Church is the renewing of the face of the earth and of the bonds between human beings, in every imaginable respect.

And yes, we all know how little it looks like that. But our authors here challenge us all to imagine a biblical Church that, because it has all these things in the forefront of its mind and the depths of its heart, is patiently and steadily seeking to find ways of meeting, talking, even disagreeing, that look more like what God longs for, more like the profile of Christ's Body that we have sketched. Can the Anglican Communion imagine this? Well, yes, apparently, on the basis of what some of its most articulate and original young minds are thinking. All the writers here are deeply aware that what they are fundamentally talking about is the work of *God*. They are not discussing programmes that we may or may not want to take up, but exploring the nature of the great current of divine transforming love in which we are swept up and which sustains us when we fail and stumble. Because these challenging pieces stir us (stir me) to think about – quite simply – what a Christ-centred Church looks and feels like, I welcome them with profound joy and appreciation; and I hope many others will do so too.

The Most Revd Dr Rowan Williams
Archbishop of Canterbury

PREFACE

It was a privilege to be asked to edit this volume and to work with the contributors to compile it. It has been a long and committed journey to arrive at this destination. Each of the young Anglicans who write on the Five Marks of Mission were at the Edinburgh 2010 conference in June of that year. They subsequently returned home and wrote their articles. These were then reworked at a workshop in Toronto a year later. Everyone came prepared with their articles written, every article was subject to robust discussion and challenging questions by the group and everyone willingly committed to rewrite parts of the work. This can be a difficult thing to do. I think it is an indicator of their level of discipleship that each person not only graciously received the feedback but also acted upon it. So what you read here is the fruit of much labour, writing, rewriting and reworking. These articles are also open and honest reflections from a range of young Anglicans in a variety of contexts. Here we see a glimpse of the strengths and struggles of the Anglican Communion. There is no space for complacency. Jonathan Sacks, Chief Rabbi of Britain and the Commonwealth posed this pertinent question in his superb book, *The Dignity of Difference,* when he wrote, "Can we live together? Can we make space for one another? Can we overcome long histories of estrangement and bitterness? … Can we find, in the human 'thou', a fragment of the Divine 'Thou'?"[1] We still have a long way to go as we try to learn what it means to live together.

The title of the book created much discussion. I still remember the excitement we all felt when KK, our first contributor, from Hong Kong, explained to us the meaning of the Chinese character for 'life-widening.' We all thought that this captured the essence of how we long for mission not only to be but also to be experienced; as life –widening. Our God is a God of love, life and spaciousness so we long for the *missio Dei* to be practised and received as life-widening. The richness of this metaphor became the theme for our week together.

For me, the book represents a bitter-sweetness, a poignancy. My mother died, in New Zealand, on the last day of our week together, Ascension Day. The group was very supportive and loving as I grieved the loss of my mother. I was strengthened by the comfort and assurance of knowing that my mother could now finally meet and know our life-widening God in all God's fullness, comfort and glory.

So we hope that this book may disturb, challenge, comfort and enrich your life. We think it will disturb and challenge as you read of the hardship and injustices experienced in many parts of God's world and creation

---

[1] J Sacks, *The Dignity of Difference,* (London:Continuum, 2002), 17.

today. We think it will comfort and enrich as you read stories of change and renewal, and as you meet the writers through their writings.

I am writing this Preface a few days before Christmas, 2011 in the season of Advent. It is a season of waiting, expectancy and preparation not only for Christmas, but also for the Second Coming of Christ. In a sense, this is how we should live all our days – living in hope, aware of the groaning of creation, but anticipating the new day. May this volume afford you some glimpses of what is and of what will be.

Cathy Ross
Advent, 2011

INTRODUCTION

THE STORY OF THIS BOOK

Janice Price

Snapshots of the Process

Gathering for the first time at Edinburgh and getting to know each other across cultures and age differences. Sitting on the floor, talking with the Archbishop of Canterbury and being served a meal by the Bishop of Edinburgh and his wife and recognising servant leadership. Sharing Eucharist in the Wycliffe College Chapel surrounded by windows telling one part of the stories of mission in Canada. Visiting a shoe museum and a baseball game together in Toronto. A moment of recognition and solidarity as we saw each other making our different contributions at Edinburgh 2010.

These snapshots are just a few of many memories that spill into my mind when I think of the Anglican delegation to Edinburgh 2010. Such memories are too many to count but are part of a rich tapestry of being and relating that this book expresses and of which it is the visible but by no means the only fruit.

The context which frames these experiences has three components. The reason for our coming together as an Anglican delegation was the Edinburgh 2010 World Mission Conference 'Witnessing to Christ today'. Our being together was forged and expressed in an ecumenical context. We were representing the Anglican Communion but we were also part of the larger Body of Christ coming together at Edinburgh. Through this we learnt important lessons about identity. For us and for many different reasons we find our spirituality expressed in the Anglican way though for some of us not exclusively. At Edinburgh, however, there was always a tangible, physical bigger picture represented by hundreds of other Christians within which we were living, working and worshipping. Our Anglican identity was not an end in itself; it was part of something bigger – Christ's body on earth. All of the delegation had responsibilities at Edinburgh 2010 beyond being part of the Anglican delegation. Some were involved in worship, others in the nine Study Themes, others in communications.

The second component of our being together was our shared identity as Anglicans. This was not about uniformity. The delegation expressed the rich variety and diversity of the Anglican Communion with delegates from Kenya, Brazil, Canada, Zambia, South Africa, England and Hong Kong. At times, particularly in the writing workshop in Toronto where we gathered for the second time, we grappled with such difference. Differing concepts were understood differently in different contexts. Such differences, however, were a source of strength and never of division. Prior to and following the Edinburgh Conference and again at the Toronto Writing Workshop our shared Anglican identity took expression in our worship. In the delegation were people with highly developed gifts in liturgy and music, art and image and all brought rich experiences to be shared in word and sacrament. Worship became the heart of our life together as we encountered God through the liturgies and languages of our various parts of the Anglican Communion.

The third component of our coming together was the fact that in so many different ways we are committed to and passionate about our participation in God's mission in the world. When we considered how this could be expressed, the Five Marks of Mission became the focus. So, they provide the framework – but not the straitjacket – through which we see our experience of participating in God's mission.

Themes in the Book

This book arises from a particular context of which it has been a privilege to be a part for all of the delegation. The process of compilation began with submitting drafts which were then subjected to rigorous scrutiny at the Toronto Writers' Workshop. All of the papers were then redrafted in the light of the discussions and submitted again to the editor. It is a mark of the maturity of the group that we were able to engage in rigorous scrutiny of our arguments involving considerable vulnerability without any sense of superiority.

What are the common themes that emerge from these contributions? The first thing that strikes this reader is passion. Each of the essays has clarity of vision and an unmistakeable message. Each is passionate about involvement in God's mission. At times disturbing and unsettling, these essays from younger Anglicans challenge the resignation to circumstances and inevitability that can sometimes be a feature of older age. However, none of the contributions is simplistic as each is argued carefully and is clearly the fruit of thorough research and deep learning from experience. This is passionate scholarship combined with profound spirituality. These essays represent an integrated approach combining elements that are personal, academic, Biblical, contextual and Anglican.

This introduction will now give a taster of the various approaches and draw together some common themes. The approach adopted by each writer is distinctive. Some writers have used one of the marks of mission to focus on a particular issue, using the marks as a lens through which to address a pressing issue. Others have interpreted the mark in the light of their experience, ministry and context. A vision for holistic mission emerges clearly from each of the contributions. Shalom as a vision for wholeness of life emerges in different ways in each contribution.

The Five Marks

Kwok Keung Chan, a young priest from Hong Kong, illustrates the first mark of mission concerning the proclamation of the Good News of Jesus Christ with two powerful images from his own context. The first is the approach to mission in the Anglican Church of Hong Kong known as the 'Three Horse Chariot'. The three horses represent the church, schools and social welfare. Kwok Keung Chan emphasizes that it is in all three horses working together that the Good News is proclaimed. The effect of this is that there is wholeness in the Good News holding together church, education and social provision. The importance of wholeness is found throughout these contributions and has much to say to Western Christians where divisions between proclamation and social action have severely hampered the proclamation of the Good News.

The second image concerns the young people's mission trips which Kwok Keung Chan took to Toi Shan for several years. He uses the term 'life-widening' to describe these visits to a different part of China for young people to experience different ways of living. When God sends people into mission to proclaim the Good News of Jesus it is a life-widening experience bringing hope and enrichment. Kwok Keung Chan, like all the writers, emphasizes the importance of young people in God's intention for God's mission in the world as he describes the post-80's generation in Hong Kong as,'prophets in the modern time.'

In a wide-ranging and deeply perceptive contribution Andy Thompson from the Episcopal Church of the USA reflects on the Second Mark of Mission, 'To baptise, teach and nurture new believers.' He sets these callings or vocations of the church in the context of the whole Christian community and its participation in God's mission in the world. Therefore, he argues that the 'church's theology of baptism must go beyond initiation to liberation for God's mission'. This is the mark of mission that 'depends upon and defines' the community of Christ's followers. The Second Mark of Mission he advocates is to call, initiate and form believers in the mission of God in the world following Jesus Christ who was himself formed in a community of faith but fundamentally redefines that community through his baptism and nurture in the new order of the Kingdom of God. Throughout, Thompson redefines or reorientates baptism, teaching and nurture into participation in God's mission in the world. He seeks to work against the natural propensity of human communities to focus inwards and says that in these foundational ministries of the church we find the roots of our participation in God's mission in God's world.

If baptism is liberation into participation in God's mission, then teaching is likewise concerned with building believers who witness to Christ through their lives in the world rather than adherence to a set of creedal statements. It is about living the habits of a moral life as participation in the mission of God and for this reason has to be contextual.

With the ministry of nurture Thompson warns against the tendency to see nurture as only concerned with retreat from the world rather than participation in the world. Calling on Moltmann, Thompson locates the biblical base of the nurture of believers in the friendship of Christ. This echoes an emerging theme in mission theology – that of friendship providing the model for world mission relationships. Friendship extended to the margins of society, as in Jesus' own ministry, provides a radical view of God's mission.

In an important critical emphasis on the second mark of mission, Thompson identifies the use of the term 'new believers'. His helpful emphasis uses Paul's use of the term 'new self' in Colossians 3:10 as meaning the new self in Christ that all believers are growing into rather than an unhelpful dichotomy between older and newer believers.

Vincentia Kgabe looks at The Third Mark of Mission 'Respond to human need by loving service' through the lens of the place of young people in the church. She describes the Edinburgh 2010 conference as a microcosm of the church of today throughout the world in the lack of listening to the voice of young people. Her passionate cry is that young people are the church of today not the church of tomorrow. She links the third mark of mission to young people through giving examples of where young people have been active in fulfilling the mark and the ministry it describes and defines human need in this context as the various and diverse needs of young people. She describes young people as the recipients and agents of mission – just as all Christians are. That is the nub of the issue. Young and old are not different people and all are equally loved and accepted in Christ. However, the way they experience different cultures can be different. Young people cannot be treated as a uniform group as it often the case in church settings. As one of the Edinburgh delegates described, 'young people have multiple identities depending on background and culture and they are as diverse as any population.'

Another of the Anglican delegation raised the issue of the risk of objectifying young people. In other words putting them so much in a category of their own that they become 'other'. Kgabe urges that the church should not fall into this trap and some would argue it has been in this trap for far too long. Her default position is not to treat young people as other but as receivers of God's generous grace and participants or essential agents in God's mission in the world.

Irene Ayallo, a young priest from Kenya, presents a stirring and moving piece on mission as transformation. She applies the fourth mark of mission primarily to her home context of Kenya and also enriches her argument with examples from a wider sphere most notably the Indigenous peoples of Australia. Her arguments, in essence, advocate mission as transformation towards the shalom of God which is justice and wholeness for all people. The justice-making action of God's mission in the world will never cease until all people can experience God's gift and ultimate intention of shalom for all. However, she warns, 'It is the kind of transformation which inherently destabilizes the status quo. It is not inclined to maintain the present order of things. This is holistic mission'.

This raises disturbing and life-changing questions for the materially rich North and West. Are Christians in the North and West prepared to undergo sacrifices for the empowerment of others to live in wholeness? Ayallo speaks and writes passionately about the image of Africa in the world. To re-shape the negative image of Africa is an important aspect of mission relationships as many in the West are resistant or even blind to the presence of the Kingdom of God in African culture and don't believe they have anything to learn from such rich and resilient cultures. One example of this is the way that the separation of mission as evangelism or proclamation and mission as social action pervades many mission discussions and does not lead to life-widening or life-enriching experiences of the power of the Gospel in contemporary Western cultures. Ayallo emphasizes how no such separation or division exists in Kenya as she writes, 'The more I dialogue in mission with these congregations, the more I am always challenged by the way in which they often bring their lives and conditions into the gospel message and allow the gospel message to speak into that.'

Mission as transformation is an active and not a passive reality. Human dignity is an essential ingredient of shalom and as such is discovered when those who have the 'courage to be and the courage to hope' are active agents of their own transformation. Above all this paper stretches the imagination and gives a vision of shalom.

John Kapya Kaoma stresses the urgency of the fifth mark of mission 'to safeguard the integrity of creation. He objects to the optional nature that issues of earth care seem to take on the missiological agenda at Edinburgh 2010 as well as in forums of the Anglican Communion. His essay gives a sense of passionate urgency and he has no hesitation in arguing that safeguarding the future of the earth must be the priority in mission in the 21st century. 'This crisis demands comprehensive attention' he pleads. He bases his thesis on a platform of missiological, theological and economic arguments. The chapter argues that Earth-Care stems from two moral propositions: our God given mandate to care for Sacramental Earth (Gen1:26), and our moral obligations to future generations.

Kaoma argues that Christians should address the environmental crisis because creation is God's. He re-examines the doctrine of dominion and the *missio Dei.* He emphasises the sacramental aspect of creation and the impact of the environmental crisis on the earth community and says that economic justice is essential to safeguarding the integrity of creation. He also provides various creative examples of how Christians can take action that impacts the earth for good. He suggests an ecological Christology as, drawing on his own African respect for the ancestors, he sees Jesus as the 'ecological ancestor of all life' and as the 'knot that holds all life together on planet earth.' He challenges the anthropocentric focus of much mission discourse by arguing that, 'mission is an invitation to participate in God's purpose for the entire created order' and the *missio Dei* should be understood and expressed as the '*Missio Creator Dei'* because of the need to respect and live out the covenant between God, all life and the earth as an act of Christian witness.'

Kaoma also challenges the commonly cited argument that Christian involvement in the environmental crisis is important because it oppresses the poor out of all proportion to its effect on the rich nations. He has direct experience of their interrelationship, however, defending the integrity of the earth forms an essential part of Christian witness because the earth is the Lord's.

He addresses a possible tension between the mark concerning meeting human need and the mark concerning the future of creation by arguing that they are the same thing. To take action to safeguard the earth is to address human needs at their most fundamental level. He too uses the concepts of shalom as 'God's salvation as an advent of the new creation where all creatures will live in perfect shalom' and holistic mission where the interconnectedness of creation is honoured. The scandal that demands economic justice is that, 'As long as 20% of the world population continues to consume more than 80% of the earth's natural goods our dream for a better world is a fallacy.'

Feminism

Another lens that was adopted by Caitlin Beck was that of feminism. In a powerful and passionate paper she critiques the Edinburgh 2010 conference in its treatment of gender and women. Setting her comments against the published target of Edinburgh 2010 for 50% of conference participants to be women she finds the outcomes significantly wanting. In the event only 95 women participated out of a total of 290. She makes the salient point that given the position of women at the time of the Edinburgh 1910 conference then with 200 women participating out of 1200 the 1910 conference was ahead of its time. Her main point is that gender at Edinburgh 2010 was concerned with women. A considerable failing, she argues, is that there is no examination of the effect of male gender on mission. In many places it is acknowledged that women are the main practitioners in mission but there is little or no deeper examination of the place of men in mission and how this affects receptivity of mission in different cultures. Citing one of the African women participants at Edinburgh 2010 she points to one of the key issues in women's place in mission particularly in Africa. Those in the West will often cite the fact that the church is growing in the global south but that this is also where most of the challenges are posed for women such as domestic violence, the effects of HIV/AIDS on families, poverty and human trafficking. Caitlin also directs her comments to the Anglican Communion, 'the Anglican

Communion must still deal with the legacy of the colonial imposition of social norms for gender.' This could be applied to the wider issues surrounding colonialism. While some parts of the Communion have dealt with these issues directly, for the majority sending church, the Church of England, these issues of colonialism have not been faced. They need to be. In relating this critique of Edinburgh 2010 to the Five Marks of Mission she asks particularly of Mark One concerning proclamation 'who does the proclaiming, what do they proclaim and who is able to hear it?' Her conclusion is that issues of mission and gender are largely overlooked but will need deeper consideration if the good news of God's love is to reach many more women and men.

Image and Worship

Luiz Coelho addresses the issue of the use of imagery as an effective tool for mission in a postmodern context. The first part of his thesis concerns the postmodern loss of meaning of the image in global cultures that are bombarded with images. He goes on to rebuild the use of the image full of gracious spirit and meaning in the context of worship. His paper moves through analysis of the problem of loss of meaning of images to the rebuilding and recreation of image-making as part of the worship of the local Christian community. Luiz's contribution to the Edinburgh 2010 Study Theme Mission and Postmodernities came in the form of his own Stations of the Cross of Globalisation. He asks the question as to whether there should be an additional Mark of Mission focusing on, worship full of imagery and symbolism. Others have highlighted the lack of any explicit reference to worship in the Marks of Mission.

A common theme which Coelho joins is the nature of mission as holistic and, in common with all the writers, is passionately committed to the integrated nature of God's mission as embracing social action and evangelism. The making of the image, he suggests, is a powerful way of bringing about such integration. The power of the image in mission moves away from an adherence to creedal statements as the meaning of the image cannot be controlled because each encounter makes meaning differently depending on context, personality and experience. This process is in the hands of a gracious and generous God who is about freedom and not control.

Conclusion

To conclude, the rich tapestry which these contributions present arises from both the unity and diversity of the experience of young Anglicans at Edinburgh 2010 and the quality of the relationships experienced there. Their interpretation of the Five Marks of Mission serves to focus or sharpen the vision of what participation in God's mission means for today and what it might look like in the future. Above all these contributions stress the importance of relationship as experienced at Edinburgh 2010. They point to relationships in mission as the future of God's church on earth today. As Kwok Keung Chan describes this process of working towards God's future: 'relationship + networking = the future of Anglicanism and ecumenism'.

The Five Marks of Mission

THE FIRST MARK OF MISSION: TO PROCLAIM THE GOOD NEWS OF THE KINGDOM OF GOD

Kwok Keung Chan

Introduction

The year 2010 marked the celebration of the centenary of the 'Edinburgh 1910 World Missionary Conference'. I was most grateful to the Anglican Communion office for inviting me as one of the official delegates to attend the conference from 2nd to 6th June, 2010 at, Edinburgh, Scotland. One hundred years ago, only three Chinese Christians were present in the meeting[1]. In 2010, Revd Dr. Ying Gao, Revd Ge Wen, Dr. Yi Sun, Revd Eric So and I were the five official Chinese delegates who were present at this historic occasion. It was indeed my privilege to have a dinner with the Chinese delegation and share our Christian life and witness during the precious time we spent together. One point that impressed me most was that all Chinese delegates, including myself, were very enthusiastic about missionary work in China and that we all shared a common vision of preaching the gospel of God throughout all places.

As a Hong Kong born Chinese Christian, I have a deep sense of obligation to proclaim the gospel in China. So, in this chapter, I will attempt to discuss and reflect on the first mark of mission suggested by the Anglican Communion – to proclaim the Good News of the Kingdom of God.

Learning the First Mark of Mission From the Scriptures

The Great Commission of our Saviour Lord Jesus Christ is definitely one of the most influential biblical verses concerning the proclamation of the gospel:

> Therefore go and make disciples of all nations, baptizing them in the name of the Father and of the Son and of the Holy Spirit, and teaching them to obey everything I have commanded you. And surely I am with you always, to the very end of the age. (Mt. 28:19-20)

---

[1] Revd Cheng Jingyi, Professor Dong Jing'an and Zhang Tingrong were the three official Chinese delegates present in Edinburgh 1910.

According to Benedict T. Viviano, O.P., 'this brief ending is so rich that it would be hard to say more or greater things in the same number of words. It has been called an anticipated parousia, a partial fulfillment of Daniel's vision of the Son of Man. Its genre combines elements of an Old Testament enthronement pattern with an apostolic commissioning.'[2]

The promise of Jesus Christ being with us always to the very end of the age is a great encouragement to Christians. With the second coming of Christ in mind, one is confident that God's salvation is never far away from us. We are assured of the love and care from our Lord Jesus Christ because He promised to be with us always until the very end of age. Because of His never-ending love, how can we resist sharing the good news with others? How can we receive the love only by ourselves? The answer is simple: we must work out the commission of Christ – to proclaim the good news of His Kingdom.

Four actions are involved in the Great Commission: to go, to make disciples of all nations, to baptize them in the name of the Father, Son and the Holy Spirit and to teach them everything Jesus has commanded. From the rich sharing in Edinburgh 2010, I heard different mission workers going to various parts of the world, making the people who did not know Jesus Christians, baptizing and harvesting in the name of the Trinitarian God and teaching them all the truths about the Christian faith. These were all done out of the command given by the Lord. The Edinburgh 2010 Mission Conference not only reminded all participants of the Great Commission of Jesus Christ but also it was a great opportunity for delegates to refresh themselves in terms of their devotion and dedication to proclaim the gospel for the sake of our loving God. And the various stories shared on mission encouraged delegates to continue preaching the gospel for God.

When I began to prepare writing this paper, I used a search engine to find out the meaning of the 'Good News'. I typed in the Chinese translation of the Good News: 好信息 and had the following results found from the Chinese Concordia Bible. One scriptural verse from the Old Testament reminded us of the real good news from God. 'When someone told me, "Saul is dead," and thought he was bringing good news, I seized him and put him to death in Ziklag. That was the reward I gave him for his news!' (2 Sam 4:10) In this verse, the dead person thought that he had brought good news. Yet, he did grasp the bigger picture of the situation and therefore he was killed. So, we need to ask: what is the 'good news' of the Kingdom of God?

From the Old Testament we read: 'Like cold water to a weary soul is good news from a distant land. (Prov 25:25)' The good news of the Kingdom of God should be something that can comfort people, can fulfill the needs of the needy, can bring caring and love, and can let the dry be

[2] Raymond E. Brown, Joseph A. Fitzmyer and Roland E. Murphy (eds), *The New Jerome Biblical Commentary* (Englewood Cliffs: New Jersey, 1990), 674.

moistened. The most typical answer to the question is that we can refer to what Jesus did in His three years of ministry before His passion. 'Jesus went throughout Galilee, teaching in their synagogues, proclaiming the good news of the kingdom, and healing every disease and sickness among the people.' (Mt 4:23) 'Jesus went through all the towns and villages, teaching in their synagogues, proclaiming the good news of the kingdom and healing every disease and sickness.' (Mt 9:35). It is clear that the good news cannot be detached from Jesus Christ. No matter what He was doing, such as healing the sick or casting out demons from people, Jesus Christ was proclaiming the Good News. In 1 Thessalonians we see the believers affirmed for their faith and love, 'But Timothy has just now come to us from you and has brought good news about your faith and love. He has told us that you always have pleasant memories of us and that you long to see us, just as we also long to see you.' (1 Thess 3:6) In this passage, Timothy was not only proclaiming the good news about the salvation of Jesus Christ. So, in a broader sense, the good news of the Kingdom of God may not be narrowly confined to the message about Jesus, but may also include the witness of different brothers and sisters in Christ.

The verb 'proclaim' in the first mark of mission is significant. From the New International Version of the English Bible, there are 167 verses using the term 'proclaim', 114 of which are from the Old Testament and 53 are in the New Testament. Whether it was in the Old Testament or in the New Testament time, proclaiming the good news was imperative. One further reflection is that we should not only proclaim with our mouths; our behaviour and thoughts can also be a very good means to proclaim the good news. And, as an Anglican, the first obligation is to proclaim the good news because this is set as the first priority of our five marks of mission.

The concept of the 'Kingdom of God' is widespread in the New Testament and there are 68 references throughout the Bible. 54 of them are found in the four gospels while the rest are all from the other books of the New Testament. Interestingly, there was not even one mention of this phrase in the Old Testament. Therefore, this concept of the Kingdom of God was initiated at the beginning of the New Testament time. God loved the world so much that He sent His only son Jesus Christ to teach us and show us about His Kingdom. Jesus' rich teachings revealed the Kingdom of God to people who were willing to follow and believe in Him. From the New Testament times until now the Kingdom of God is always somewhere Christians are very eager to arrive at. During my college years, one of my most valuable lessons was that the Kingdom of God was not somewhere I could only arrive at only after my death. It should be a place among us, where we Christians can love one another as God loved us. So, the Kingdom of God is not a remote and distant place. It is, indeed, a concept about 'here and now'. Our Christian faith means that we need to live out our Christian witness so that the Kingdom of God will be revealed in our midst.

Mission: Bold Humility!

When we proclaim the good news, we should bear in mind that stereotyping must be avoided. The reason behind this is that all people in the world are different from one another. The way one perceives the gospel of God is not necessarily the same as or similar to that of another. So, one should bear in mind individual differences when proclaiming the good news.

Does mission mean telling the good news to one who has not heard about Jesus Christ? The answer is yes and no. With reference to my personal experience, the term 'mission' is a kind of sharing of treasures in life. I have spent nine years teaching English as a second language in an Anglican primary school in Hong Kong. Throughout these nine years of teaching, I tried to perform well in terms of my professional work as a teacher of language. Besides that, I also tried hard to nurture my students. I attempted to share my life as a Christian. I also tried hard to express the beauty of Anglican liturgy in my school when we had daily noontime prayers. During weekends, I helped to lead the primary students' fellowship so that these young people could be fed spiritual food in church. All this has formed part of my understanding and interpretation of 'mission'.

Do not be afraid to voice out the name of our Lord Jesus Christ. Do not be a Christian who does not tell the good news. If we do not speak up about the gospel, people around us will be unable to benefit from our sharing of the good news about Jesus Christ. As Jesus Christ demonstrated in His three years of mission work, He never gave up any opportunity to share the good news with those He loved. Therefore, as Christians, we should also try our best to proclaim the good news, both by our mouths and by our hearts. 'Silence is golden' was a very popular song during the 60's and this wise saying is still true when we are proclaiming the good news of God's Kingdom. This would be particularly true when we are dealing with some difficult controversy. Nevertheless, I would insist that we must try our best to verbalise the good news. We should make our gospel heard by others, including our neighbours, our colleagues, our schoolmates, our friends and also our family members. This is our obligation to God.

I read in Rick Warren's book, 'I took a job I hate in order to make a lot of money, so someday I can quit and do what I love to do.'[3] Rick Warren thought that was a big mistake. One should not waste his / her life in a job that doesn't express one's heart. He asked us to remember that 'the greatest things in life are not things'. Meaning is far more important than money. The richest man in the world once said, 'A simple life in the fear of God is better than a rich life with a ton of headaches.' (Prov 15:1). From the experience gained in Edinburgh 2010, I found this to be true. People from around the world shared about their lives of mission in various contexts. A

---

[3] Rick Warren, *The Purpose Driven Life* (Grand Rapids:Zondervan, 2002), 239.

woman from Jamaica shared about her witness of preaching the gospel. Seeing her beauty in terms of her devotion in proclaiming the gospel, I was deeply touched that she had overcome her disability, which prevented her from walking comfortably. She treated her physical disability as a trial in life and, most importantly, she did not give up easily. A brother from India also discussed the difficulty he was facing when doing the mission work among young people in his country. However difficult it was, he tried his best to carry on with his mission work for young people in India. These brothers and sisters are not rich in terms of their earthly wealth. Yet, regarding their wealth in life, I am very sure they both found the true meaning of living a worthwhile and meaningful life for God.

Humility is the key for leadership in proclaiming the good news of His Kingdom. When I looked back to the different speeches or addresses given in Edinburgh 2010, I discovered that most Church leaders shared in a manner of humility and invited brothers and sisters in Christ to serve God with a similar attitude. One of the key questions I am always asking myself throughout my ministries is: 'Am I enjoying myself in the presence of God, listening to the voice of God, appreciating the beauty of God and connecting to the truth of the incarnate God?'[4] For sure, humility cannot be found without humbling ourselves and letting God be in charge. The humility demonstrated by various Christian leaders from around the world, especially the Archbishop of Canterbury from the Anglican Communion, should be appreciated. Humble, in a sense that we are all equal, with Christ being the first among equals, is the very first thing I learnt from the world Christian leaders. The washing of feet done by Jesus Christ on Maundy Thursday evening was a classic example of humility. Similar practices by other Christians were done all over the world every year on Maundy Thursday. Jesus Christ has demonstrated to all Christians a special kind of leadership, Servant Leadership. He taught us that the more humble we are, the closer we are to God.

'Whatever your hand finds to do, do it with your might.' (Eccl 9:10a) One of the reflections I have from the Edinburgh 2010 Mission Conference was to learn from others, especially the young people and children. On Friday 4th June, 2010 the Conference began with a common prayer in the morning. This was a very special morning for me as we had a group of guests with us during the prayer time. Students from primary six class of St Mary's (Leith) Roman Catholic Primary School were with us and led the hymn singing. Their angelic voices and innocence in leading the worship is still clear in my mind today. The important point about the presence of these children with us is the reminder of the significance of 'humility'. David Bosch reevaluated the 'superiority of the Christian religion' when

---

4 Henry Nouwen, *In the Name Of Jesus, Reflections On Christian Leadership* (Chinese translation) (Hong Kong: Logos Publishers, 1992), 32. Translator: Lee Lo Ming.

discussing paradigm changes in missiology[5]. The children in Edinburgh were important in reminding us of the simplicity and purity of heart that they have. The melody and gestures of the songs they taught me still surround me while I write this article.

I always share with university students the following saying, 'If you think you are somebody, you are nobody at all; if you think you are nobody, you begin to be somebody now.' My godfather taught me this when I was still at secondary school. He emphasized the importance of humility for a Christian. Now, as I have to be responsible for campus ministry in various universities, I continue to convey this message of humility to my brothers and sisters in Christ.

The 'Post 80s' in Hong Kong

A big issue for young people in Hong Kong today is the term called the 'Post-80s'. This term 'Post-80s' is generally used to describe the group of young people who were born in the years 1980-1989. Some critics from the media complained that this group of people has been too radical and emotional when participating in social movements. Yet, on Palm Sunday this year, I encountered some 'Post-80s' who were really keen in leading a youth gathering and their performance impressed me greatly. The meeting was organized by the Joint-Committee on Youth Ministries from the three dioceses and one missionary area of Hong Kong on Palm Sunday afternoon at All Saints' Cathedral in Western Kowloon. What really impressed me most was that these 'Post-80s' young people had done a lot of preparation work for leading the small group sharing. The well-planned tasks in small groups included video shows, group games, short dramas, article sharing, etc. I was particularly impressed by a group discussing the domination by several land developers in Hong Kong. Unlike those media reports criticizing the 'Post-80s' for being irrational and, sometimes, even violent, these young people from the Anglican Church of Hong Kong tried hard to remain neutral and keep themselves objective during the process of sharing. This is really what I want to see from the young people who are the future leaders of Hong Kong.

The 'Post-80s', both within the Church and in the secular world, were well-known for their willingness to insist and press on for the core values of Hong Kong. They fought for social justice and so they helped to protect the Choi Yuen Village and the villagers living there. They wanted to uphold the legal system of Hong Kong that we are enjoying now and therefore they opposed the suggestion of a substitution system in case any legislative councillor needed to quit his post. What they agreed to was that we should hold a substitution election for what is being practised right now.

---

[5] David J. Bosch, *Transforming Mission: Paradigm Shifts in Theology of Mission* (Maryknoll: Orbis, 1991), 189.

The 'Post-80s' are also very concerned about the right attitude and judgment towards historical events such as the June 4th Tragedy in 1989. Every year on this day, they attend candle-light vigils to remember those who died twenty-two years ago in Beijing. To a certain extent, I would regard the 'Post-80s' as prophets for the modern time. They are all very ready to speak up and they have a strong demand for the betterment and a higher degree of democracy for the future of Hong Kong.

This is my prayer: I pray that people can continuously serve God with all the blessings that we possess, not just part of them. Like these 'Post-80s' young people, everyone has specific kinds of spiritual gifts from God. These young people are gifted in voicing out their ideas and suggestions. We, as Anglicans, also have our own gifts and we can humbly offer what is given from God to the Church. I also pray that parishioners are able to proclaim the good news all the time, not just at times when they are free or when they feel good at doing so. When I look back to what the 'Post-80s' young people did in Hong Kong, I can really feel their passion and willingness to sacrifice their time and energy.

Paradigm Shift in Mission: From 'West to East' to 'South to North'?

One of the most commonly heard comments during mealtime talks in Edinburgh 2010 was the shift in paradigms of mission. A century ago, the basic understanding of mission was from the west to the east, or from the developed countries to the developing places. After one hundred years, things have changed. Most delegates at Edinburgh were aware that mission is from anywhere to anywhere.

Bryan Stone, a systematic theologian from the School of Theology at Boston University, discussed and re-structured the meaning of evangelism. According to his analysis, the emphasis of evangelism should include the understanding of one's calling in every Church, every place and every time: 'To announce peace and to bear faithful, public, and embodied witness to God's reign in its own context.'[6]

Unfortunately, what is puzzling some Western, and even Eastern, churches today is that they still have a memory of the good old days of the old Christendom model. Historically speaking, the Christian Church has been closely related to political, economic and cultural authorities. Therefore, the Church really had a central role and enjoyed her special position as well as rights of speech. Nevertheless, as time goes by, the position is now very different from that of the past. Taking Hong Kong as an example, when we were still under the rule of the British colonial government before the year 1997, the Anglican Church had a say in the

---

[6] Bryan Stone, *Evangelism After Christendom: The Theology and Practice of Christian Witness* (Grand Rapids: Brazos Press, 2006).

consultation of various policies involving the public, such as education, housing and medical care. Things are very different now. We may find ourselves in a place somewhat similar to the Jewish remnant in the Old Testament.[7] Therefore, the Church cannot assume that she is still in a similar context for brothers and sisters to perform the function of 'producing Christians'. Places once seen as the home base of Christianized regions or countries are no longer the same. The feeling of 'home' is becoming weaker and weaker. Therefore, as Christians, the real question that we should ask is whether we are still making ourselves at home in a situation like this? Are we still faithful if we have been positioned in a marginalized place?

In Edinburgh 2010, the voice about 'mission from the south to the rest of the world' was frequently heard. Analyzing the true environment of mission, this call may be true. However, I am not in favour of jargon like this. This jargon may have been good in boosting morale. Yet, this may also lead us to the trap of labeling others. If we declare that mission is from the south, Christians from the north may not be happy about that. Similarly, when we refer back to Edinburgh 1910, critics might say that Christians were under the 'imperialistic influence of the Church from the west'. To me, whether mission originated from the south or from any other direction is not the most important matter. What matters most is the kind of spirit that we possess so as to help us along the way of mission for God.

During the mission conference in Edinburgh 1910, there was a profound concept of superiority in the mindset of the missionaries. Mainstream western churches were continuously thinking of where their missionaries should go. The concept of doing 'mission to' the different parts of the world, especially to Asia and Africa was prevalent. Back to the present age, in Edinburgh 2010, the concept of 'mission to' was critically redefined and the idea of 'mission with' has been newly established. We are no longer asking whether mission should be done from the West to the rest. Neither are we trying to say that mission should be done from the south to the north. In a broader sense, with necessary humility rooted deeply in one's mind, there should be no more mission from here to there. Rather, as bodies of one Church in general, we should try our utmost to build up a world without boundaries. A world without boundaries is a perfect idea for building up the Kingdom of God. Nowadays, the human-made boundaries including the various theological orientations cause very diverse opinions or thoughts in Christian faith. Boundaries also include the lack of humility by various Christians so that someone may think that I am strong and you are weak! I was especially impressed to learn about the humility of Archbishop Rowan Williams when we met him in the Bishop's House in

[7] After their exilic life, the Jewish remnants were in a condition that they lived in a dispersed manner amongst various Gentile lands. They were no longer playing a central role in the community but were on the periphery of where they were located.

Edinburgh. His Grace tried to introduce himself to us by having one knee down to the ground and to actively stretch out his hand for shaking. I was stunned! Yet, this is really the essential quality for the mission of evangelism to prevail.

If 'mission to' is no longer the right attitude in the Christian world today, what should be the right attitude then? In my opinion, 'love' is the key element in the Kingdom of God. One who loves will not think that he is superior to others. One who loves will also try to think in the position of others rather than thinking of oneself only. And one who loves will surely put God in the first place in the priority list of one's life. So, if 'mission to' fails today, the mindset of 'mission with' may be the right track to follow. As a Christian who loves God, we are trying to do mission with the people around us. We are trying to walk with others, serve with others and pray with others. Most importantly, we are doing mission not only with others, but we are also doing mission together with God. In his famous book *Transforming Mission*, Bosch once again reminded us to return to the work of God. If we want to ask what theology is, I would say that it is the connection with God through prayer and biblical teachings. Even though the importance of missiology has been downgraded in the past, we, as faithful servants of God, should still bear in mind the Great Commission given to us by our Lord.

The Three-Horse Chariot: Mission Model in the Hong Kong Anglican Church

The term 'Three-Horse Chariot' is used to describe the way and the method the gospel of the Kingdom is proclaimed in Hong Kong. The idea is that the Anglican Church in Hong Kong cannot stand by herself in meeting the real everyday life needs of the citizens of Hong Kong. One of the earlier bishops during the colonial days, the Rt. Revd Ronald Owen Hall[8], had emphasized the importance of the social gospel to be practised in Hong Kong so that the Anglican Church in this place was really working out the true love of God. Thus, the 'Three-Horse Chariot' literally means that the Church is not alone, but working collaboratively with schools (the second horse) and social welfare units (the third horse) in Hong Kong so as to proclaim the good news of Christ our Lord.

In his book entitled *Incarnation: Charles Gore's Anglican Theology*[9], the Revd Samson Fan described Bishop R.O. Hall as one of the practical bishops in terms of working out the good news of Jesus Christ in Hong

[8] The Rt. Revd R. O. Hall was one of the most remembered Anglican bishops during the colonial days. He was the 7th diocesan bishop of the then Diocese of Hong Kong and Macau. After his retirement and passing away, two secondary schools and a building on Hong Kong Island were named after him.

[9] Samson Fan (Chinese book), *Incarnation: Charles Gore's Anglican Theology* 2009, 53.

Kong. He shared his view as follows: 'Bishop R.O. Hall, the 7th bishop in the Diocese of Hong Kong and Macau, was deeply influenced by Charles Gore, who was a typical representative of Liberal Catholicism.' Until today, the spirit of both Bishop Charles Gore and Bishop R.O. Hall is still being actively worked out in the Anglican Church of Hong Kong. We try our best not to forget the incarnation of Jesus Christ, who demonstrated how the salvation and love from God are shared with everybody on earth. As Jesus is the model, so we Christians are His followers. The following is a short description of how the 'Three-Horse Chariot' functions for the proclamation of gospel in the Anglican Church of Hong Kong.

Doing mission through the Church: During the sixties of the last century, most Hong Kong citizens were new immigrants from the mainland China and they were, generally speaking, quite poor. Basic life necessities became the most important things they were requesting. Therefore, the Anglican Church of Hong Kong tried to distribute rice, milk powder, canned food and other daily necessities to these people in need so as to allow them a very basic level of living. As time went by, more houses were needed by the large amount of immigrants coming from China each day. Bishop Hall also helped in organizing the Hong Kong Housing Society so that more public housing estates could be built to fulfill the requests of Hong Kong people.

Doing mission through education: Another important part of mission in the Anglican Church of Hong Kong is education. Nowadays, several Anglican secondary schools have become the most popular and renowned schools in the region. One of the reasons for their popularity is the long history of these schools in Hong Kong. Diocesan Boys' School is one of the oldest boys' schools in Hong Kong with a history of more than 140 years.[10] Lots of Anglicans were graduates from these secondary, primary schools and kindergartens. They started to have their first encounter with Jesus Christ during their days of receiving education in the Anglican educational institutions in Hong Kong. Today, the collaboration between churches and schools is close. We try to work hand in hand so that mission work can be done very smoothly. Unlike the situation in most Western countries, the government in Hong Kong has never attempted to stop or hinder any religious activities in Anglican schools. On the contrary, we can organize gospel week or evangelical activities to convey the message about the love of God. We hold Bible study groups and fellowship gatherings for students in Anglican schools. During the summer holidays, gospel camps are also held for students from Anglican primary or secondary schools. This has contributed to a young and energetic Anglican Church in Hong Kong.

---

[10] Diocesan Boys' School was founded in 1869. The first principal was Mr. William M. Arthur.

Doing mission through social service: In the Gospels, Jesus Christ demonstrated to all Christians the loving care He had towards the sick and the poor. If the good news is not only a monopoly to the rich and the privileged class of the society, we should definitely remember the teachings of Jesus to show concern to the needy people in the world. Based on this, the Anglican Church of Hong Kong has always been conscious of the need to care for the poor, the sick, the elderly and the marginalized in the society. There was a disaster when a building collapsed in Hung Hom on 29th January 2010. The building was very close to the parish where I am serving. When the government officials phoned a colleague of mine to request that a community hall allow the victims temporary residence, I agreed immediately. They lived in my church building for eight nights before there were arrangements for them to live in a public housing estate. This was exactly what my predecessors had done in the past, helping the poor, providing food and clothes, and shelter. The spirit of serving the society has become well-known for the Anglican Church of Hong Kong. The Anglican Church Welfare Council is now the third largest non-government organization serving in Hong Kong.

Today, the Anglican Church of Hong Kong does not only mean the three dioceses and the missionary area, it also includes all the educational institutions as well as the social service units. These three fields were closely linked together and the summation of all the three forms of the present Hong Kong Sheng Kung Hui, the Anglican Church of Hong Kong. Without this 'Three-Horse Chariot', the development of the Anglican Church of Hong Kong would not be possible. Surely, in the way ahead, the 'Three-Horse Chariot' will still lead the church, the schools and the social service units to work together and help proclaim the good news of the Kingdom of God.

Life-Widening Mission Trips to China

In two consecutive years, 2008 and 2009, I was honoured to lead mission groups of Anglican young people to Toi Shan, Guangdong Province. Toi Shan is a town lying in the western part of Hong Kong. It took about two to three hours to travel from Hong Kong to Toi Shan by coach. The Church we contacted with some Three-Self Church units, is monitored and financially supported by the government officials in China. The trip itself was a five-day trip with the major focus on church visits and serving the local community. Participants were all young people from the Diocese of Eastern Kowloon, Anglican Church of Hong Kong. Some of them were having their first visit to a Three-self Church in mainland China. They were given two training and briefing sessions before the trip started.

The brothers and sisters in Christ from Toi Shan possessed the characteristics of traditional Chinese. They were very hospitable towards the guests whom they were serving. They were very enthusiastic, caring and warm when we were at their place. The warm welcome we received made me think of the emphasis of traditional Chinese on treating our guests with enthusiasm and warmth. On the first day when we arrived at the Tai Kong Village, evangelist brother Wong and warden madam Liu led us to the hotel and then immediately took us out for lunch in a nearby restaurant. I can still recall the warm welcome they gave us. Such hospitality is essential when we are in the process of proclaiming the good news. When sharing the good news with people who encounter the Christian faith for the first time, we should be able to show that we are passionate and eager to show the best thing in our lives to them. Before we left Toi Shan for Hong Kong, the chairman of the Christian Council in Toi Shan, the Revd Yan Yue Ching invited us for lunch to bid us farewell. We had never thought about that before because he was such a busy person and that day was his weekly day-off. Obviously, these brothers and sisters from Toi Shan did not think that we were only a group of young people and neglected us. On the contrary, they demonstrated the hospitality in accordance to the teaching of Jesus Christ in the gospel: "Truly I tell you, whatever you did for one of the least of these brothers and sisters of mine, you did for me." (Mt. 25:40)

If I were asked to use a word to summarize the gains in the Toi Shan Mission trips, I would say that my spiritual life has been 'widened'. The term 'widened' translated into Chinese is the same as the two syllables of the pronunciation of 'life'. Honestly, these two trips were an experience for the young people to widen their horizons and to enrich their lives. Whether it was the time when the young people were chatting with elder brothers and sisters in the remote village, or when they were making friends and sharing with some young factory workers coming from all the very distant provinces in China, I believe that these young people from Hong Kong have learnt a lesson in life. The exposure to different layers of the society, the different dialect they spoke in Toi Shan, the different background that Toi Shan brothers and sisters were from… All these have brought the Hong Kong Anglican young people into a deeper, wider, more dynamic perspective of life. I am quite sure that such an experience would be beneficial to the future development of these young people.

If one is asked about the benefits of a mission trip, I will answer by saying that it is not the people in Toi Shan who gain most. I would rather share that it was the people who were going all the way from their own familiar places to a new and strange corner on the earth who benefited the most in their lives. The Toi Shan trips ended two years ago but I still hear from the sharing of the participants about their spiritual progress after the trips. Praise the Lord! These life experiences helped brothers and sisters from Hong Kong to get a more genuine picture of how the front line of mission work is done in China. They taste it and feel it by their own eyes and their own minds. The serious attitude towards Christian faith, the devotion and dedication to Church life, and the willingness to commit one's life are all the points Hong Kong Anglican young people have learnt through the trips. The lives of these young Anglicans have definitely been widened and enriched. And, I am confident that these were only the enzymes that began the chemical process of changes in their lives. In the long run, these ideas could definitely benefit those who would share these unforgettable experiences with others.

Relationship + Networking = The Future of Anglicanism and Ecumenism

One of the most impressive things I have learnt from the Edinburgh 2010 Mission Conference is the friendship and relationship that I can treasure for the rest of my life. Not only have I made friends with Anglicans all around the world, but I have also been able to make friends with Christians from other denominations and traditions. The building up of these inter-personal relationships is important for the future development of both the Anglican Communion and the whole Christian world at large.

An African idiom points out the main gist of cooperation and collaboration: 'If you want to walk fast, you walk alone; but if you want to walk farther and longer, you walk with others.' This is particularly true when we are pointing to the future of mission work. What I have learnt and reflected from Edinburgh 2010 about 'proclaiming the good news of the Kingdom of God' was that I needed to build up a good inter-personal network with brothers and sisters from around the world so as to maintain the relationship for continuing dialogue and contact. With a profound relationship as the basis, one can then help in the local or global level of mission.

With the advancement of scientific technology and the Internet, the world is brought much closer together than one hundred years ago. When I was attending the Edinburgh 2010 Mission Conference last summer, the live broadcast of the Closing Ceremony made it possible for various Christians, without the boundary of different geographical locations, to know exactly what was happening in Scotland. The use of the social network on the Internet has also been a great help for proclaiming the gospel. Ten to twenty years ago, when I finished a youth camp, I would exchange my home phone numbers for further contact only. Nowadays, we exchanged our MSN, e-mail addresses as well as our Facebook account names so that we can keep in contact with others. It is important to make use of technology to help proclaim the good news of God. Facebook can be one of the ways to convey the message from the Heavenly Kingdom. I could still remember the time when we were gathering in the Pollock Hall conference rooms waiting for the beginning of several sessions, some Anglican delegates, including me, uploaded the latest news about the Edinburgh 2010 conference onto our Facebook walls so that brothers and sisters from our own countries could know what was going on almost simultaneously.

In the Province of Hong Kong Sheng Kung Hui, one of the dioceses has formed the Diocesan Committee on Information and Communication.[11] The Revd Stephen Hung, the diocesan officer responsible, has been using Facebook as a network for nurturing and pastoral care of his parishioners.

One possible drawback about the use of Internet tools or networks is that we cannot ensure whether the information from these sources is true or not. Such a disadvantage can be minimized by both prevention and education. If we take Facebook as an example, we can choose carefully who our friends are. If we are cautious enough, there should be no strangers in the list of friends in our Facebook account. On the other hand, I would say that the effect of education is significant when we advise our fellow young people in Church how they are supposed to use these Internet devices. I always demonstrate on my own Facebook account about how a positive message, a scriptural verse or some reflections from Church gatherings can benefit others through the Internet. This becomes one of the effective ways for me to communicate with my young people in Church.

When we look at the Anglican Communion today, some parishioners may worry about our future because of the issue of human sexuality and same-sex marriage blessings. Yet, if we can keep ourselves in a good relationship and continuous conversation with different Anglicans from around the world, I can see a future for the Anglican Communion. Similarly, for the various denominations and traditions of the present Christian world, continued dialogue and never-ending networking will keep us together, regardless of the different understandings of Holy Communion or of the Scriptures. With relationships and networking being continued, I am convinced that the future of Anglicanism as well as Ecumenism can prevail.

Widening Young People's Lives

When talking about equipping young people, one suggestion will directly be encouraging them to study theology. Here, I am not requesting all the young people to devote themselves to full-time ministries, i.e. to become a priest, an evangelist or a monk in a convent. What I want to point out is that some basic knowledge about the Christian faith is necessary when we are trying to share the good news of the Kingdom of God towards other people. We may also need to understand what the Kingdom of God means, how important it is for Christians to proclaim, and what the good news really means. We may need to know more about our liturgical tradition as an

[11] This Diocesan Committee belongs to the Diocese of Hong Kong Island. It is the first established committee at diocesan level to promote the use of information technology as well as communication tools for evangelistic work.

Anglican. We may need to have a more profound knowledge of our Holy Bible. And we may need to know some church history. All these may need to be systematically taught by courses organized by theological colleges, universities or cathedrals.

As an Anglican, we have a very good tradition of perpetuating the intellectual as well as logical ways of thinking. The way we put 'reasoning' as one of the three pillars in Anglicanism is one example. To continue with our tradition, we should not forget the importance of continuing education. The earlier we start to learn about our Christian faith, the better we can absorb the various fields of studies. Therefore, I would sincerely encourage youth members of our Church to start studying our Christian faith as soon as possible. Remember, we don't need to have all-round scholars or PhD degree holders all around our Church. What I am encouraging young people to do is to engage in lifelong learning.

For the situation in Hong Kong now, some youth workers who are serving full-time in Anglican Churches are pursuing their theological studies in an in-service diploma course organized by the SKH Ming Hua Theological College. Other youth leaders or young adults are trying to take some short-term courses in the Chung Chi College Divinity School or the Lutheran Seminary. This is very good preparation work for a young Christian to enrich his/her life. And, with this trend being encouraged by more priests and church leaders, I can foresee that more young people from the Anglican Church in Hong Kong will start their learning paths to enrich their Christian faith. In the long-run, the lives of these studious young people can be widened by the input of knowledge and attitudes towards Christian faith.

E-mission is the name of a group of brothers and sisters from the Diocese of Eastern Kowloon in Hong Kong. The name E-mission can mean three things, at least. First, brothers and sisters of E-mission have in mind a mission to help proclaim the good news in the diocese, be it schools or social service units in the Eastern Kowloon area. Second, they all want to be a kind of powerful force (emission) from their own parish church to the rest places in the diocese. Third, since we all live in the era with electrical and electronic devices, these brothers and sisters want to be innovative and creative in the ways of doing mission. Why did we form this group of E-mission in our diocese? One of the most important reasons was to support the Anglican primary and secondary schools in the diocese so that they could convey the messages of our Christian faith more effectively. Before the establishment of the E-mission, the writer has heard from different school heads requesting if there were any kinds of help for mission work in their schools. Some principals are really enthusiastic in proclaiming the good news in their schools but it was a pity that they only had one pair of hands and therefore could not do all the work all the time. With their repeated demands for external assistance in terms of mission work, the diocese decided to form the E-mission project. And I am most privileged to be invited as the Chaplain of the E-mission.

Young people play a very important role in the formation of the E-mission. About eighty percent of the members are university students who can spare time for evangelistic gatherings in the mornings or afternoons when most adult parishioners need to go to work. The other twenty percent were retired parishioners who are still very healthy and want to be used by God in any way.

Since its inaugural service in November 2009, the E-mission has been invited to more than twenty places for sharing and performances. Programmes include hymn singing, gospel magic shows, drama shows, group games and prayers. Some schools invited the E-mission to help organize an Easter Evangelistic Rally or a Christmas Service before the school holidays began. The feedback received from these gatherings was overwhelmingly positive. Looking back to the summer in 2009 when the chairman of the E-mission and I were discussing the possibility of forming the group, it was really through the grace of God that we could decide to start the ball rolling. And the pilot scheme of this missionary model will surely be carried on through the continuous prayers and efforts put in by the young people in the Diocese of Eastern Kowloon.

Conclusion

From the flight departing from Edinburgh to London Heathrow, then one week later from Heathrow back to Hong Kong[12], the long journey was quite a tiring one. In terms of the time spent, I am sure I have already saved many hours in comparison with the return trip of the Revd Cheng Jingyi, Professor Dong Jing'an and Zhang Tingrong one hundred years ago. Surely, the spirit of continuing to proclaim the good news of the Kingdom of God has never been changed, be it in 1910 or now. Pray that more and more lives can be widened. May God be honoured and praised!

Discussion Questions

1. When the term 'life' is pronounced in Cantonese, it also means 'widening'. To what extent is your life widened in your experience of involvement in mission?
2. Some 'Post-80s' young people in Hong Kong were criticized for being too radical while others were acknowledged as neutral and objective. What are young people of your place like and why?

[12] The team of Anglican delegates stayed in London for another week to follow up on the potential mission work to be done in the whole Anglican Communion.

3. If technological advancement is a help for the proclamation of the Good News of God, how far is it practised in your church as well as in your town?
4. The author suggests that good relationships and effective networking are important for the development of Anglicanism and Ecumenism. How far do you agree with this and why?

The Second Mark of Mission: To Teach, Baptise and Nurture New Believers

Andrew Thompson

Introduction

I am excited to have the opportunity to reflect on the second mark of mission in the Anglican Communion – to teach, baptise, and nurture new believers – for two reasons, one very personal and the other academic. The personal reason is that, as I write this, my wife and I are preparing for the baptism of our three-month-old son (our first). Indeed, a good deal of this essay has been written with him in my lap, or in my arms, or lying beside me, and even when he has not been physically present, he has been very present in my thoughts throughout the writing. I have therefore felt more urgently the importance of the ministries of teaching, baptism, and nurture and the need to understand these ministries within the context of God's radically transformative mission in the world. I want the community with which my son will soon be formally joined to be one worthy of the divine mandate entrusted to it, and I hope to offer some contribution to that effort.

Academically, I find this project exciting because these ministries – teaching, baptism, and nurture – are fundamentally and integrally connected with the identity and life of the Christian community, the church.[1] The life of the community as it enacts its witness to God's mission is a perennial interest of mine. As graduate student, a teaching fellow at an ecumenical seminary and a lay leader in the Episcopal Church in the United States (and as the husband of an Episcopal priest), I am committed to helping to strengthen the public witness of the church in response to social problems by bringing together the complementary inquiries of ecclesiology, missiology, and ethics.[2] These areas of thought as they relate to the life of the mission community were prominent in the proceedings of the Edinburgh 2010 World Mission Conference, as participants sought to

---

[1] For the purposes of this essay, I use the phrases, 'Christian community', 'missionary community', and 'the church' interchangeably, in part to avoid too narrow an identification with the institutional church or any particular incarnation of it.

[2] In my studies at Yale University, I focus this inquiry on the church's response to one particular social issue, mountaintop removal mining in the Appalachian region of the U.S.

understand and clarify both the global mission community and individual local communities. The second mark provides an opportunity to reflect further on how the life and witness of the missionary community are shaped, in particular by the three specific ministries named.

In this essay I will argue that the community of God's transforming mission requires theologies and practices of baptism, teaching, and nurturing that are equally transformative, capable of challenging the alienating and oppressive beliefs and behaviours of the world. Through these ministries the community of Christ's followers works to anticipate and approximate God's eschatological community. After preliminary attention to the unity of these ministries and their relation to the community of those liberated by God, and to the implications of the phrase 'new believers' in the second mark, I will consider the three ministries themselves, beginning with baptism. I will describe the role that each ministry plays in defining and shaping the community: baptism liberates believers for life in the community as it participates in God's mission; teaching shapes the witness of the community in its cultural context; and nurture both sustains that witness and constitutes part of that witness to the reconciled relationships of God's eschatological community. While I do not intend these interpretations to be iconoclastic, they are admittedly challenging. I believe a more robust understanding of God's transformative mission and the participation of the church in that mission calls us to more radical interpretations of the ministries of the second mark of mission.

Three Ministries, One Mark

A natural way to address the three-fold mandate of the second mark of mission would perhaps be to treat each of its ministries – teach, baptise, and nurture – individually in detail, and I intend to offer such discussion. This treatment would be misguided, however, if it failed to emphasise the unity of these three ministries within the one mandate. Teaching, baptising, and nurturing new believers are not three separate marks of mission, nor is any one of these three ministries given priority over the others. For this reason, I begin and end my reflections on the second mark of mission with the unity of the three ministries: teaching, baptising, and nurturing.

What fundamentally binds these ministries as one mark of mission, distinct from the other marks, is the centrality of the Christian community. It is the community that teaches, baptises, and nurtures new believers, and it is in and through this teaching, baptising, and nurturing that the community is shaped, given continuity, and expanded. More than any of the other marks of mission, the second mark depends upon, and in turn defines, the community of Christ's followers. Certainly the existence and activity of the community is implicit in the proclamation of the Gospel, loving service, transformation of society, and the protection of creation; we fail to understand these marks if we do not see them as functions of the entire community. Yet it is in the ministries of the second mark of mission that God gives shape to the community of God's people. Through the church's teaching, the identity and distinctive life of the community are formed; in Baptism, the community of Christ's followers is continually expanded and made more inclusive; and with the nurture of new believers the Christian community cares for and maintains itself. In these ways, the Christian community is fundamental to the second mark of mission, and vice versa. Put simply, the second mark is *about* the community.

This is perhaps to put it *too* simply, however. We misunderstand both the second mark and the nature of the Christian community if we see that community as an end in itself. After all, the second mark of mission is *about* mission, as is the community it describes. The Christian community is called into being in the service of God's mission; it exists to proclaim God's Gospel of renewal and reconciliation of the world and to invite others to participate in God's kingdom. The separate ends of teaching, baptism, and nurturing – the formation, initiation, and care of believers in the community – are secondary to the ultimate end of that community, its participation in God's mission. It is the character of this mission, therefore, that defines the community that teaches, baptises, and nurtures.

With Jürgen Moltmann, I understand the church to be the community of those liberated and called by Christ, in the power of the Holy Spirit, for God's unifying and transforming mission.[3] As the church testifies to God's history with the world and the eschatological future that consummates that history, it mediates the new creation in history.[4] It is, therefore, neither wholly a part of its culture nor wholly countercultural; it is an expression, however incomplete, of the eschatological transformation of all culture into God's kingdom. It is, as Miroslav Volf puts it, a community neither of outsiders seeking to become insiders nor of outsiders striving to remain outsiders, but rather of 'insiders who have diverted from their culture by being born again'; it is a new creation 'precisely within the proper space of the old'.[5] This community is bounded neither by the visible, institutional church, nor by the creeds or scriptures of the Christian tradition (though both are indispensable means of its participation in God's mission); it is circumscribed only by God's unpredictable and inscrutable grace. It exists wherever God's Spirit empowers and upholds human participation in God's mission in community.

Understanding the church this way, in light of its ultimate foundation in God's mission, is particularly important given the current turn toward the notion of community as a social panacea. In numerous areas of contemporary thought, from theology to sociology to political science to

[3] Jürgen Moltmann, *The Church in the Power of the Spirit: A Contribution to Messianic Ecclesiology* (1st ed: New York: Harper & Row, 1977), 33-36.
[4] Ibid., 35.
[5] Miroslav Volf, 'Soft Difference: Theological Reflections on the Relation Between Church and Culture in 1 Peter', *Ex Auditu* 10 (January 1, 1994), 18-19.

ecology, 'community' is being appealed to as the solution to societal and spiritual ills. Certainly Christians should to some extent welcome this turn, since community in some form is undeniably a central feature of our faith tradition. Yet without further definition and, more importantly, a more fundamental end on which to ground community, the concept can be at best vacuously nostalgic and, at worst, oppressive and homogenising.[6] For this reason, rather than the idea of community itself, the defining value of the Christian community is God's mission.

Since these three ministries are united in the shaping and expansion of the community of Christ's followers for the sake of God's mission, it follows that none of the three is an end in itself. Neither the care of believers, nor their formation, nor – most notably – their inclusion in the community through baptism, is the goal of this mark of mission, or of mission more generally. This is the error into which many practical theologies of mission fall, and one that a certain interpretation of the second mark may invite: we proclaim the Gospel to new believers in order that they might consent to join the church through baptism. We often evaluate the success or failure of our missionary activity on the basis of the number of the newly baptised or received. Certainly, every initiation into the Christian community is to be celebrated. God's mission is universal, and the more inclusive our community, the more closely it follows the will of its Creator. Every baptism is potentially a step toward a more universal community. Nonetheless, these steps toward greater inclusivity are one aspect of the growth of the community in service of God's mission. New believers are initiated – and educated and nurtured – not to expand church rosters and add to the ranks of Christians, but to invite them to share in the proclamation of God's good news and the life of God's kingdom.

We do not educate and nurture new believers in order to baptise them, nor do we baptise in order then to instruct and care for the baptised. Rather, we engage all three of these ministries in order to expand, shape, and uphold the Christian community for the sake of its participation in God's mission. The unity of the three ministries involved in the second mark of mission consists in their common purpose, furthering the spread of the Gospel, and in their common location, the missionary community.

A Note on 'New Believers'

The phrase 'new believers' in the second mark is problematic, because it implicitly establishes certain unacceptable dichotomies: between 'old' and 'new' and between 'believers' and 'non-believers'. The first unnecessarily separates recent converts from those who have been a part of the church for a longer period. This is salutary insofar as it calls attention to the

---

[6] Iris Marion Young, *Justice and the Politics of Difference* (Princeton, N.J: Princeton University Press, 1990), 227-236.

continuing expansion of the church and challenges the inertia that would be satisfied with maintenance and stability rather than proclamation and growth. Yet an exclusive focus on 'new believers' suggests that there is some other class of 'old believers', established and settled. These believers are apparently no longer in need of the nurture, teaching, and baptism mandated on behalf of new believers, and it is therefore incumbent upon them to do the nurturing, teaching, and (indirectly) baptising.

Even more problematic is the second term, believers. Certainly the term can be variously understood; belief need not be restricted to doctrinal assent. Yet this is how the term belief is commonly used, and thus the implication seems to be that teaching, nurture, and baptism are contingent on some kind of orthodoxy. This is too restrictive a condition. To begin with, the church, as the community of Christ's followers, is identified by a way of life, rather than a set of beliefs (though, as I will argue with respect to teaching, the beliefs are foundational to that way of life). Thus it is more appropriate to focus the ministries of teaching, baptism, and nurture on those whose lives strive to express God's transforming mission in the world. Yet, second, we can never presume to place even these limits on the Christian community. What finally constitutes the Christian community is God's grace. Accordingly, if the ministries of teaching, baptism, and nurture are the ways in which we shape, expand, and care for the community of Christ's followers, we must be prepared to extend these ministries wherever the Spirit of God's transformative mission is in evidence.

Nonetheless, the phrase 'new believers' is not necessarily contradictory to this understanding of the Christian community, if it is differently interpreted. I suggest that we understand the phrase 'new believers' in the same sense as the Pauline image of the 'new self' (Col 3.10): those whose lives are transformed by God's grace to reflect God's kingdom. Here the emphasis is on God's action, rather than a person's creedal adherence, and on the renewal that action creates in the lives of all persons, rather than simply newness in relation to the community. So understood, 'new believers' refers not to one group within the Christian community, but rather to all members of the community insofar as their lives are renewed by God's grace to reflect God's eschatological reality.

Moreover, the image of the 'new self' or, in the present context, the 'new believer', can be taken not to refer to individual members of the community, but to the community as a whole. As theologian José Comblin argues, this image refers to communities, and specifically to communities that recover, 'in our present historical context, an inspiration that lay at the basis of primitive Christianity and that has been reborn ever and again throughout history': the mission community.[7] This community challenges

[7] José Comblin, *Retrieving the Human: A Christian Anthropology* (Maryknoll, N.Y: Orbis Books, 1990).

relationships of domination and subjugation, as well as the conflict between the individual and collective, by a model of freely willed service and mutual commitment in *agape*. For the purposes of this essay, I propose that we understand the phrase 'new believers' to refer first to this missionary community, created by grace, that testifies to God's mission of transformation in the world, both the subject and object of the teaching, baptism, and nurture of the second mark of mission.

This new interpretation of 'new believers' is crucial for a truly missionary understanding of the second mark. If we fail to challenge the distinction between 'us' and 'them', 'in' and 'out, that is too often implicit our use of the phrase 'new believers', our language of liberation, inclusion, and mutuality degenerates into empty self-congratulation. However radical our intentions, today as in the past, in our zeal to bring God to others, we forget that God is always already there. If we are really to participate in God's transformation of the world, we must see God's universal grace at the foundation of all mission, and therefore be willing not only to baptise, teach, and nurture, but to *be* baptised, taught, and nurtured.[8]

Baptism for Mission

With the unity of the three ministries of teaching, baptism, and nurture firmly in mind, I turn first to baptism. I begin here not because baptism is first in importance (as noted above, none of the three ministries has this priority), nor because it comes first temporally (though practically speaking it often does). Rather, I begin with baptism because, as the sacramental symbol of inclusion in the Christian community, baptism and our understanding of it carry implications for the formation and life of the community – for teaching and nurture. In this section, I will suggest a theology of baptism as liberation for, rather than simply initiation into, the community of Christ's followers and the kingdom of God proclaimed by that community.

Baptism is most often, and most plainly, understood in terms of initiation into the Christian community.[9] At its best, this initiation represents a commitment to a certain way of life, within a specific community. Accordingly, baptism of new believers is appropriately an event to be celebrated, and a worthy mandate to be included under the rubric of this second mark of mission. The inclusion, radical community, and commitment to others that may be expressed in this view of baptism have the potential to be a challenging witness to a world where these values are often sorely needed.

---

[8] Thanks to the Right Reverend Mark MacDonald for bringing this to my attention.

[9] James M Gustafson, *Treasure in Earthen Vessels: The Church as Human Community* (Louisville: Westminster John Knox Press, 2009), 16-17.

Yet each of these features has the potential to work against mission: Inclusion in the church, when such inclusion is too closely circumscribed by orthodoxy, can become exclusion. Community, similarly, can become homogenising and suffocating. Rather than inviting others to enrich the community, baptism can be used to compel them to conform to it. Finally, commitment purely for commitment's sake becomes onerous. In all these cases, when the community, and inclusion in it, becomes an end in itself, our theology of baptism can undermine, rather than uphold, God's transforming mission. For this reason, I argue that the church's theology of baptism must go beyond initiation to liberation for God's mission.

In my (and Moltmann's) ecclesiology sketched briefly above, the life of the church is the experience and practice of the eschatological anticipation of the kingdom of God. It mediates the new creation in history. In its telling and retelling of God's history in the world, it creates freedom, liberating its hearers from the worldly and sinful stories, myths, and compulsive actions of their societies and inviting them to reconceive their lives in the liberating context of God's eschatologically oriented history.[10] Baptism is an expression of this invitation to freedom.[11]

Baptism reflects the liberation of the baptised from the structures of society – its dominant myths and patterns of behaviour. More importantly, however, it expresses their liberation *for* God's eschatological community, in the presence of the Holy Spirit. Believers are freed through baptism to live in the radical openness and universality of God's reconciled future. The repentance and forgiveness of baptism, the step of turning from old ways, is not for its own sake, but because the kingdom is at hand (Mt 3:1-2). The baptised are freed *from* sin – their own and society's – *for* new life in this new reality. Rightly understood, this is not a symbolic claim, nor merely a proclamation of future freedom, though it is that. It is a real transformation, liberating the baptised to live, as a community, in that future freedom in the present. Baptism calls believers to reconceive – and thus really to renew – their lives in the context of God's liberated future. At Jesus' baptism, heaven opened and the Spirit came (Lk 3:21-22); today, God's eschatological future is similarly opened to those liberated by the power of the Spirit in baptism in the missionary community, and they are freed to continue in Jesus' proclamation of that future.

A young Anglican clergywoman in Africa tells of one of her first acts as a priest, the baptism of one hundred children born out of wedlock. Because of the stigma associated with their birth, these children had previously been excluded from baptism. Their baptism, then, celebrated their freedom, by God's grace, from the oppression of that stigma, for new life in the community that testifies to God's kingdom.[12]

---

[10] Moltmann, *The Church in the Power of the Spirit*, 35.
[11] Ibid., 232-236.
[12] I am grateful to the Reverend Irene Ayallo for offering this example.

This freedom is a challenging prospect. The present maintains its hold on our lives, and the future must exist in tension with it. The new person must operate with and within the old, seeking the movements and moments of transformation in the midst of an ambiguous world.[13] Yet as José Comblin argues, the very existence of this community of the 'new person', though it be persecuted and challenged at every step, is itself a powerful witness to God's new world.[14] In baptism, new believers are liberated for this witness.

Moltmann identifies the particular power of story to effect this liberation: '[B]y virtue of its remembrance of the story of Christ and its hope for the kingdom of man, [the community] liberates men and women from the compulsive actions of existing society… freeing them for a life which takes on a messianic character'.[15] This may happen more indirectly and generally, as when the baptised are freed from conceptions of social hierarchy and inequality. In some cases, though, it can take place quite directly and specifically, through the telling, hearing, and redeeming of individual stories. One study of baptism preparation in the United Kingdom looked at the use of story in lieu of more traditional classes in that preparation. The study showed that those who shared and reflected on their own personal stories, including stories of struggles and difficulties, found more meaning in their baptismal commitment than those who took classes focusing on doctrine.[16] Another example, that of Urban Rural Ministries Canada, will be considered below. With or without the sacrament itself, these ministries are powerful examples of baptism as liberation.

These examples remind us that baptism, as a sacrament, is not in itself the graced initiation and liberation it expresses. That is, while baptism is an outward sign of the inward, liberating grace of God's eschatological future, it is that grace, through the Holy Spirit, that frees persons for the new way of life; baptism does not effect this freedom. Thus the community of those liberated for God's future is not limited to those who receive the sacrament of baptism; it exists among all those whose lives testify to God's transforming and reconciling intention for the world, be they members of the institutional church or practitioners of other faiths altogether. Baptism does not create or define this liberated community; it recognises and celebrates the creation of this community by God's Holy Spirit. Baptism for mission, therefore, expresses sacramentally God's initiation and liberation of persons for life in the community that anticipates the eschatological future.

---

13 Comblin, *Retrieving the Human*, 41.
14 Ibid., 29.
15 Moltmann, *The Church in the Power of the Spirit*, 225.
16 Thanks to Janice Price for this example.

Teaching for Mission

Baptism represents persons' liberation into the community of God's mission; yet we should not imagine that this graced transformation immediately and inevitably leads to renewed and reconciled lives. As Comblin argues, the life of the 'new person' of the community of the people of God must be lived in the midst of and in tension with the old. This requires careful discernment, which, in turn, requires formation in the life of faith. The witness of the missionary community depends on its ability to shape persons capable of discerning God's transforming action in the world and living in ways that affirm and proclaim that action.

This recognition that mission may be as much about witnessing through the way of life of a community as it is about proclaiming creedal truths is one of the more exciting directions in contemporary mission, and was very much in evidence at Edinburgh 2010. In a postmodern context, with legitimate concerns about neocolonialism and epistemic violence, such a paradigm seems to have more potential for pluralism and cultural sensitivity. Yet writing a century ago, missionary Roland Allen argues that this was precisely the mission paradigm of the most successful Christian missionary, St. Paul. In Paul's preaching and instruction Allen finds great sensitivity to the diverse cultural contexts in which he operated and an approach of mutual instruction.[17] Paul understood both the challenge of the Gospel message and the importance of trusting the message itself, and his teaching therefore sought to empower communities to discern the implications of the Gospel in their particular situations. Allen believes that Paul trusted so thoroughly in the power of the Gospel that he was willing to empower community leaders to discern its truth in their own context. While Paul was willing to circumscribe that freedom at times in the name of the purity of the Gospel (and to do so more aggressively than Allen seems willing to acknowledge), he finally trusted in the communities, the Holy Spirit, and the message itself. The truths of the Christian faith, Allen argues, are not primarily intellectual assertions, but are encountered in experience. The diverse experiences of faithful communities therefore enrich, rather than threaten, doctrine.

All scepticism toward Allen's generous interpretation of St. Paul aside, he presents a compelling model of education for mission: moral, contextual, and community-based. First, it is moral, meaning that mission education is concerned with the actions and decisions of the community. Allen argues that the lives of Christians, more than any doctrinal teaching, are what will compel new believers: '[W]hen [people] see a change in the lives of their neighbours…[t]hen the people are face to face with the Holy

---

[17] Roland Allen, *Missionary Methods: St. Paul's or Ours?* (Grand Rapids: Eerdmans, 1962), 62-64, 84-90.

Ghost.'[18] One goal of education for mission, therefore, is to form communities of believers whose lives reveal the Holy Spirit.

Ethical traditions centre on virtue and the virtues highlight this process of education for moral witness. Authors in these traditions understand the moral life to depend on habits and patterns of behaviour – referred to broadly as virtues – transmitted by communities, instilled in agents, and nurtured by practice. In place of a more typical emphasis on abstract values and discrete issues, these approaches focus on the role of education and the community in the formation of moral agents. In this vein, theologian Stanley Hauerwas compares moral formation to the learning of a craft: the goal is objective – morality is, at least to some extent, independent of our desires and opinions – and reached only by being formed in the skills and practices of a tradition.[19]

Education in the missionary community, then, is moral, in that it is concerned with shaping communities whose lives and actions reflect God's transforming mission in the world. This is not to suggest, however, that education is not also concerned with belief and doctrine. Rather, as ethicist James Gustafson argues, the foundation of the moral discourse of the community is its interpretation of its beliefs in its social context.[20] The community's beliefs about what God has done and wills to do in the world – the *missio Dei* – frame its own interpretation of its moral actions in its own context. For this reason, education in the missionary community must be contextual; that is, not wholly determined by relative contextual circumstances, but rather always seeking to interpret that context in light of God's mission in the world. God is always enacting God's mission in and through the agents and structures of the world, and one of the church's theological tasks is to discern that action in its own context. As Allen asserts, the truths of the Gospel are encountered in and strengthened by the diverse experiences of the church in the world; education must prepare the community for this encounter.

The process of shaping a church capable of encountering and discerning the truths of faith in its experiences, emphasises openness over orthodoxy, and discernment over dogma. This kind of contextual education is exemplified by ministries like the Appalachian Ministries Resource Center (AMERC) in the Appalachian Mountain Region of the United States. AMERC works with seminaries to provide future ministers with training in contextual theology in Appalachia. As director Lon Oliver says, the church's job is to discover 'what God is up to' in a given situation, and

---

[18] Roland Allen, *The Ministry of the Spirit: Selected Writings of Roland Allen*, ed David M. Paton (Grand Rapids, MI: Wm. B. Eerdmans, 1960), 100.

[19] Stanley Hauerwas, *After Christendom? How the Church is to Behave if Freedom, Justice, and a Christian Nation are Bad Ideas* (Nashville: Abingdon Press, 1991), 93-111.

[20] James M Gustafson, *The Church as Moral Decision-Maker* (Philadelphia: Pilgrim Press, 1970), 86-88.

what it can do to contribute.[21] To fulfil this mandate, AMERC immerses seminary students in the local culture to learn about theological themes like creation and sin in those contexts. Through such openness to God's action in concrete situations, Oliver believes the church can help develop the trust and community necessary to seek creative solutions to the pressing problems facing that region.

Finally, education for mission is community based. Chief among the various experiences and agents in which God's action is encountered are the institutions and communities in which we find ourselves; as the community devoted to discerning and affirming that mission, the church is a primary *locus* for that encounter.[22] God acts in and through the traditions, customs, and relations of the Christian community. Community is fundamental to God's mission and our participation in it. Education, then, must affirm and build on the relations existing in and around the church community. For Allen this means working, as Paul did, to allow 'local prophets' to speak, and to empower independent communities in the care of local leadership.[23] In other contemporary contexts it may mean seeking, in our education efforts, to strengthen lay and diaconal leadership, and building on connections with local communities and ministries. Above all, it means learning to hold one another accountable as a community before God, rather than depending upon a handful of chosen (or ordained) leaders.

Community-based education may not be complicated or dramatic. As a missionary of the Episcopal Church, I worked in Sitio de los Nejapa, a poor community in rural El Salvador. In reflecting on passages such as Matt 11:25 ('I thank you, Father…because you have hidden these things from the wise and the intelligent and have revealed them to infants') community members, mainly women, began to overcome the self-doubt that came from decades of marginalisation and recognised their ability to speak for themselves. This new self-awareness, in turn, has empowered them to collaborate with leaders of the church and community to develop other activities, beginning with a weekly sewing class. In this modest example, local leaders are beginning to arise as a result of gathering as the church in the context of their community. Here, then, is teaching for mission: the formation of a community capable of discerning God's action in its own context and responding with a common life that affirms and testifies to that action.

Nurturing for Mission

Just as baptism can be understood too narrowly as initiation or commitment, without a sense of graced liberation, and teaching can

---

[21] Interview with Lon Oliver, Berea KY, 10 August 2010.

[22] Ibid., 73-76.

[23] Allen, *Missionary Methods*, 84-90.

overemphasise propagation of doctrine at the expense of the lived experience and witness of the community, the concept of nurturing lends itself to distortion. Indeed, it may be the most easily misconstrued of these three ministries. In what Gustafson refers to as alienated society, where persons are perceived as disconnected from one another and from the centres of public power, and the church seems to have equally little influence over these centres of power, the role of the church becomes primarily pastoral and therapeutic.[24] In this context, nurture would seem to refer only to the care of individuals in the face of this alienation. This private ministry apparently has little to do with transformation of the public world, and can indeed be seen as being complicit in the present order, for better or worse. At best, the church becomes an enclave of interpersonal care, an escape from the anonymity of the modern world; at worst it becomes a source for vague, superficial self-help. This understanding of nurture seems to have little to do with God's transformative mission in the world.

Yet it is equally distorting for the church to ignore the pastoral ministry of care for its members in favour of prophetic public ministries. At the root of these twin distortions, according to Gustafson, is an unwarranted division between private and public, between ministries of care and the realms of social power. Contrary to this dichotomy, the nurture that shapes persons and envelops them in a community of mutual commitment can be a significant force for cultural and even political transformation.[25]

Feminist theologians and ethicists in particular have insistently decried the separation of public and private and the relegation of care and nurture to the private realm of interpersonal relationships. Care, active loving response to the concrete needs of particular individuals, is contrasted with, though not inconsistent with, impartial concerns for justice or universal love. Feminist authors point to the practices of care without which the development and sustenance of capable moral agents would be impossible.[26] The moral agents that exercise political power and influence public issues remain particular persons with irreducibly particular needs. It is incoherent to imagine that the public realm in which they act, and the manner in which they act in it, can be abstracted from those needs and the supposedly private institutions that respond to them with care. This is not to suggest that there is no distinction between the private realms of nurture and the public realms of social action; it is rather to argue for the undeniable connection between the two.

---

[24] Gustafson, *The Church as Moral Decision-Maker*, 63.

[25] Ibid., 64-65.

[26] Eric Gregory, *Politics and the Order of Love: An Augustinian Ethic of Democratic Citizenship* (Chicago: University of Chicago Press, 2008), 165-175; Seyla Benhabib, *Situating the Self: Gender, Community, and Postmodernism in Contemporary Ethics* (Cambridge: Polity Press, 1992).

From a missiological perspective, this means that care for believers is an integral, rather than incidental, feature of participation in God's mission. As one of the three ministries of this second mark of mission, the nurture of believers is not a private affair, distinct from the public commitment of baptism and the moral witness of education. It is a central feature of the formation and sustenance of the community that testifies publicly to God's transforming mission in the world.

Not only is nurture necessary for sustaining and upholding the witnessing community, however; it is also a part of that witness: The community that testifies to God's transformative mission is, among other things, a community wherein people care for one another. This is an aspect of a ministry of nurturing that the pastoral/therapeutic view described above gets both somewhat correct and emphatically wrong. On the one hand, that view recognises the potential for the church to be a *locus* of caring interpersonal relationships in a world bereft of such communities. This kind of care is a feature of God's future reign, and so the community that genuinely realises relationships of this sort is, to that extent, fulfilling its missionary mandate. For the most part, however, what passes for relationships of care in church communities falls far short of the radical nature of God's eschatological community. The liberated community described by Moltmann, under Christ's lordship, cannot help but reflect aspects of the society around it; it must not, however, perpetuate the biases and existing power dynamics of that society.[27] The realisation of the liberated community is, as he puts it, 'a continual problem and a continual opportunity'; it is challenging. Relationships within the community push boundaries and challenge assumptions.

The biblical foundation for the caring relationships of the Christian community, according to Moltmann, is the friendship of Christ.[28] Indeed, Christ's role as friend subsumes and elevates the meaning of his other titles – priest, prophet, and king. Jesus' friendships with his disciples (Jn 15:12-15) and with tax collectors and sinners (Lk17:34) brought those people into a new kind of relationship with God, a relationship of freedom and intimacy. Friendship with Christ, and thus the friendship of the community of Christ's followers, is a relationship of genuine freedom, liberated from all forms of domination or privilege. It is the foundation for the domination-free reign that Christ initiates.[29] Above all, it is a public relationship: Jesus' own friendships were a public declaration of his intimacy with those at the edges of society, and an expression of the messianic feast; the friendships of his followers must likewise represent a public challenge to the exclusion and domination of society in the face of God's radically inclusive fellowship.

---

[27] Moltmann, *The Church in the Power of the Spirit*, 105-106.
[28] Ibid., 114-121.
[29] Ibid., 116.

The church I attend in Hartford showed me a compelling example of this challenging and public care for one another. Faced with the difficult decision of whether to leave the building the congregation had known for decades or to remain and face certain financial catastrophe, the bilingual, multicultural congregation met to deliberate. During the conversation, a member of the English-speaking group (perhaps 10% of the congregation) stood and said, 'There are so few of us, we just want to be sure whatever course we take is best for the Spanish-speaking group'. Later in the meeting, and apparently not prompted by the earlier statement, a Spanish-speaker (representing the other 90% of the congregation) argued that as the larger group, they knew that they (the Spanish-speakers) would be fine in a move, and were only concerned that the decision be in the best interests of the English-speakers. Contrasted with the rancour that often accompanies cultural and ethnic interactions in society, and had in fact characterised this very congregation in earlier times, this is indeed radical, public care.

The relationships of care that characterise the missionary community are therefore no lukewarm feelings of other-regard, nor vague concern for others of the same social, economic, or ethnic status. They are difficult, unsettling, boundary-crossing relationships. If it is truly to live into its identity as a new creation or new person, the community must transgress and radically transform the norms of the world around it, rather than simply offer alternatives within those established parameters. In this way, the nurture that sustains the missionary community in its witness also constitutes a part of that witness, the caring friendship offered by Christ and fulfilled in the messianic future.

Edinburgh 2010 and the Second Mark

In the context of God's transformative mission, the second mark can and should challenge – sometimes radically – how we engage the ministries of teaching, baptism, and nurturing. Edinburgh 2010 provided helpful examples both of missionary efforts that reflect God's liberating intention for the world in some of the ways I have described, and of the ways we, as a church, continue to 'miss the mark', so to speak.

To begin with, Edinburgh's emphasis on mission and unity, and the conscientious effort made to include voices from a wide array of traditions, regions, and ethnic groups, were indications of the inclusivity of the missionary community. The participation of mission practitioners from grassroots ministries around the world gave expression to the importance of witnessing through actions, rather than merely words. Moreover, the sense that mission in the twenty-first century must be involved in and aware of its cultural context, and seek to live its witness in and around that context, rather than in spite of or in ignorance of it, was an important theme in discussions about mission and postmodernity, power, and community.

Both the structure and the substance of the conference fell short, however, of the transformative community entailed by God's mission. The dominant voices were often those of institutional and ecclesial leaders, rather than laypeople and practitioners. Many of the marginal voices that had been so conscientiously included in this centenary, in contradistinction to the first Edinburgh World Mission Conference, remained nonetheless marginal: the global south, women, and young people, to name a few. In this way, the values of freedom, equality, and inclusion were at times overpowered by hierarchy, domination, and exclusion. The conference too often took its cues from the societal norms around it, instead of challenging those norms. Rather than a criticism of the conference itself, these shortcomings are an important reminder of the limitations of all human efforts to live into God's transformative future.

Inevitable human shortcomings notwithstanding, there were many powerful instances of the missionary community, forged in baptism, shaped by education, and upheld by nurture. In a parallel session on Mission and Subaltern Voices, we discussed the compelling example of the Urban Rural Mission Canada (URM-Canada), a grassroots network of people gathered from indigenous, agricultural, and immigrant communities.[30] The network has its origins in the story circles of First Nations cultures, and uses these circles as a foundation for other organising and development projects.[31] By telling and hearing one another's stories of struggle and oppression and juxtaposing them with Gospel stories of liberation and hope, groups engage in a carefully cultivated process of dialogue in order to work for constructive solutions.

This process of storytelling and transformative action exemplifies many features of the missionary community as I have described it. The power of the story circle is its cathartic capacity to free persons from oppressive relationships and dynamics – racism, marginalisation, poverty – and to resituate them within the liberative context of the Gospel. Individual stories become instructive for the life and action of the larger network, and the structures and processes of the circle are carefully cultivated for mutual respect and care. Here, then, is an example of baptism as liberation for the messianic community, teaching as formation for public witness, and nurture as a public relationship of care.

Conclusion

In this essay I have argued that the three ministries of the second mark – to teach, baptise, and nurture new believers – are properly treated together as the ministries that shape, establish, and sustain the community that participates in and reflects on God's transforming mission in the world.

[30] http://urm.visiontech4u.com/home.html.

[31] http://urm.visiontech4u.com/eventPgStuffs/events/sept2008/stories/speakers.php.

After emphasising this unity, I treated each of the three individually to consider the particular implications of each for the community: Baptism is understood not only as initiation, but more significantly as liberation from the oppressive dynamics of society for the community of God's mission. Teaching shapes the life of the community as it seeks to embody that mission in its particular social context. Nurture both sustains the witness of the missionary community, and, as a public relationship of care, represents a part of that witness to an inclusive and genuinely caring community.

To conclude, I wish once again to take the three ministries together. For what they together describe is a community whose intention is always beyond itself, in the universal *missio Dei*. If taken seriously, this mark reminds us that the Christian community exists, and forms itself, and sustains itself not for its own sake, but always to proclaim and strive for the ever more inclusive, ever more universal community of God's kingdom. It calls us always to question the ways in which our churches have remained content with initiation rather than expansive liberation, doctrinaire education rather than formation in community, and self-preservation rather than public relationships of radical care. It urges us to greater inclusion, a more faithful lived witness, and more public friendship.

As I prepare to celebrate the welcoming of my son into this community, and into the relationships of mutual instruction and care that are features of the community, I pray that the church may continue to seek the foundation of its teaching, baptism, and nurture beyond itself, in God's transformative mission in the world.

Discussion Questions

1. Does your church approach the ministries of baptism, teaching, and nurture in a unified way? If so, how do these ministries reinforce one another? If not, how might each be strengthened by a more unified approach?
2. Which practices surrounding baptism reflect an understanding of its liberative power? Which practices undermine such an understanding? How could the latter be made more liberative?
3. What aspects of its social context (i.e. local, national, and global issues) should the church address in its education programmes? How might it do so? What theological themes speak to those issues?
4. What makes a relationship public or private? What are examples of these kinds of relationships? Do these examples reinforce or challenge exclusion and domination?
5. What examples have you seen of baptism, teaching, and nurture for mission, as the essay describes them? What are the strengths and weaknesses of these examples?

The Third Mark of Mission: To Respond to Human Need by Loving Service

Vicentia Kgabe

Introduction

In this chapter I will be exploring how young people can be equal partners in mission in their respective local churches. I will dispel the myth that says young people are the church of tomorrow, when there are visible signs that they are the church of today. This myth has been used in some cases to discourage and disempower young people from taking active and leading roles in the church. I will unpack the third Mark of Mission from its traditional understanding and explore how it can be used by the local church and young people to work and minister as equal partners in engaging in mission.

At the 2010 Centenary Celebration of the 1910 Edinburgh Mission Conference I was astonished by the under-representation of young people, even though one of the transversal topics was on youth and mission. The voice of the young people was not fully heard and they were barely seen, in terms of presenting papers or responding in large plenary sessions. The Anglican Communion had a good representation of young people at the conference – out of nine delegates, six were young people which was a balanced representation of the Communion. We not only had a good representation but we also had two of our delegates involved in writing and multimedia competitions hosted by the conference. Andy Thompson's essay '*Communities of the Spirit: The Missiology of Roland Allen in the Twenty First Century*' was selected by the panel as the most innovative approach to the study theme. Luiz Coelho's multimedia work best illustrated '*The Changing Face of Mission*'. These two contests were organized in an effort to increase youth participation and foster creative thinking within the Edinburgh 2010 process.

The Third Mark of Mission and Young People

The Third Mark of Mission is, '*To respond to human need by loving service.*' The churches have a long tradition of care through pastoral ministry and Christians are called to respond to the needs of people locally and in the wider human community. Traditionally this mark has been identified with works of compassionate service to those in distress and need, and it has also taken a form of social responsibility responding to the needs of those less fortunate. Bishop David Walker wrote,

> the Marks of Mission are not restricted to the description of the activity of some small core religious group directed towards the world outside. Rather they guide the Church towards identifying programmes of action to which all who would self-identify with the Christian faith can be called both the agents of mission and the objects of Mission.[1]

Acknowledging the traditional understanding of the mark, the question that arises from the Mark for me is whether the mark can only move us to respond with compassionate service to those in distress and need? What about those who are not in this situation; how does the Mark address them and their needs? I would like to suggest another way we can look at the Mark besides its traditional understanding. As a young person I have felt for some time now that not much is being done to involve young people fully in the life of the local church. Now young people are calling on the local church to respond and embrace them as equal partners in mission.

I have wondered how many members of the worldwide family of the Anglican Communion, especially young people, know about the Marks of Mission and for those who know about them; how have they integrated them into their worship, church life and witnessing in the communities to which they belong? I imagine the answer will vary from province to province, diocese to diocese and parish to parish. In my context, when I mentioned the Marks of Mission and asked how many knew about them including clergy, I was met with silence followed by questions of clarity and requests to explain myself. It seemed that many were hearing about the Marks of Mission for the first time when I shared them. I am encouraged to hear and read that in other parts of the Communion a lot has been done to incorporate the Marks of Mission into the life of the church. I am most excited by young people who are embracing the Marks of mission. An example is of the Episcopal Youth Event, ECUSA, where the young people pledged that, 'with the Anglican Marks of Mission as our charge, we will strive to engage the passion and energy of faithful youth, to embrace their call to ministry and to empower them to put their faith into action'.[2] The challenge facing us is not just to 'do' mission but 'to be a people of mission'. That is, we must allow every dimension of church life to be shaped and directed by our identity as a sign, foretaste and instrument of God's reign in Christ. And our understanding of mission needs to make that clear.

---

[1] D. Walker, 'Marks of Mission and ways of belonging: shaping the Anglican agenda for occasional churchgoers in the countryside', *Journal of Anglican Studies,* Vol 9, (August, 2010), 101.

[2] www.ecusa.anglican.org/eye2011 accessed, July 2011.

Avis states that mission 'is the good news of God's love, incarnated in the witness of a community, for the sake of the world.' [3] The working definition he gives for the mission of the church is, 'mission is the whole Church bringing the whole Christ to the whole world.' Working on this chapter I came across a number of definitions for mission. Here are two which capture something of my understanding: 'mission is the total action of God in Christ by the power of the Holy Spirit, creating, redeeming, sanctifying for the sake of the whole world.'[4] And 'mission is the creating, reconciling and transforming action of God, flowing from the community of love found in the Trinity, made known to all humanity in the person of Jesus, and entrusted to the faithful action and witness of the people of God who, in the power of the Spirit, are a sign, foretaste and instrument of the reign of God.'[5] I am of the opinion that the mission of the local church finds its roots in the 'Great Commission' (Matt 28: 16 – 20). In the Great Commission we read of three activities that Jesus commanded: making disciples, teaching and baptizing. Jesus had already shown the way, modelling all three tasks. He had called his disciples who came from different socio-economic backgrounds and now the whole world is to be called to discipleship both young and old.

Avis claims it is a common misconception that mission is a separate, discrete function of the Church, an activity in which it engages over and above its basic, bread-and-butter tasks.[6] It is often assumed that this triple ministry (word, sacraments, pastoral care) takes place independently of the Church's mission, as though mission were something added to the continuous, ordinary life of the body of Christ, rather than the outworking, the leading edge of its very existence. The biblical *locus classicus* of missiology, the 'Great Commission', suggests a rather different perspective – that mission is seen as the cutting edge of the total life of the church. That life is made up of many activities such as; prayer, worship, confession of faith, teaching and preaching, celebrating the sacraments, especially baptism and the Eucharist, providing pastoral care and oversight, enjoying Christian fellowship, bearing one another's burdens, bringing prophetic critique to bear on unjust social structures, and communicating the love of Christ to the suffering through compassionate service.

The definitions given are inclusive in their nature, but do all members of the community of faith especially young people feel welcomed, belonging, included and active participants in the mission of the church? In trying to find answers to this question, I looked back at some of the young people who participated at the Edinburgh 2010 Mission Conference. Jec Dan

---

[3] P. Avis, *A Ministry Shaped by Mission* (London: T&T Clark Ltd, 2005), 1.

[4] Lambeth Indaba Reflections, para 19, www.lambethconference.org/reflections/document.cfm.

[5] E. Johnson and J. Clark (eds), *Anglicans in Mission: A Transforming Journey* (London, SPCK 2000), 21.

[6] Paul Avis, *A Ministry Shaped*, 1.

Borlado from Asia wrote a paper on 'Mission, Youth and Power.' He wrote:

> today we are here in Edinburgh. Today, we are at our crossroads as the global church representing our own respective local congregations. The fullness of God's time has come to pursue new and fundamentally better participation in God's Mission in the world. Essential to this road towards new and better things is the young person; the young person being both a recipient and potential agent of the Mission.'[7]

Another young participant at Edinburgh 2010 Mission Conference Vineeth Koshy from India wrote,

> Youth is a state of life and mind when there is quality of thinking, predominance of courage and appetite for adventure. However, one of the alarming features of today's youth participation and leadership in the church is that the younger generation is in the 'exit-phase' and there may be various reasons for justifying the exit. We are forgetting that the gifts of the Holy Spirit are distributed equally and widely in the church. Therefore it is quite essential that the spiritual experience and expertise of every member must be recognised and drawn into the common spirituality of the local congregation. Thus the concern for the church must be broad-based involving the youth, women and children.[8]

Lerefolo from South Africa believes that, 'youth tends to be marginal in most proceedings and that results in their voices being silent.' She believes that it is 'high time we [church] move forward and identify youth as the mission practitioners of today. Without the voice of the young people the trends for the future mission will not be perceived soon enough for the church to act in light of the Gospel.'[9]

The State of Young People's Ministry in the Local Church

In my context (suspecting that this may be similar elsewhere) the ministry of young people and instructing them on what the church and mission is about, has been left to young people themselves or to someone who loves youth. If you are in a financially well-off parish this ministry will be the responsibility of a youth pastor. By doing this the local church abdicates its responsibility and sits back to judge how well the youth pastor or the volunteer is doing with the youth ministry. Martinson emphasises this observation by pointing out that, 'youth ministry belongs to God through the ministry of God's whole church. Youth ministry is the responsibility of the entire congregation through its elected, volunteered or paid representatives, the congregation as a whole needs to support the life and

---

[7] www.edinburgh2010.org/en/resources/papersdocuments.html
[8] Ibid.
[9] Ibid.

mission of young people in the church and community.'[10] The involvement of the whole church in maturing and supporting youth ministry will be helpful as young people in our churches come from such different situations. The social standing and the quality of the education they receive can vary enormously; some come from two parent homes while others are from single parent homes and we also have those who come from child headed homes due to HIV/AIDS and poverty. Many parishes in an urban setting will have young people on their own or with their families from rural or small towns who have migrated to those areas in search of a better life.

There is also a category of young people in our churches who have migrated from their countries due to socio-economic and political issues. Wild-Wood writes, 'migration is widespread on the African continent, but its relationship with Christianity has had little attention. Migration brings or hastens change by providing migrants with a new set of life experiences and negotiating an altered identity. In this interaction religious identity provides migrants with a framework for stability and flexibility during migration. Thus migration alters religious identity.'[11]

Doing Mission with Young People

Wild-Wood shares a story of a Tabu boy from the *L' Eglise Anglicane du Congo;* when he was growing up there were no groups for young people and participation in church affairs was considered to be the preserve of adults and young people were marginalised.[12] For Tabu and his counterparts things changed when they contested for change, the activities of the youth movement in their church produced a variety of reactions among those who were in leadership so that some embraced changed and others were less reluctant. In my opinion, there should be an intentional effort from those in church leadership to groom and expose young people to a greater scale of doing ministry and mission. Ward has challenged local church youth workers to enter the various subcultures of youth. He describes several groups of teenagers in his town of Oxford, England, who are distinct in their dress, music, and interests, and shows how they each must be reached from within their particular culture rather than from without.[13] Ward distinguishes between a theology of young people and a theology of youth ministry. He says,

---

[10] R. D. Martinson, *Effective Youth Ministry: A Congregation Approach* (Augsburg Publishing House: Minneapolis, 1988).
[11] E. Wild-Wood, *Migration and Christian Identity in Congo (DRC)* (Leiden: Brill, 2008), 1.
[12] Ibid.
[13] P. Ward, *Youth Culture and the Gospel* (Grand Rapids: Zondervan 1992).

> When groups of young people begin to speak of their encounter with God that's where a theology which is indigenous to them can begin to emerge. A theology of youth ministry, on the other hand, seeks to demonstrate how our understanding of God shapes and influences the practice of youth ministry…a theology of youth ministry must seek to be a distinctive expression of the gospel in light of the current social situation.[14]

Nel defines youth ministry in this manner, 'youth ministry is to, with and through the young people.'[15] This is an attempt to grant the youth their self-reliance and maturity as part of a local church. This understanding can be used in conjunction with the third mark of mission to say '*doing mission to and through the young people*', responding to their human needs and challenges, (the challenges may be local or international) such as social, spiritual, relational, ecological, financial, technological, cultural and gender related. A good example is of a group of young people in the Diocese of Johannesburg; calling themselves 'Transformers'. They gather monthly to minister, train and develop other young people in the diocese in areas of Christian leadership and spiritual formation. They help them grow from 'world performers' to 'God's Transformers'.[16] They also deal with social, political and economic issues that they are faced with as young people and seek a Christian way to respond to them. For an effective mission, the church must understand the soul and spirit of today's youth.

So what is the local church? The Edinburgh 2010 Report on Theme 5 defines it as, 'the people of God in the local context.'[17] The commonly known structure of the local church for both the Protestants and Roman Catholics is in the form of a parish. Yet there are emerging new forms that try to bind together the original apostolic core with new imaginative, less structured forms gathering in cafes, dance clubs, on riverbanks etc. Ward agrees with this to a point, especially on the emergence and need by other members of the body of Christ to develop new forms of a local church.[18] He advocates for a need to preserve the 'family' feel of the local congregation. He implies that the church is where people of all ages and types gather to worship God and fragmentation into different 'congregations' or churches flies in the face of the biblical emphasis on the power of the gospel to bring people together.

However, there is still a majority of Christians who are caught up in a model of a church which meets in a building that has been consecrated for worship with all the components of church housed under one building or on

---

[14] P. Ward, *Youth Work and the Mission of God* (London: SPCK, 1997), 25-27.

[15] M. Nel, *Youth Ministry: An Inclusive Congregational Approach* (Pretoria: Jeugbediening Publishers, 2000), 65.

[16] Young people aged 18-26 who are in leadership roles in their local parishes in the diocese of Johannesburg.

[17] D. Balia & K. Kim, *Edinburgh 2010: Witnessing to Christ Today* (Oxford: Regnum Books 2010), 117.

[18] Ward, *Youth Work*, 116.

the same hectare of land. And if we are to involve young people in doing mission, we have to reconsider what their views and perceptions are on what church and mission is and where it congregates and how it worships.

Young people dream of a church fully catering to their needs as church in the new and evolving context of 'common global culture'. As much as they are active participants in the life of a local and global church; the church continues to see and refer to them as the 'church of tomorrow…the church of the future' missing out on the value they add and as active participants of the church of today. Sandvig adds that, 'it has been said that youth are the future of the church. This may be true, but it is important to realize that while youth will eventually become the Church of tomorrow, they are also intricately involved in the formation and development of today's Church.'[19] Young people are not only the church of the future; they are a significant part of today's church. Young people have their perspectives, enthusiasm, energy, and gifts which are crucial if Christian ministry is to be inclusive, faithful and effective. The words of St. Paul to Timothy ring true when he said 'let no one despise your youth, but set believers an example in speech and conduct, in love, in faith, in purity (1 Tim 4:12). Young people who are involved in youth ministry are there to be prepared for adult church leadership.

The United Nations defines those persons between ages of 15 – 24 years as young people/youth.[20] It is estimated that 1.8 billion adolescents and youth in the world today account for nearly a third of the world's population, with just below 90 per cent living in developing countries, a proportion that will increase during the next 20 years. Archbishop Thabo Makgoba in his Charge at the 32nd Sitting of the Provincial Synod of the Anglican Church in Southern Africa (ACSA) made this statement:

> Did you know that about a quarter, 27%, of the world's population is aged 15 or under? Within ACSA though that figure is only 19% in the island of St Helena, elsewhere it ranges from 32%, about a third, in South Africa, rising to 46%, close to a half, in Angola. The youth are not merely the church of tomorrow; they are the church of today. Nurturing our young people, not only spiritually, is therefore a vital priority. This goal must inform every debate we have. Frankly, Synod is appallingly unrepresentative on this score![21]

The Anglican Church in North-East Congo is a ray of hope – in the year 2000 the church was predominately a young church.[22] It was young not simply because children under nineteen made up the majority of the congregation, not because it was constantly spreading to new areas, but because young people were influencing change within it. They were taken

---

19 www.edinburgh2010.org.

20 www.un.org/apps/news (United Nations website).

21 www.anglicanchurchsa.org/view.asp?ItemID=330&tname=tblComponent1&oname=News&pg=front.

22 Wild-Wood, *Migration and Christian Identity in Congo (DRC)*, 196.

seriously and seen as equals in doing mission; their numbers gave them a voice and turned their voice into positive outcomes for the church.

If the local church is to involve young people intentionally as missionary partners they must start at the local level, because it will be familiar, easy to identify with and relevant. And we need not seek resources outside of ourselves as there are plenty within and amongst us just waiting to be tapped. As we contextualise the mission among young people we need to be aware that economic, social, cyber and political issues have a great bearing in the way we do mission involving young people. Young people must be recognised and participate not only as followers but also as leaders.

Empowerment of the Next Generation

There is no clear definition of the concept of empowerment, especially one that could cross disciplinary lines. Empowerment can mean the following: 'to equip or supply with ability', 'to enable the process of increasing the capacity of individuals and groups to make choices and to transform those choices into desired actions and outcomes' and 'increasing the spiritual, political, social or economic strength of individuals and communities.'[23]

Empowering the youth starts with the realisation that they have a role to play and that they too possess the gifts and talents that will be integral for the mission of the church. Ward points out that children and youth are at the centre of attention in many of the stories the New Testament tells about the ministry of Jesus and the emergence of the Early Church. Nel affirms this when he says that, 'young people are part of the total congregation; ministry and mission and are not a separate entity.'[24] The local congregation should never think of the faith, the life and experience of young people as something separate from the faith, life and experience of the adult members. People need not reach a certain age before God becomes interested in them and starts working with and through them. The young people are part of the local church service to God because they share in God's relationship with God's people and are incorporated into the local church. Young people are not a separate group in the congregation. Even though they are unique and have a distinct character they are not apart from the rest. The relationship of God with believers and their children, as well as the nature of the local church as something created by God, make this impossible. Therefore, although young people, because of their distinct nature, require and should receive specific attention, they should still be approached and ministered to as an essential part of the local church.

---

23 William Morris (ed), *The Heritage Illustrated Dictionary of the English Language* (American Heritage, Publishing Co, 1973), 429.

24 Nel, *Youth Ministry*, 77.

Nowhere in the congregation can young people be neglected or ignored. The local church and her mission cannot consist only of adults, as it cannot consist only of young people. The young people have to be incorporated into every line of thought and received into every part of the ministry. They have to be taken into account, regardless of ministry on the agenda. The young people are the local church's responsibility and this responsibility is inalienable and non-transferable.

There are three steps that Borthwick suggests could be used to empower young people as equal partners in mission.[25] His suggestions are close to how we should practise the Third Mark by responding to human (young people's) need by loving service. The three steps are Modelling, Memories and Doers of Mission:

Modelling

Jesus' discipleship ministry might be summarized in the phrase 'follow me'. He built his ministry to his twelve chosen ones on the principle that experience is the best teacher. He never told them to do something that he did not exemplify for them. The adults and those in leadership of the local church are to model both the Christian life and Christian compassion for young people and others. Such modelling leaves a lasting impression on the spirit and hearts of the young people.

Memories

Teenage and adolescence stages are the most crucial periods for forming memories. Adults and local church leaders need to work hard to build an environment where positive memories for young people about God, church and her mission can be formed.

Doers of Mission

Participating at the Edinburgh 2010 Mission Conference, I realized that the future of mission work for the next century lies with the young people. Reaching and influencing young people should be part of our mission strategy. The seeds of desire need to be planted in the hearts of young people and this will help them grow into amazing servants of Christ both in the local and worldwide church. By exposing young people to the goals, visions and experience of mission, the church can influence young people to make plans for their future education and careers. Then young people can develop a deep sensitivity to the needs of mission work, mission workers and the needs of the poor and marginalised.

---

[25] P. Borthwick, *Organizing Your Youth Ministry* (Grand Rapids:Zondervan, 1988), 51.

Conclusion

Through our participation at the Edinburgh Mission Conference 2010, many of us have been exposed to a wide variety of schools of thought and interpretation on what is mission and how to do mission especially in the 21st century. However, the voice of the young people was not vocal enough. As a Communion we were present and well represented, and it is from this premise I feel that we need to carry this further, so that when we talk about *doing mission* and our actions being a measure of our response to Christ, we should do this as an inclusive family. In a paper she presented at the Edinburgh 2010 Mission Conference, Wendy Strachan, Children's Ministry Coordinator for Scripture Union International, said,

> a world fit for children [young people] cannot only be the mandate of the United Nations. It is surely the mission of the church in the next decades. When the next Edinburgh Mission Conference is held to explore how different ways of that mission are impacting our world, will children [young people] be prominent on the agenda? Will children [young people] be active and equal participants at the conference?[26]

Mission is the good news of God's love, incarnate in the witness of a community for the sake of the world; and as we respond to human need by loving service we do so too, with and through the young people, adults and the local church being our launching pad.

Discussion Questions

1. Read Joel 2:28; where do you situate the ministry of young people in the life of your local church.
2. Young people dream of a church fully catering to their needs; as much as they are active participants in the life of the local and global church, the church continues to see and refer to them as the 'church of tomorrow'. How is your local church currently preparing them for the leadership roles?
3. How can the local church develop and its young people be equal partners in Mission?
4. Young people have become missionaries of social and political transformation; how evident is this in your local church?
5. The Third Mark of Mission calls the church to respond to human needs by loving service. Cite examples of how you or your church has responded to the Mark.

---

[26] Wendy Strachan, 'Welcoming Children', in Anderson and Kim (eds), *Edinburgh 2010: Mission Today and Tomorrow* (Regnum Books, Oxford 2011), 287.

The Fourth Mark of Mission: To Seek to Transform Unjust Structures of Society

Irene Ayallo

Introduction

This is a reflection on mission as transformation. This understanding of mission is expressed in the fourth mark mission – to seek to transform unjust structures of society. My thesis challenges a perspective of mission which makes a distinction between evangelism and work for social change. In any cases and circumstances where people struggle with the 'courage to be' and the 'courage to hope', I argue that holistic mission entails transformation. It challenges all injustice which destroys God's intention of well-being for human beings and creation. Christian mission is primarily God's actions in everyday life (in its totality), corporate and individual. Mission is not a 'special' responsibility so that it is the work of just a few people and organisations. Rather, it is the responsibility of all Christians in dialogue with God. This encounter with God touches every part of our lives. It leads to 'holistic transformation'. Conceptually, I link holistic transformation to justice.

I illustrate such a holistic understanding of mission in two main sections. In the first section, I explain that a holistic understanding of mission begins with God's intention for human beings and for the world. In the Bible, this intention is expressed in many notions. For this essay, I appeal to the notion of *shalom*. Based on my understanding of the way *shalom* is used, I contend that God (in whose mission we are engaged) is concerned with all aspects of our lives. God refuses to come to term with 'anything'[1] which disturbs *shalom*. In the second section, I illustrate the holistic and transformative nature of mission by asking what is being transformed and citing some everyday experiences which affect the totality of people's lives. Poverty, discrimination, inequality, and 'politicised ethnicity' affect the spiritual, social, and psychological well-being of people. These experiences

[1] Unlike the fourth mark which only mentions 'structures', I use 'anything' to include behaviours, actions, ideologies, and institutions which destroy people's well-being and requires transforming.

seek transformative and liberating images of God, so that those directly affected by these injustices may reclaim *shalom*.

My perspective that mission is transformative, justice oriented, and holistic has been shaped mainly by my experience of serving in rural congregations in Kenya and by my experience of participating in the Edinburgh 2010 Mission Conference as an Anglican Communion delegate. Since I was made deacon in the Anglican Church of Kenya in 2004, I have served mostly in rural parishes and engaged with grassroots communities. The more I dialogue in mission with these congregations, the more I am always challenged by the way in which they often bring their lives and conditions into the gospel message and allow the gospel message to speak into that. For the majority of these men, women, and children, there is no element of their lives that is beyond the reach of the gospel message. The gospel message transforms their views of God, of Jesus Christ, and of the Holy Spirit. Likewise, they look to the gospel message to empower and enable them to have the necessary skills to meet their day-to-day needs such as education, health, food and proper shelter. To put it simply, the gospel message has to be holistic and transformative. These two elements of mission go together. I now turn to explain briefly my use of the notions 'transformation' and 'holistic'.

Definitions: Transformation and Holistic

The two most common definitions of the word 'transformation' in English Dictionaries are: it can describe an act and process of transforming. It is also a state, which indicates a change in form, appearance, nature or character. The *Oxford English Dictionary* is emphatic that this change is especially 'a radical' and a 'marked change'. It does not imply any predetermined outcomes. As such, I believe it is important to distinguish 'transformation' from 'development'. This is because 'development' is widely conceived and characterised by the belief in set goals, progression, or some predetermined quantitative outcomes. I use 'transformation' in this essay in a number of ways; it describes a process of 'marked' 'substantial' and 'radical' change. Transformation requires some form of 'doing' or action from the object (person, structure, or institution) doing the transforming and from the object being transformed. Through transformation an object moves from one point or state to another point or state. However, I ask further questions. What is being transformed and as compared against what? This, I believe, is the question that has caused the compartmentalization of mission, into either evangelism or social change. My simple answer to the question is that this transformation is 'holistic'. It includes and involves all of something, especially all of a Christian's physical, spiritual, mental, and social conditions. Transformation is both spiritual and material.

I am in accord with the Archbishop of Canterbury, who in his presidential address at the 1998 Lambeth Conference[2], said that God's mission is the transformation of life, not only of individuals but also of society. There are three important relationships in the life of a Christian. These are one's relationship with the self, their relationship with God, and their relationship with one another and with the rest of creation. Every institution, structure, people, and belief which significantly shapes these relationships is open to transformation. The transforming gospel of Christ, therefore, addresses both the personal and the corporate. The process of transformation begins by the fact that we are in Christ, and this knowledge needs to continue to reshape ourselves, our communities and our institutions. This shaping is what 'holistic transformation' is all about. We reshape them so that they closely reflect the purposes of God. What then is the purpose of God?

Primarily, holistic transformation involves asking some big questions: What is God's intention for human beings and for the world? What disturbs God's intention for the world? How can we, in dialogue, with God restore God's original intention for the world? These questions should be asked simultaneously. This is because they all contribute to God's intention for us and for the world.

Mission as 'Holistic Transformation'

The story of creation gives the picture of God's intent for creation.[3] In both the Old Testament and in the New Testament, a cluster of words are used to express the many dimensions and subtle nuances of this intention. Examples of such notions include love, justice, and righteousness. In this section, I argue that there is no distinction between these notions, they all express parts of the whole. The 'whole' is God's desire for *shalom*.

In the 21st century, each of the notions above, expressing God's intent, has been associated with certain perspectives of mission. For instance, the very many ways in which God's intention is expressed in the Scriptures has fuelled debates about whether mission should be about winning souls (often associated with righteousness and love) and establishing churches or whether it should be about identifying the work of the Spirit in the contemporary world (often associated with justice). I do not view these perspectives as two different commissions. However, it was my observation at Edinburgh 2010 that this tension was not only caused by the different expressions of God's intention for the world in the Scriptures but also it was shaped by hermeneutical, historical, and doctrinal debates. As

---

[2] The Archbishop's presidential address is available at www.lambethconference.org/1998/news/lc023.cfm.

[3] Robert George Bellingham, 'A Biblical Approach to Social Transformation' (DMin, Eastern Baptist Theological Seminary, 1987).

such, individuals and groups overemphasised some aspects of mission to the detriment of others.

In the seventies the two dominant, often opposing, perspectives of mission were widely described as the evangelism mandate and the creation mandate.[4] Subsequent debates on the same have revolved around understandings of the notions of love, justice, and righteousness. For instance, David Bosch implied that mission should focus more on the idea of love than justice because a focus on justice risks being purely political.[5] Arguments such as those advanced by Bosch suggest that love is a religious ethic while justice is a mere rational ethic. My contention is that, love and justice are closely related. One cannot stand without the other. Love is the root of doing justice, and doing justice is a way of loving. On the one hand, justice may be seen as providing the necessary conditions for loving and enabling love. On the other hand, justice is always done in a loving fashion. Duncan Forrester argued that love without justice is in danger of becoming sentimental and irrelevant. Justice without love easily becomes judgemental and uncaring. I agree with Forrester that doing justice and loving are complementary descriptions of the same kind of mission. Where justice is denied, love is also denied.[6] Evangelism is not just about preaching the gospel, winning souls and planting churches. It speaks with its clearest voice when it directly engages concrete socio-political issues in society such as advocacy, social empowerment, and solidarity with the poor.

In the past years, a number of documents have been produced to counter the separation of God's mission. Examples of such writing include those produced by the Consultation on the Church in Response to Human Need in Wheaton in 1983[7], the 1982 World Council of Churches' Ecumenical Affirmation of Mission[8], and the most recent Lausanne Conference 2010[9]. A similar argument is also found in the majority of literature by liberation theologians, Christian agencies of social development, and human rights action groups. Liberation theology, in its many forms, confirms that mission unavoidably has to deal with the questions of the poor and unjust socio-political structures. God is not removed from problems of suffering and injustice.

---

[4] John R. W Stott, *Christian Mission in the Modern World* (Downers Grove: IVP, 1975); Ronald J. Sider and John R. W Stott, *Evangelism, Salvation and Social Justice* (Bramcote: Grove Books, 1977).

[5] Willem Saayman, 'David Bosch – Some Personal Reflections', *Mission Studies: Journal of the International Association for Mission Studies* 26, no. 2 (2009).

[6] Duncan B. Forrester, *Just Sharing: A Christian Approach to the Distribution of Wealth, Income and Benefits* (Augsburg: Fortress, 1987), 77-78.

[7] Document available at www.lausanne.org/transformation-1983/overview.html.

[8] Statement available at www.religion-online.org/showchapter.asp?title=1573&C=1525.

[9] Statement available at www.lausanne.org/documents/CapeTownCommitment.pdf.

A broader interpretation of evangelism and social change is more authentic and sustainable than an extremely narrow perspecptive. For instance, defining evangelism as purely preaching the gospel or food-for-faith would be irrelevant to the concrete needs of rural communities such those which I have served. Similarly, social action such as solidarity, empowerment, and advocacy are strategic ways of engaging in opposing unjust social and political structures at all levels of society but can be ineffective if they are not articulated and implemented hand-in-hand with the preaching of the gospel. I believe that the gospel provides Christians with goals and values. These are important because often unjust structures are the result of wrong or misdirected goals and values. Holistic mission takes place only when there is expansion of freedom and removal of all types of un-freedoms, and where there is a process of marked and radical change in our societies. However, my perspective does not deny the problematic nature of notions of justice and love in the Scriptures and in their modern usage.

In explaining such difficulties, it is easy to separate key elements of mission. For instance, the meaning and the practice of justice is contentious. The dilemma is not easily resolved given the hundreds of biblical texts in the Old and New Testaments which speak explicitly about justice and hundreds more which refer to it implicitly.[10] Osborn Booth states that, in the Old Testament only there are eleven possible meanings associated with justice.[11] But, despite its many usages, it is widely accepted that justice is primarily an attribute of God. All true acts of justice find their source in the person of God, therefore carrying with it God's demand. It is rooted in God's character (Ps 37:30) and God requires that justice be done (Mic 6:8). Because justice is rooted in the very being and actions of God, Nicholas Sagovsky contends that justice is the very foundation of which there is a world at all, God intended the well-being of human beings and of the world.[12] Miroslav Volf and Duncan Forrester also acknowledge the

---

[10] For more reading on the problematic nature of 'justice' in Scriptures, see Walter Brueggemann, 'Old Testament Theology and the Problem of Justice', in *Theology of the Old Testament: Testimony, Dispute and Advocacy* (Minneapolis: Fortress Press, 1997). Walter J. Houston, *Contending for Justice: The Ideology and Theology of Social Justice in the Old Testament*, Library of Hebrew Bible/Old Testament Studies (London: Continuum, 2006). Karen Lebacqz, *Justice in an Unjust World: Foundations for a Christian Approach to Justice* (Minneapolis: Augsburg, 1987); Christopher D. Marshall, *The Little Book of Biblical Justice: A Fresh approach to the Bible's Teachings on Justice*, The Little Books of Justice & Peacebuilding (Intercourse, PA: Good Books, 2005).

[11] Hemchand Gossai, *Justice, Righteousness and the Social Critique of the Eighth-Century Prophets*, vol. 141, American University Studies Series VII, Theology and Religion (New York: Peter Lang, 1993), 6.

[12] Nicholas Sagovsky, *Christian Tradition and the Practice of Justice* (London: SPCK, 2008), 32.

difficulty of justice in the modern or non-religious usage of the concept.[13] Volf argues that there is no easy solution to the problem of 'clashing justices'. Everyone who asks a philosopher today, 'what is just?' must reckon with the counter question, 'whose justice?' and 'which justice?' But when justice struggles against justice, at least one must be false.[14] For my reflection, the true justice is the one which is in accord with God's intention for human beings and for the world.

Shalom

Nevertheless, instead of furthering the divide between notions of justice and love or justifying one over the other, I emphasise *shalom* which entails all the notions above. A similar holistic expression of mission is expressed in the New Testament, in the coming of the 'Kingdom of God'.[15] *Shalom* reaches out to feelings, intuitions and actions. It reaches out to what makes a person. *Shalom* embraces all of human life, and the life of the world. It reaches out to singing, crying, laughing and hoping. *Shalom* reaches out to food and hunger, water and thirst, fatigue and sleep.[16] It reaches out to nakedness and clothes, sickness and health, hopelessness and seeds of hope. Simply *shalom* is for everyone, to be experienced everywhere. It is a gift of God given to everyone. Ideally, any concept of mission founded on *shalom* is holistic. It is also against any power which destroys God's intention for wholeness, peace and harmony of creation. *Shalom* is a notion which embodies justice, love, and righteousness. *Shalom* is a concept involved in the maintenance of relationships within the community and with God. It is enacted and implemented concretely in human practice as the overall intent of God for the world,[17] as I seek to show using the following examples from the Old Testament and from the New Testament.

Shalom permeates Old Testament themes for transformation. First, God intended *shalom* since the foundation of creation. This aspect is mainly expressed in the book of Genesis. There are three relationships described in Genesis which preserve *shalom*. These include the relationships between people and God, between individuals and society, and between humans and

---

[13] Miroslav Volf, *Exclusion & Embrace: A Theological Exploration of Identity, Otherness, and Reconciliation* (Nashville: Abingdon Press, 1996). Duncan B. Forrester, *Christian Justice and Public Policy* (Cambridge: Cambridge University Press, 1997).

[14] Volf, *Exclusion & Embrace*, 197, 202.

[15] The notion/concept of the 'Kingdom of God' is already significantly explored by my colleague – the Reverend Kwok Keung Chan.

[16] Valdir Raul Steuernagel, 'To Seek to Transform Unjust Structures of Society (i)', in Andrew Walls and Cathy Ross (eds), *Mission in the Twenty-First Century: Exploring the Five Marks of Global Mission* (London: Darton, Longman and Todd, 2008), 63.

[17] Brueggemann, 'Old Testament Theology and the Problem of Justice', 66-67.

the world. Each of these relationships has implications for the mission of God. These are that people and the world are God's creation, people can commune with God, and that men and women are responsible to God. Because people and the world are God's creation, they do not exist independently and God is interested in, concerned for, human life and welfare. God's mission, therefore, concerns the totality of life. The relationship between individuals and society is also vital in the fulfilment of God's intention for the well-being of the world. In Genesis 2, God's desire is that equity and harmony characterise the relationships between individuals and their societies. As such, beliefs and practices which make some people second class citizens and/or second class human beings are unbiblical and disturb *shalom*.

Second, God expresses *shalom* through the Exodus event. Chapters 1-15 of Exodus are narrative accounts of an event which begins with the biblical nation Israel crying out to God for the suffering they were experiencing at the hands of the Egyptians. An entire nation was kept in slavery, they were oppressed by hard labour, they were mercilessly beaten and they were killed. God responded to their call by engaging with them, raising up a reluctant leader among them and eventually rescuing them from their suffering. In this event, God refuses to make peace with any kind of power which destroys well-being. The experiences of oppression in Egypt inhibited Israel's ability to develop and exercise their capacities, express their needs, thoughts and feelings. The Egyptians exploited the Israelites' labour, they marginalized them and they made them feel powerless.[18] These socio-political dimensions of reality experienced by the Israelites, which express the absence of *shalom,*[19] are countered by the revolutionary character of God who refused to accept the disturbing of *shalom*. God restored *shalom* by setting the nation Israel on course to establish itself as a nation and to be the subject of its own history.[20]

The main force of the Exodus 'event', according to Brueggemann, is to restore wholeness by establishing justice. God, in whose mission we are engaged, is shown to be a resilient and relentless advocate and agent of justice. God's justice entails the reordering of power arrangements on earth. God's justice is implemented and enacted concretely in human practice, and not in some kind of a vacuum. The Exodus event exemplifies an understanding of mission which advocates inclusivity and a radical redistribution of social goods and powers. It acknowledges the existence of an unequal and destructive distribution of various forms of goods in the world, and that the well-being of the household of God requires that social goods and power be shared. It is the kind of transformation which

[18] Cf. Ex. 5.

[19] Cf. Mic 2:1-2; Am 4:1; 5:14-15; Isa 1:16-17.

[20] Brueggemann, 'Old Testament Theology and the Problem of Justice', 741.

inherently destabilizes the status quo. It is not inclined to maintain the present order of things. This is holistic mission.

A third example in the Old Testament of God's intent for *shalom* is expressed in the making of laws. These laws are mostly found in four sections.[21] The Ten Commandments give the basic requirements God set for His people. The Book of the Covenant includes instructions about justice and compassion for the poor. The laws in Leviticus mostly contain instructions for the priests. And the Deuteronomic Law contains the preaching of Moses on how to live to please God and help one another. There are cases when these Old Testament laws contradict one another, and because of this they are highly debatable. Nevertheless, the purposes of these laws can be grouped into three headings. These include laws to restrain and protect the poor and vulnerable. These laws are contrasted with the autocratic disregard for human life in Egypt. A second category of laws could be said to have existed to create a common good. The poor and vulnerable had to be protected to allow the common good which is intended by God to flourish. In particular, these laws were established to enable, create and sustain a just and equitable society. For instance, disparity between rich and poor was to be resisted because everything belonged to the community, all bore the image of God, and all were valued by God. The concentration of wealth in the hands of one person or group posed the dangers of that person thinking they were of more value than others and therefore misusing the power which such wealth gave them. Third, the laws provided a model. They described what an ideal society, relationship, or behaviour should be like. Holistic mission recognises that even laws can protect and disturb *shalom*, depending on how they are established and implemented. Just laws contribute to the preservation of *shalom* because they establish justice in society and protect vulnerable people from across the different strata of society.

Fourth, the perspectives of the Old Testament prophets express God's intent for human beings and the world. In the face of oppression, God raised up the prophets to plead the cause of the poor and to remind those in power of the standards of God's justice.[22] The prophets combined the call for spiritual renewal with the demand for social justice. They were concerned with the use of property, individual rights, and the abuse of institutional power. For instance, Isaiah describes what God wants to see happen in human community.[23] God desires a community in which children do not die, old people live in dignity, people who build houses live in them,

---

[21] These include the Ten Commandments (Ex. 20:1-7), The Book of the Covenant (Ex. 21-23), and The Levitical Law (Leviticus), The Deuteronomic Law (Deut. 5:6-22).

[22] Cf. Am 2:7, 4:1, 5:11, 5:12; Joel 3:2; Isa 1:23, 10:1-2, 41:17, 58:6-10; Jer 5:28; Ezekiel 22:29; Mic 2:2, 3:11, 6:10-11, 7:3; Zeph 3:1, 3:4.

[23] Raymond Fung, *The Isaiah Vision: An Ecumenical Strategy for Congregational Evangelism* (Geneva: WCC, 1992).

and those who plant vineyards eat the fruit (Isa 65:20-23). As Fung states, the vision of such a just community is not about paradise. It has to do with human history, with the here and now. To work towards this end, where people live in dignity and their needs are met is to do God's will. To work for the 'Isaiah Agenda' is to help make God known to the world, and to let God reveal himself in the world. Children dying, old people disregarded, and workers and peasants going hungry are simply not acceptable in the eyes of God. The claims of these people are divinely legitimate, and their voices have to be heard. Holistic mission includes hearing and giving voice to the marginalised.

There are also examples of holistic transformation in the New Testament. In the New Testament, the gospel message is centred on the ministry of Jesus Christ. In him and through his life, death, and resurrection, Jesus is bringing about the restoration of human beings' relationships with God, with each other in society, and with the whole creation. Also, the gospel announced by Jesus in his words and actions is the gospel of the Kingdom. This gospel speaks against all evils which alienate people from God, and which spoils God's original intention of wholeness for people and the creation. There are five signs generally associated with the presence of the Kingdom of God. They are: Jesus in the midst of people in their cultures and communities, the preaching of the gospel, miracles of healing, the miracle of conversion and new birth, and the fruit of the Spirit in the lives of Christians (Galatians 5).[24] These signs and features should be present in any programme or movement seeking to extend and demonstrate the presence, the reality, and the priority of the Kingdom of God in human communities. Moreover, Jesus linked the good news inescapably with the poor. He described the good news as especially good news for the poor and the vulnerable. It had special relevance to them because their very position of marginality disturbs *shalom*. Therefore Jesus announced, demonstrated, and implemented the good news by identification and solidarity with the poor and vulnerable.

The examples above from the Old Testament and the New Testament demonstrate that holistic transformation is a joint enterprise between God and humanity in history. It is not just a mechanistic or naturalistic process. Oppression and injustice, alienation, poverty and other social and institutional ills destroy God's purpose for creation. For this reason, transformation is required. Transformation does not root people out of their contexts, but changes their circumstances as well as themselves. Ideally, the people are given the power, abilities, and opportunities to change their situations. Wayne Bragg suggests some helpful ways of reflecting on holistic transformation in mission.

First, mission as transformation is life sustaining. Mission must provide people with adequate life sustaining goods and services. Second,

[24] Bellingham, 'A Biblical Approach to Social Transformation'.

transformation is also about freedom. Throughout history, people have struggled to change their societies by seeing their goals in terms of freedom from subservience and slavery. Christian mission must work to liberate people from bondage, and also from the bondage of themselves (Jn 8:36). Third, transformation is about participation. Mission as transformation requires that affected people play a meaningful and active part in their own transformation. True transformation comes about only when people are able to act upon their own needs as they perceive them and progress towards a state of wholeness in harmony with their own context.[25]

With these characteristics of transformation in mind I now turn to highlight examples, conditions and encounters which beg an understanding of holistic mission. Because this essay is a reflection, I do not seek to offer step-by-step ways of dealing with the cases of injustice which I am highlighting. It is my belief that such an exercise is contextual. Ways of achieving transformation are effective if developed in dialogue between God, churches or agencies, and those directly affected by those injustices.

What is Being Transformed?

As a participant at Edinburgh 2010, I observed that there were differing understandings of mission among participants. As I stated at the beginning of this essay, some of these perspectives would have even been contradictory. I noticed that a perspective of mission as holistic transformation was, however, readily and best understood within contexts where people struggle with 'the courage to be' and 'the courage to hope' because of their circumstances. Samuel Kobia, while explaining the meaning of these phrases which were first suggested by Paul Tillich paid particular attention to an African context. Kobia explained that these phrases are animated in contexts where circumstances prevent people from affirming themselves, their life and their community, where people are anxious and face conditions which generally mitigate against this essential self affirmation.[26] How then does mission cause people to act out of hope, to be forward looking, to turn fear into hope, and to acquire positive attitudes that free them from reliance on the past as a place of retreat?

At Edinburgh 2010, examples of injustice and the urgency of a transformational understanding of mission was offered under the theme of 'Mission and Power'. For instance, Graeme Mundine discussed the experiences of Australian Aboriginal people. Mundine compared the biblical story of Lazarus (Jn 11: 43) to the experiences of Aboriginal

---

[25] Wayne G. Bragg, 'From Development to Transformation', in Vinay Samuel and Chris Sugden (eds), *The Church in Response to Human Need* (Grand Rapids, Michigan: William B. Eerdmans, 1987), 44.

[26] Samuel Kobia, *The Courage to Hope: The Roots for a New Vision and the Calling of the Church in Africa* (Geneva: Risk Books, 2003).

people. In particular, Mundine explained that Australian Aboriginal people are still 'entombed'.

> They are entombed by poverty; by violence; by the effects of colonization; the legacy of missionaries; by exclusion; by racism; by more than 200 years of having land taken and culture trampled and by policies and practices from Governments, Churches and others which are designed literally, and metaphorically, to keep us bound and hidden, out of sight, behind the tomb stone.[27]

For the Australian Aboriginal people, mission as transformation involves asking questions such as how to go about the necessary work of setting people free from the yoke of imperialism and colonialism. Additionally, it requires a critical examination of resources that are available for indigenous people to be part of the mission and vision of setting them free. This process is important because when indigenous people suffer from the twin 'isms' (imperialism and colonialism) the entire church suffers, as well as their respective nations. Mundine concluded that Australian Aboriginal people are looking to churches to walk with them as they throw off things that oppress them. They are looking to be empowered. They are looking for a change of paradigm of living out the church experience. Mundine noted that the 'White Western European Church' does not have all the answers and is not the only way to experience and live church. Indigenous people are equal partners in the creation of the community of church in the present and the future. 'We need the mainstream church to listen – not to impose; to learn – not to dictate. Open your hearts and minds to what indigenous people offer and then we can walk together to live the life (to which) Christ has called each and every one of us.'[28]

Similarly, in most African contexts, particularly in Kenya, mission faces issues such as politicised ethnicity (commonly known in Kenya as tribalism). Tribalism and ethnicity do not necessarily constitute a negative connotation or identification.[29] Defined in a traditional sense, ethnicity simply implies a group of people sharing common consciousness based on language, culture, and common ancestral heritage. It is a cultural, economic, political as well as a religious issue. Ethnic identification in Kenya and most African countries is quite strong such that various ethnic groups consider themselves distinctive and would like to maintain their identities. These are reflected in how individuals associate in social, cultural, political, religious, and economic spheres. However, recent developments in Kenya that led to tribally inspired genocides and violence

---

[27] Graeme Mundine, 'Mission and Power', (a paper presented at the Edinburgh 2010 Mission Conference 2010). This paper is available at http://ncca.org.au/files/Natsiec/Mission_and_Power_Edinburgh.pdf

[28] Mundine, 'Mission and Power'.

[29] Thanks to Bishop Mark McDonald for explaining to me that 'tribalism' and 'ethnicity' are in fact liberating concepts for communal cultures and for Indigenous people.

have demonstrated the dangers of 'tribalism' and 'ethnicity', particularly when they are politically manipulated.[30] Groups and individuals continue to deliberately mobilise tribal awareness to achieve political and economic objectives. They remind tribes of their differences, and they tell the tribes that these are irreconcilable. In Kenya, as in most African countries, tribalism has been the home of oppositional politics. It has and directly continues to determine access to national resources, public participation in national issues, allocation of burdens and benefits, and access to major decision making bodies. Tribalism is a major contestation of power in almost all spheres, including in churches. Tribalism continues to destabilise societal harmony in Kenya, and our mission with God. In 1992, it was estimated that 1, 500 people died and over 30,000 were displaced across the country as a result of what was dubbed 'ethnic clashes'.[31]

Mission as holistic transformation encounters tribalism, and makes it possible for people in contexts such as Kenya to transcend 'tribalism' which has imprisoned their mentality. But the situation is further complicated by the revelation that historical mission activities have contributed to politicised ethnicity. Mwaura explains that due to comity agreements that were signed to deal with denominational proliferation in countries such as Kenya, Zambia and South Africa, certain mission agencies were allocated geographical areas that coincided with ethnic boundaries. Therefore these missions and their African churches acquired an ethnic face. Nevertheless, Kobia argues that mission as transformation challenges people to venture beyond their tribal boundaries towards the wide horizons and open spaces where the rest of humanity may be encountered and appreciated.[32] Mission as transformation encourages freedom and reconciliation, so that people can interact and enjoy unrestricted exchange of ideas. The more people interact with the other outside tribal confines, the more they will learn to appreciate the commonality of their aspirations and social interests. 'Otherness ceases to represent the unknown, to be feared and resisted, and becomes instead a gateway to new opportunity and unimagined beauty.'[33] Mission as transformation is 'life-widening'.[34]

Mission also meets conditions of indignity and worthlessness. For instance, the continent of Africa is often summarised in pictures of gloom; people die of hunger, children are suffering and are diseased, men and

---

[30] Nic Cheeseman, 'The Kenyan Elections of 2007: An Introduction', *Journal of Eastern African Studies* 2, no. 2 (2008).

[31] Philomena Njeri Mwaura, 'Christian Identity and ethnicity in Africa: reflections on the gospel of reconciliation', in Diane B. Stinton (ed), *African Theology on the Way: Current Conversations* (London: SPCK, 2010), 129, 31.

[32] Kobia, *The Courage to Hope*: 5.

[33] Cf. Gal 3, Eph 2.

[34] The concept of 'life-widening' has been discussed by my colleague, the Rev Kwok, in the chapter on the First Mark of Mission in this volume.

women fight against one another, and young people run aimlessly on the streets holding machetes killing almost everyone along their way. It is the dark, if not dangerous, continent where death and disease are almost taken for granted. Foreigners who dare to visit or to make Africa their home are either brave or foolhardy. It is where corruption is endemic and savage brutality is to be expected. It is a place where almost nothing works, where positive news is almost a miracle. While it is a fact that Africa struggles with crucial issues of poverty, corruption, poor leadership and HIV/AIDS among other diseases, it is also true that the continent struggles with the dark and hopeless image that the world knows; the continent struggles to show her countless blessings, riches, diversity, happy moments and unique contribution to the household of God where ideally every member and all faith communities are equal. It is not about being wrong or right but the failure to recognise that there are occasions when Africa laughs because of its peoples' own efforts. This negative image is detrimental to the place, integrity and dignity of Africans and African churches in mission on the global stage. In practice, this image affects the continent's role as a partner and agent of mission.

Kwame Labi's words best describe this unbalanced relationship. He claims that Africans and people of African descent are still placed on the lowest rung of the race ladder. There is hardly any race that does not somehow consider itself a little better than the African.[35] Because of the dehumanisations which result from such stereotyping, the overwhelming majority of Africans suffer from a certain sense of inferiority. It has gone on for so long so that a majority of Africa's masses have grown to believe that they are inherently inferior to other people. This is a feeling that cuts across a wide spectrum of Africa's populations and is deeply embedded in the psyche of the people. In the past, in mission partnerships Africa has always been the recipient and the perpetual receiver. Undoubtedly, it has promoted unequal and unhealthy models of relationships. It has promoted partial rather than mutual vulnerability.

Conversely, mission as transformation is life affirming and life-widening. It involves a complete change of attitudes and relationships, such as that of the giver-receiver kind of relationship. It entails enabling, complete renewal of mind and freedom that comes with being a child of Christ. And a true account of transformation has to be based on a balanced and critical socio-historical analysis, not a biased one. The question of human dignity and worth of a person is best understood in terms of the nature of being created by God, as a human being. Thus mission as transformation in the African context becomes a restoration of people's dignity and sanctity of life. It is the call to awaken the hearts and minds of Africa's people, giving hope for a new life of abundance and fulfilment. A

[35] Kwame Labi, 'Transforming Ecumenism in Africa in the 21st Century', *Ecumenical Review* 53, no. 8 (2001).

controversial African economist calling for the withdrawal of developmental assistance in Africa has rightly noted that Africa suffers from a severe PR problem. Consequently, Africa cannot become an equal partner in any circles, including mission, at a global level until this problem is addressed.[36] Mission as transformation will provide solutions to encounter the PR problems that Africa suffers. We will promote relationships based on concepts of networking and partnerships – not pity. These concepts will restore dignity and self-worth.

Mission also encounters the 'youth crisis'. In a Kenyan context, youth is defined more by socio-cultural factors such as rites of passage and less by chronological age. As it is, response to youth issues is significantly influenced by cultural representations (which vary from tribe to tribe) often ordering the relations between age groups and generations. These are rooted in worldviews, social memories, values and ritual performances and are manifest in spheres such as gender relations. It is common to find these values transplanted to relationships in church settings. However, for legal purposes youth include those within the age groups of 18-35 years. Globally, mission with youth is shaped by the 'bigger picture', that is youth experiences within the wider society. A United Nations report provides this picture by describing that there are over 200 million youth living in poverty, 130 million youth are illiterate, 88 million unemployed and 10 million youth living with HIV/AIDS.[37] Moreover, youth interventions are driven by negative stereotypes of young people, including delinquency, drug abuse and violence. Concretely, youth in Kenya face a myriad of challenges.

Youth is an ambiguous category to discuss, mainly because of the dynamic nature of this group and the ever changing social spaces within which they participate. Nevertheless, youth are the majority in Kenya – over 50%. But this demographic dominance often disguises the fact that youth are vulnerable to a host of factors which affect their self-identity and security. Youth are located at the centre of the country's opportunities as well as at the centre of the challenges cited above. The struggle for limited resources in Kenya exacerbates their vulnerability. Additionally, the population of young people continues to increase within a context of a malfunctioning state, which has generally led to decline in their well-being and social advancement. Consequently, youth are over-represented in risky behaviours and activities such as criminal activities, to which they are easily recruited. Nevertheless, I have observed youth in Kenya show tremendous efforts to survive. The number of youth groups, formed for socio-economic reasons, are increasing. They are attempting to empower themselves through educative programs and by creating income generating

---

[36] Dambisa Moyo, *Dead Aid: Why Aid is not Working and How There is Another Way for Africa* (London: Penguin Books, 2009).

[37] United Nations, 'World Youth Report 2005', (2005). This report is available at www.childoneurope.org/issues/child_participation/b_39.pdf.

activities. Within the Anglican Church of Kenya, about one quarter of the priests in most dioceses and those going for ministry formation are youth. However, this figure is still not proportionate to the youth who are members of the church. The youth are undeniably speaking out.

A common discourse in most circles in Kenya is that 'youth are the leaders of tomorrow'; that they will at some point in time take up leadership positions in social and political life. However, this remains an ambiguous statement both in theory and in practice. First, it seems to imply that this transition comes with various stages of life – the young will be leaders when they cease to be young. Second, it could mean that the youth will rise up to claim power as youth and therefore be the leaders of tomorrow. Well, the former is the dominant understanding of this statement. Conversely, I wonder whether the handing over of power will be done willingly and trustingly, or through acts of rebellion. As the situation stands, even within church circles, it seems the handover may be regrettably a complete overhaul. Barbara Trudell concludes that the desire to overturn established authority and break the mould of tradition is a powerful and natural urge of the young.[38]

Likewise, in most societies youth or youthfulness is admired and at the same time considered problematic and in need of rescuing. Consequently, youth are often excluded and/ or exclude themselves from leadership positions, decision-making bodies and self-governance because of presumed lack of confidence and skills. My ministerial experience as a young female priest reinforces these observations. There is a widening gap between people of different age groups within the Church. In the Anglican Church, this gap is reinforced by a system commonly known as departments. Most Provinces and Dioceses have separate departments for youth, women, children, and men. Indeed, these institutionalised groupings enable churches easily to handle the interests and age-appropriate developmental issues of each group. However, from an ideological perspective, they have also been used to exclude others from the centres of power within the churches. Departments have become sites for power struggles. Such struggles can be deduced from stereotypes and statements one group uses to describe the other group. For instance, on many occasions I have heard youth refer to older members of the parish as outdated, buffers to freedom and, at the extreme, social enemies. Likewise, older members can view the youth as rebellious, dependent, and at the extreme, socially inferior. Additionally, materials for mission to the youth are often based on 'how to' models as Michael Hughes has convincingly

[38] Barbara Trudell, 'Introduction: Vulnerability and Opportunity among Africa's Youth' in Barbara Trudell et al. (eds), *Africa's Young Majority* (Edinburgh: Centre of African Studies, University of Edinburgh, 2002), 2.

explained.[39] In my opinion, such thinking will also affect mission to these groupings. Yet mission as transformation seeks to reveal and address structures that promote mishandling of power.[40]

The examples that I have cited above all show how the spiritual transformation of the Gospel goes hand in hand with the material transformation – love and justice as inseparable aspects of mission. Moreover, mission entails day-to-day experiences. These experiences affect every being and elements of people's lives. Mission as transformation, as I have argued throughout, establishes conditions where human beings and the world may enjoy wholeness of life.

Conclusion

I began this paper by stating that in mission, we cannot separate evangelism from social work and social work from evangelism. To make such a distinction equals misunderstanding the mission of God. I illustrated the holistic nature of God's mission in two sections, arguing that mission begins with God's intention for human beings and for the world; in *shalom* God desires that all people may be whole, live in peace and in harmony. I also illustrated citing real life experiences such as tribalism and marginalisation that we cannot place our lives into compartments, such as the spiritual and the social. In contexts such as in Kenya where people constantly struggle with the 'courage to be' and the 'courage to hope', injustices touch the very being of people; and God in mission meets people in the totality of their lives. The transformation in mission changes all aspects of life.

My reflection in this paper has, in principle, shown that mission is holistic. Holistic mission entails transformation, which is a marked and radical change. Mission as holistic transformation makes no distinction between evangelism and social change. These are key concepts of mission. They cannot have a life of their own. This is because whenever social change is attempted it cannot be done without relation to God in Christ. It cannot be accomplished without reference to and relation to what Christ offers to people. Mission as transformation is a commitment to change it in the direction of abundant life, justice, righteousness and love. It is a commitment to return to *shalom*.

---

[39] Michael E Hughes, *Young Hearts Be Free: Christian Youth Ministry and a Theology of Liberation* (Auckland, New Zealand: Churches Youth Ministry Association, 2004).

[40] The issue of youth and power in mission has been addressed by another author in this book – the Venerable Vicentia Kgabe.

Discussion Questions

1. Is transformation in and through mission important to you or to your church? Why?
2. What does transformation mean in your context?
3. Who does the 'transforming', and how?
4. What happens after transformation?

The Fifth Mark of Mission: To Strive to Safeguard the Integrity of Creation and Sustain and Renew the Life of the Earth

Kapya John Kaoma

The Face of the Earth in 2110

For three days, in June 2010, 297 delegates to Edinburgh 2010 – representing all major Christian traditions – wrestled with what it means to witness to Christ amidst various challenges of post-modernity. Among the many issues addressed was the impact of the ecological crisis on human life and the Earth in general. No better words prophetically captured the urgency of problem than the phrase "See you in 2110," which flashed on the screen on the final day of the conference. Judging by the age of the delegates at the conference, nobody is likely to live into the next century, much less 2110. In this regard, those words could have been meant to be a simple joke. However, amidst the occurring ecological crisis, they have serious eco-social and theological overtones.

The future of the natural world in the 22nd century will be determined by human attitudes towards Earth. Thus, how God's Earth looks in 2110 depends on how humanity will relate to planet Earth. Theologically, the Christian community ought to proactively respond to the worsening depletion of life-supporting planetary systems because the Earth is the Lord's. In addition, Earth is a sacramental 'place of divine mystery,'[1] hence another form of divine revelation. From these two theological observations, negative attitudes towards Earth are sins against the Creator Spirit. Irresponsible attitudes that have led to extreme deforestation, air and water pollution, land degradation, uncontrolled population growth and many other ecological predicaments are all sinful acts that call for immediate *metanoia*. But there is another reason for safeguarding Earth's integrity. Ethically, we are obliged to safeguard Earth as our only life sustaining home, and the home to countless future generations. Most importantly, the destruction of Earth will lead to a definite annihilation of all life on Earth.

[1] Elizabeth Johnson, 'Losing and Finding Creation in Christian Tradition,' in D.T Hessel and Rosemary R. Ruether (eds) *Christianity and Ecology* (Cambridge: Harvard University Press, 2000), 3.

How then can Christian mission, theology and ethics help in safeguarding the future of life?

The following themes do not by any means address all eco-social theological issues involved in answering the above question. Nonetheless, they provide some theological and moral basis for Christian involvement in safeguarding the Creation. The chapter argues that Earth-Care stems from two moral propositions: our God given mandate to care for Sacramental Earth (Gen1:26), and our moral obligations to future generations.

First, the chapter makes a case that Christians should address the ecological crisis because creation belongs to the Creator God. Second, it attempts to re-examine two important theological propositions from an ecological perspective; the doctrine of dominion and the concept of *Missio Dei.* Third, it examines the sacramental aspect of creation and explores the impact of the environmental predicament on Earth's community. Finally, the chapter advocates economic justice as essential in addressing the recurring ecological crises and suggests some practical steps that can aid Christian ecological witness today.

The Earth Belongs to God

The belief that all creation exists through and for the Creator is fundamental to Christian faith. Heaven and Earth are not products of chance but creations of the loving God, who declared the entire created order as 'very good' (Gen 1:26). Despite our self-promoted belief that we are different from Earth, the Bible maintains that humanity is a product of the dust or clay of Earth (*adamah*, the Hebrew for clay; Gen 2:9). Human dependence on Earth is reiterated in the biblical story of the Fall: 'For Earth you are, and to Earth you will return' (Gen 3: 19). Old Testament writers did not treat Earth, humanity or any other creature as above God. 'Doing so would be considered idolatry. Neither did they present Earth as something outside God's realm due to their belief that the Creator cared for every creature, big and small.'[2]

The Old Testament conviction that Earth belongs to a caring Creator is carried over into the New Testament, where the supremacy of Christ is linked to creation. The gospel of John asserts that Creation is the product of *logos* (John 1). Similarly, the letter to the Colossians identifies Christ as 'the firstborn over all creation and in him all things hold together' (Col. 1:15-20). The declaration that Jesus Christ is both the source and goal of life finds expression in other biblical books as well. Writing to the Romans,

[2] Kapya J. Kaoma, 'Missio Dei or Missio Creator Dei: Witnessing to Christ in the Face of Occurring Ecological Crisis,' in Kirsteen Kim and Andrew Anderson (eds) *Edinburgh 2010: Mission Today and Tomorrow* (Oxford: Regnum Books, 2011), 302.

Paul argues that 'For from Him and through Him and to Him are all things' (Rom 11:36) and in Christ, 'are all things.'(1 Cor. 8:6).

The above understanding invites a paradigm shift in Christology (Col 1:17-20). In essence, by virtue of being the source of life and ultimate life-self, Jesus can be said to be an ecological ancestor of all life. Being an ecological ancestor, Christ is not only connected to every creature but also is present in the same. Unlike a human ancestor whose life-giving power is limited to living descendants, Jesus is the origin-ancestor of all creation; visible and invisible. In other words, Christ is an ecological ancestor of all life. In Christological terms, Jesus is the knot that holds all life together on planet Earth. This Christology (which is informed by the African respect for ancestors) is crucial in safeguarding the creation. For Christ is not only the origin of human life; he is the life (cf. John 1:4) that holds the natural world together.[3]

Revisiting the doctrine of dominion

How does the above theological basis of Earth-care square with the much preached doctrine of dominion – the concept that advances the hypothesis that humans have a God-given mandate to exercise unlimited control over the natural world – which has been employed to dominate, exploit and abuse Earth, the poor and all life?

In his attempt to trace the historical root of the occurring ecological crisis, Lynn White Jr blamed the Christian doctrine of dominion for the exploitation of planet Earth and the ensuing ecological catastrophe. White argued that this doctrine informed Western social-economic and technological developments that regarded unlimited exploitation of the Earth's natural goods as divinely sanctioned. Despite his damning critique of Christianity, White argued that the solution to our ecological crisis must 'be essentially religious, whether we call it that or not.'[4]

Whether one agrees with White or not, religion is crucial to forming human values. But to blame the entire crisis on Christianity is to ignore Christian history, which reveals diverse religious attitudes towards Earth. Presenting a historical analysis of Christian missionary engagement with Earth-care, Dana Robert argues that each Christian generation has engaged 'nature in accordance with its own knowledge and values.'[5] Robert shows that while some Christians have destroyed nature, others have shown reverence to the natural world. For example, desert fathers (and mothers) such as Mar Paul, also known as the Prince of the Monks who was fed by a

---

[3] I have argued that the creation exists for Christ, who is the sole *telos* of creation. Ibid.

[4] Lynn White, Jr., 'The Historical Roots of Our Ecological Crisis,' www.uvm.edu/~gflomenh/ENV-NGO-PA395/articles/Lynn-White.pdf (accessed 1.11.2010).

[5] D. Robert, 'Historical Trends in Mission and Earth Care', *International Bulletin of Missionary Research,* 35, no. 3, July 2011, 123.

raven, the animal loving Abba Theon,[6] St. Francis of Assisi, missionaries such as David Livingstone[7] and Albert Schweitzer and contemporary missionaries, among them Marthinus Daneel, founder of African Earthkeepers in Zimbabwe, employed their Christian faith to care for Earth.

If Robert's argument, that 'knowledge and values' affect Christian attitudes towards nature, is valid, then we may ask how can our current knowledge about the workings of the planetary systems and the interconnectedness of life change the human – nature paradigm?

Although this knowledge has not yet found full expression in Christian circles, the impending ecological disaster has forced many Christians to re-visit human-nature relations. In 1979, Pope John Paul II brought the issue to the centre of Roman Catholic theology when he declared St. Francis of Assisi a patron Saint of ecology. Eleven years later, the Pope presented a moral argument when he insisted that the environmental crisis was a moral issue that had 'assumed such proportions as to be the responsibility of everyone.'[8] In 1989, the World Council of Churches established the relationship between peace, justice and the integrity of creation.[9] In the Anglican Communion, both 1998 and 2008 Lambeth conferences affirmed the Fifth Mark of Mission – 'to strive to safeguard the integrity of creation and sustain and renew the life on earth'[10] – as central to Christian identity. Edinburgh 2010 equally paid attention to addressing the exploitation of Earth. In Evangelical circles, the protection of Earth was equally addressed at 2010 Third Lausanne Congress of World Evangelization in Cape Town (2010).[11]

Despite this paradigm shift, in most parts of the world, the doctrine of dominion continues to influence human values towards the natural world.

---

[6] For detailed discussion on the Desert Fathers' attitudes to nature, see James Nash, *Loving Nature: Ecological Integrity and Christian Responsibility* (Nashville: Abingdon Press, 1991), 81-83.

[7] For a detailed discussion on Livingstone, see John Kaoma, 'Earthkeeping as a Dimension of Christian Mission: David Livingstone's attitude Towards Life: A Challenge to Earthkeeping Missions', in Rodney L. Petersen and Marian Gh. Simion (eds), *Tracing Contours: Reflecting on World Mission and Christianity* (Newton Center: BTI, 2010), 74-76.

[8] Quoted in *NMCCB Statement on the Environment: Partnership for the Future A Pastoral Statement of the Roman Catholic Bishops of New Mexico.* www.archdiocesesantafe.org/ABSheehan/Bishops/BishStatements/98.5.11.Environment.html; accessed 10/01/2008.

[9] See Robert, 'Historical Trends', 123.

[10] 'The Five Marks', www.anglicancommunion.org/ministry/mission/fivemarks.cfm (accessed 26.6.2011).

[11] See 'The Pew Research Center's Forum on Religion & Public Life: Global Survey of Evangelical Protestant Leader', 22.6.2011, 20. http://pewforum.org/uploadedFiles/Topics/Religious_Affiliation/Christian/Evangelical_Protestant_Churches/Global%20Survey%20of%20Evan.%20Prot.%20Leaders.pdf (accessed 6.26.2011).

In most African and Evangelical churches for example, the doctrine of dominion controls human-nature relations. But how can present knowledge inform our understanding of dominion?

The fact that a majority of non-Western indigenous religions do not view humanity as the ruler of creation *per se* but rather as a part of interconnected forces of life can inform Christian spirituality. As we shall see below, Africans reverence natural phenomena as instruments of divine mysteries. In some cases, sacred forests, certain animals and snakes, mountains, river sources and trees can be said to be ontologically superior to humanity.[12] The presence of a python, for example, is celebrated as divine visitation among many African cultures – among them the Igbo of Nigeria and Luo of Kenya.

Sadly, these traditional ecological cosmologies were denounced as evil while the nature-exploiting doctrine of dominion was promoted as divinely sanctioned and in line with Christian civilization. So as Christianity took root on African soil, so did the negative attitudes towards the natural world. For indigenous people therefore, conversion to ecological consciousness would imply rejecting the Enlightenment tainted Earth-denying theologies in favour of their nature loving cosmologies.

Revisiting the concept of Missio Dei

As with the doctrine of dominion, the concept of *Missio Dei* – the belief that God and not the Church is the centre of mission – needs re-examining in light of the enduring ecological crisis. Whereas those who gathered in 1910 saw the Church as the force behind mission, delegates to Edinburgh 2010 followed the German theologian Karl Hartenstein's argument that mission emanates from the triune God.[13] Although Andrew Kirk follows Hartenstein, he argues that "*missio Dei* springs from God's boundless and matchless love for the universe he has created, and particularly for the beings within it that bear his image." [14] While Kirk particularizes God's love to humanity, God's love for creation has no boundaries. In short, mission is an invitation to participate in God's purposes for the entire created order.

The above understanding of *missio Dei* has influenced missiology in the Anglican Communion. In 1998 for example, Lambeth insisted that mission is God's own attribute; it is 'God's way of loving and saving the world.' [15] Because mission belongs to God, Christians are called to engage in mission

---

[12] John Kaoma, 'God, Humanity and Nature: Reflecting on the Relational Approach', *Listening: Journal of Religion and Culture* 35, 3 (Fall 2000), 224-225.

[13] David J. Bosch, *Transforming Mission: Paradigm Shifts in Theology of Mission* (Maryknoll: Orbis 1999), 390-93.

[14] Andrew J. Kirk, *What is Mission? Theological Explorations (*Augsburg: Fortress, 2000), 28.

[15] Lambeth Conference 1998, Section II, 121.

'so that God's will of salvation for all may be fulfilled.' Lambeth added that the Church is an instrument of God's mission; thus, 'to participate in mission is to participate in the movement of God's love toward people, since God is a fountain of sending love.'[16] Lambeth 2008 also repeated this conviction: 'Mission is the total action of God in Christ by the power of the Holy Spirit – creating, redeeming, sanctifying – for the sake of the whole world.'[17] The conference, however, extended this concept to Earth care when it argued that mission is oriented towards 'social justice and care for God's creation.'[18]

As with other theological formulations, contextual knowledge and values invite critical reformulation of certain theological assumptions and beliefs. Anthropocentric lenses of viewing God's mission as focused solely on humanity can lead to Earth-denying theologies. But as already alluded to, God, the owner of mission, constantly renews and sustains all life on Earth.

From a biblical perspective, however, an argument can be made that the missiological task of Earthkeeping was first pronounced in the creation account when God invited humanity to take part in the *missio* of Earth-care (Gen 1:26). While this invitation to 'serve' (as opposed to dominate)[19] Earth has been misunderstood as sanctioning domination and exploitation of the natural world, the call was to join the Creator in participating in Earth-care (Gen 3:9). If Christian mission is understood as *missio Creator Dei*, then there is need to respect the covenant between God, all life and Earth as an act of Christian witness. In other words, ensuring the wellbeing of Earth is not a side bar to Christian mission but fundamental to the *missio Creator Dei*. In a nutshell, the Creator's mission demands that we take care of Earth as God's creation. Christians ought to remember that the death of Earth, is the death of Christian Mission!

Earth as a Sacrament

The theological theme that Earth belongs to God does not only invite us to revisit the doctrine of dominion and the concept of *missio Dei* but also leads to another theological basis for Christian involvement in Earth-healing; the sacramental nature of Creation. While the Enlightenment-influenced Western societies have presented the natural world negatively – as the centre of evil forces – in spiritual terms, Earth reveals the Creator. In fact, both Hebrew and Christian Scriptures testify to the revelatory nature of Creation. According to the prophet Isaiah, the universe is 'filled with the

---

16 Lambeth Conference 2008, www.lambethconference.org/resolutions/2008 (accessed 8.2.2011).
17 Ibid.
18 Ibid.
19 This interpretation follows John Hart in *Sacramental Commons: Christian Ecological Ethics* (Lanham: Rowman and Little Publishers, 2006).

glory of God' (Isa 6:3). In ecological terms therefore, this manifestation of divine glory is revealed fully in the complex web of life. Because every creature shares and manifests 'a bit of the divine beauty,'[20] the natural world reveals divine glory. As Isaac Watts put it, 'There is not a plant or flower below, but makes thy glories known.'[21] Again Elizabeth Johnson rightly asserts, creation 'signifies that the incomprehensible holy mystery of God [that] indwells the natural and human world as source, sustaining power, and the goal of the universe, [is] enlivening and loving it into liberating communion.'[22]

Subsequently, John Hart argues that Earth

> is a revelation of the Spirit's ongoing creativity and is a place of interaction and relationship between the human and the divine....The cosmos as an integrated whole and in each of its parts can be a sign and experience of divine creativity and a revelation of the Spirit's presence; an occasion of grace and a conveyor of blessing; and a bearer of sacred creatures, all called 'very good' by their Creator.[23]

Advocating 'a creation-centered consciousness' when relating to the natural world, Hart argues that 'all creatures emerge from the dynamic cosmic processes and the evolutionary biological process set in motion at the origins of the universe.'[24] Creation-centered consciousness, he argues, 'includes Earth awareness and engagement' whereby people 'recognize their responsibilities not only to the Creator, but to each other, to all life and to Earth. They take note of the inherent elegance, goodness, value, and dignity of creation.'[25] In addition, Hart asserts that since humans are ecologically connected to all creatures, they are an integral part of the biotic community, and provide cosmic self-consciousness...within the vast universe.'[26] Thus the universe is the locus of interconnected engagement of Earth communities and the Creator.[27]

Following Pope Paul VI's argument that the poor are a 'sacrament of Christ,' Hart argues that ecological justice advocates the rights of the poor to Earth's goods and denounces consumerism and unequal distribution of Earth's natural goods. He advocates an inter-relational mode of existence that integrates creation spirituality and creation ecology and 'allows people

---

[20] U.S Catholic Bishops, *Renewing the Earth: An invitation to Reflection and Action on Environment in Light of Catholic Social Teaching* (Nov. 14, 1991), 6.

[21] Isaac Watts, 'I Sing the Mighty Power of God' in *The Hymnal 1982* (New York: Church Pension Fund, 1985), 398.

[22] E. Johnson, 'Heaven and Earth are Filled with Your Glory: Atheism and Ecological Spirituality', in Michael J. Himes and Stephen J. Pope (eds) *Finding God in All Things* (New York: The Crossroad Publishing Company, 1996), 91.

[23] Hart, *Sacramental Commons,* 12.

[24] Ibid., 17; Cf. xviii.

[25] Ibid., 17.

[26] Ibid., 18.

[27] Ibid., 62-63.

to accept their responsibilities to God, to each other, to all life and to the Earth.'[28] Thus, in the current context of 'ecological devastation, political domination, wartime destruction, and economic deprivation, the understanding of sacramental commons stimulates exploration of revelatory, prophetic dimensions of Christianity (and of other faith traditions).'[29] Therefore, the contemplation of the Creator Spirit revealed in nature ought to lead us into appreciating the sacramental value of the cosmos.

The sacramental nature of creation is equally found in indigenous cosmologies. As already observed, in indigenous thought, Earth's natural goods are not mere instruments to human wellbeing.[30] Rather they possess intrinsic value as revelators of the divine presence (sacraments). Anglican African leading theologian John Mbiti argues that Africans exist

> in a religious universe, so that the natural phenomena and objects are intimately associated with God. They not only originate from him but also bear witness to him. …[humanity] sees in the universe not only the imprint but also the reflection of God; and whether that image is marred or clearly focused and defined, it is nevertheless an image of God, and the only image known in traditional African Societies.[31]

Likewise, Anglican scholar Jacob Olupona of Harvard University argues that indigenous people have always related with nature on a spiritual level. No Africanist, he argues, can dispute the fact that 'nature is sacred in African traditional religious thought and ritual' and 'wild animals are the most pure expression of God's power.'[32] Amidst the recurring ecological crises, the revelatory power of creation should inform our mission theology.

Protecting the Dignity of Earth

In addition to the sacramental nature of Earth, the dignity of Earth should be upheld on the moral basis of intrinsic value and rights. Is Creation of value aside from its instrumental value to humanity? And why should Christians concern themselves with defending the rights of non-human beings? These questions are important to ensuring the future of planet Earth.

Lambeth 1998 indicated that ecological issues be 'given greater

---

[28] Ibid., 17.

[29] Ibid.

[30] To some extent this is also true of Western Christianity. See James Nash, *Loving Nature*; Paul Santmire, *The Travail of Nature: The Ambiguous Ecological Promise of Christian Theology* (Philadelphia: Fortress Press, 1985).

[31] John Mbiti, *African Religions and Philosophy* (London and New York: Preager, 1990), 48.

[32] Jacob Olupona, 'Comments on the Encyclopedia of Religion and Nature', *Journal of the American Academy of Religion* 77, no. 1 (March, 2009), 63.

visibility and be better coordinated across the Anglican Communion.'[33] This concern was rewarded with the establishment of the Anglican Communion Environmental Network (ACEN), whose goal is 'to encourage Anglicans to support sustainable environmental practices as individuals and in the life of their communities' among many others.[34] In addition, in 2009, the Anglican Consultative Council meeting in Jamaica, resolution 14.15 stated ACEN's support of 'the Archbishop of Canterbury in his thoughtful reflection and witness in the areas of the environment, the global economy and our support of vulnerable people and communities.'[35]

Such developments are signs in the right direction. In fact, the intersection between poverty and environmental degradation has been on the radar of theological discussions in recent years. Anglican missiologists noted that we exist in a corrupt world with systems that create wars, conflicts and many social evils that 'dehumanise the majority of people by denying them the opportunity to live purposeful and peaceful lives.'[36] It is in this context that the Church is called to 'participate in God's mission of love and justice for all.'[37] Under Mission as Solidarity with the Dispossessed, the Inter-Anglican Standing Commission in Mission and Evangelism (IASCOME) made a case for defending the rights of indigenous people to their lands. IASCOME went on to address other areas of injustice that have contributed to global poverty such as violence and HIV/AIDS.[38] Sadly despite the valuable and insightful observations, the integrity of creation was not addressed as an independent missiological issue.

This shortfall was somehow duplicated during the Edinburgh 2010 conference, where ecological issues were only integrated in major themes. Worse still, environmental degradation did not make it to the plenary. Indeed, the integration model can be applauded, but the magnitude of the crisis demands specialized and focused missiological reflections on the matter. It is saddening that while the words 'eco-mission,' 'Earth-Care,' 'environmental mission' and 'missionary Earthkeeping' have been in use for some time now, these terms did not make it to the list of 'key terms for mission and Christian unity in 2010' – missionary power, ecumenical

---

[33] http://acen.anglicancommunion.org/ accessed 20/05/2011.

[34] For a complete list of goals, see http://acen.anglicancommunion.org (accessed 20.5.2011).

[35] http://acen.anglicancommunion.org/resources/docs/ACC14_ACEN_resolution.pdf (accessed 20.5.2011).

[36] IASCOME, *Communion in Mission and Travelling Together in God's Mission, Anglican Communion* (London: AC, 2006), 79.

[37] Ibid, 79.

[38] Ibid, 80-89.

charity, budding ecumenism, mission to the North.[39] But as already observed, we can hardly participate in the Creator's mission without addressing the unprecedented ecological devastation to which Earth community is currently subjected.

While the oppression of the poor and the exploitation of the Earth are interrelated, defending the intrinsic value of Earth is essential to Christian mission. It must be pointed out that Earth's integrity is an ontological reality that needs defending in its own right. Against the long-held assumption that Earth is a reservoir of raw materials, Elizabeth Johnson rightly argues that; 'The life-giving Spirit of God, *Dominus et vivificantis*, encircles, pervades, and energizes the world, gifting it with its own intrinsic, self organizing powers that have led to magnificence beyond our imaginations, including our own human race.'[40] In this regard, doing mission involves adequately participating in the Creator's mission of ensuring the integrity of creation as an ontological entity with intrinsic value.

The intrinsic value of Creation was pronounced long before humanity set foot on Earth when God declared the natural world as very good (Gen 1ff). This declaration was renewed in God's covenant with all living things (Gen 9:11-13). While the Creator reiterated the moral position of humanity in the ecosphere, God covenanted with all life on Earth regardless of its value to humanity (Gen 9: 1-17). In the covenant narrative, Earth and all life are independent covenanted entities with indisputable intrinsic value. On the existential level, however, the covenant suggests that all life is a concern of the Creator God. Importantly, humanity, earth and all life exist in interconnected relationships with the Creator God and one another. Ethically and theologically, therefore, acts that continuously threaten the future of covenanted Earth are abominations to the Creator.

The understanding that God cares for creation and Earth as independent entities is carried over into the New Testament: 'Consider the ravens: they neither sow nor reap, they have neither storehouse nor barn, and yet God feeds them' (Lk 12.24). God equally cares for the lilies and the grass of the fields (Lk 12:27). Anthropocentrically, sparrows are of little value to the humanity, yet not a single sparrow falls to ground without the Creator's knowledge and concern (Matt 10:29).

Although God covenanted with all life on Earth, scholars are divided on the sacredness of creation. Arguing for the ethics of relevance for the entire biota for example, Albert Schweitzer argued that 'the absolute ethics must reverence every form of life, seeking as far as possible to refrain from destroying any life, regardless of its particular type. It says of no instance of

---

[39] Edinburgh 2010, 'Key Terms for Mission and Christian Unity in 2010', www.edinburgh2010.org/en/news/en/article/4645/key-terms-for-mission-and.html; accessed 20.5.2011.

[40] Johnson, 'Heaven and Earth', 86.

life, "This has no value."'[41] Schweitzer further argued that humanity is part of the wider community of life: 'we are part of life, we are born of other lives; we possess the capacities to bring still other lives into existence.'[42] Subsequently, American Episcopal feminist theologian Sallie McFague advocates respect for the sacredness of life regardless of its perceived value. Like Schweitzer, McFague argues that human life is directly linked to other beings in the ecosphere. For this reason,

> By destroying the health of nature, we are undermining our own. The ecological [society] does not support either/or thinking: either my good or yours, either our good or nature's. The good life for nature – a resilient, complex nature – is what we must have for our good life, but our good life rests on our caring for nature's well-being.[43]

Not all ecologists would accept this argument, however. The late Professor James Nash objects that 'biota egalitarianism' is a moral absurdity and an antihuman ideology. Arguing against Albert Schweitzer, Nash posits that biota egalitarianism fails to appreciate 'the unique capacities of humans to experience and create moral, spiritual, intellectual and aesthetic good. The value-creating and value-experiencing capacities of humans are morally relevant differences between us and all other species, and justify differential and preferential treatment in conflict situations.'[44]

In contrast, John Hart argues for egalitarianism. According to Hart, from a relational perspective, human beings ought to see themselves 'as one part of a dynamic biotic community living in egalitarian relationships in ecological systems.'[45] In other words, humanity is part of the interconnected cosmos. That said, the extinction of species reduces the vital force of the universe to which humanity belongs. On this basis, the reverence for life should become a Christian duty. After all, Christian love demands that we love God with all our hearts and our neighbours as ourselves (Deut 6:5; Mk 12:30). Ecologically, we are not just neighbours to our own species but to everything that God has created – from disease infected rats, mosquitoes and bedbugs to beautiful zebras, kangaroos and penguins! As already observed, since all life comes from a single source – the Creator Almighty – the exploitation of Earth's natural goods is an affront to the sacred.

In addition, the occurring ecological crisis is not just an attack on the poor but also on God's beauty in Creation, hence ensuring the integrity of creation is a spiritual issue. Our liturgies, hymns and spiritual disciplines

---

[41] Albert Schweitzer, 'The Ethics of Reverence for Life'. Originally published in *Christendom* 1, 1936, (225-39), 6. www1.chapman.edu/scheitzer/sch/reading4/html; accessed 07/16/08.

[42] Ibid., 10.

[43] Sallie McFague, *Life Abundant: Rethinking Theology and Economy for a Planet in Peril* (Minneapolis: Fortress Press, 2000), 117-8.

[44] Nash, *Loving Nature*, 149.

[45] Hart, *Sacramental Commons,* 70.

should aid our reverence for Earth as God's Creation. As Jeffrey M. Gollieher argues, to address our suicidal destruction of the web of life, 'we will need both an ecological reformation of the Church and a spiritual revolution in reverential love. The church must become God's creation in a process of renewal.'[46]

The renewal of the Church should lead to re-examining human attitudes to Earth and non-human beings. In this case, our missiological analysis should endeavor to develop a Christian basis for environmental activism in the globalized world. We should not lose sight of the fact that our God is ecologically present in the natural world as well as the Church. Just as the Church exists to worship the Creator God, all creatures are invited to participate in worship. Psalm 148, for instance, invites the ecological community to worship and praise the Creator God for their existence. Aside from presenting the interconnectedness of creation, this Psalm reveals that every creature expresses gratitude to its maker (Ps 148: 7-13; cf Ps103:20-22). While most of our Christian liturgies still limit worship to humanity, the entire universe is obliged to venerate its Supreme Maker.

The consciousness that all creatures participate in worship led many saints and mystics to perceive nonhumans as companions in holy life. For instance, St. Francis preached to diverse creatures; he invited animals and birds to praise their Creator after the pattern of Psalm 148. In *Laudes Creaturarum* (Praise of the Creatures), St. Francis illustrates the ecological praise rendered to the Creator. Composed around 1225, when his health was its worst, St. Francis invited all creatures to join him in glorifying the Creator God. To Francis, the glorification of God is curtailed without all the creatures of Earth. *Laudes Creaturarum* reflects the biblical tradition that celebrates 'the wonders of the Spirit in creation.'[47] For instance, the prophet Isaiah called on the mountains and trees to shout for joy (Isa 44:23; cf. 49:13; 55:12). Here, the assumption that Earth's value is dependent on its instrumental worth to humanity fails to address the liturgical significance of creation to the Creator. As already alluded to, the natural world reveals God to Earth community and ecological responsibility is another way of reverencing the Creator.[48] In short, our negative and irresponsible attitudes towards creation are assaults on the Creator Spirit, whose glory we diminish.

---

[46] Jeffrey M. Gollieher, 'This Fragile Earth Our Island Home: Environmental Crisis', in Ian T. Douglas and Kwok Pui-Lan (eds), *Beyond Colonial Anglicanism: The Anglican Communion in the Twenty-First Century*, (New York:Church Publishing Incorporated, 2001), 141.

[47] Hart, *Sacramental Commons*, 27. Hart argues that St. Francis linked his nature mysticism to the biblical traditions such as Dan 3 and Psalm 148. Ibid., 27-29.

[48] Ibid., 6.

Witnessing to Christ: Sustaining Life

The world is slowly coming to terms with the fact that human wellbeing is dependent on welfare of all ecological systems.[49] The *Earth Charter* warns:

> We stand at a critical moment in Earth's history, a time when humanity must choose its future. As the world becomes increasingly interdependent and fragile, the future at once holds great peril and great promise. To move forward we must recognize that in the midst of a magnificent diversity of cultures and life forms we are one human family and one Earth community with a common destiny. We must join together to bring forth a sustainable global society founded on respect for nature, universal human rights, economic justice, and a culture of peace. Towards this end, it is imperative that we, the peoples of Earth, declare our responsibility to one another, to the greater community of life, and to future generations.[50]

The Charter's observation suggests that authentic liberation is directly linked to the emancipation of entire planet Earth. The prophet Isaiah was right when he proclaimed God's salvation as an advent of the new creation, where all creatures will live in perfect *shalom*. In the new Earth (as God originally intended), the weeping of Earth, the poor and all other species will be heard no more (Isa 65: 20; Rev. 21:1-4). Because political, social, and economic oppression will have no place in God's new creation, every creature will have equal access to Mother Earth's natural goods. This understanding begs for a paradigm shift in Christian mission. Today, participating in the *missio Creator Dei* means accompanying God's mission of love towards the whole Earth and future generations of life. Amidst the recurring ecological crisis,

> Witnessing to Christ would mean addressing population growth, pollution, species extinction, climate change and human responsibility towards future generations. In other words, the instrumental view of the natural world, which dominated early missionary activities and still influences our economic theories, should be replaced with 'holistic approaches' that honour the interconnectedness of creation. In this case, the *missio Dei* should be understood as the mission of the Creator (*missio Creator)* revealed in the cosmic Christ, under whose authority, care and influence Earth and heaven now exist. Thus, all environmental issues are subjects of mission studies.[51]

As participants in the grand mission of the Creator, we are obliged to protect the dignity of Sacramental Earth as home to all life and divine mysteries. Because the Creator is the source of the *missio* and all life, we are obliged to care for the natural world (Gen 1:28). In other words, it is our duty to guard and protect mother Earth out of reverence for the Creator.

---

[49] Preamble to *Earth Charter*, 2000, www.earthcharterinaction.org/content/pages/Read-the-Charter.html (accessed 02/03/2009).
[50] Ibid.
[51] Kaoma, 'Missio Dei or Missio Creator Dei', 298.

Renewing Earth: Addressing Economic Realities

The presence of the Africans, Asians and other colonized peoples at the conference presented the double-sidedness of Christian mission. Their presence was both a celebration of missionary achievements as well as a reminder of the failures of Christian mission. For example, the presentation by indigenous people at the Conference reminded us of some mistakes committed in the name of civilization and Christianization of indigenous cultures. To a larger extent, the enlightenment-influenced missionary activities altered indigenous people's eco-spirituality and led to the de-sacralization of nature.

But Christian mission also alerts us to the fact that God is present in Creation. There is a tendency to present the Christian God as heavenly. Yet the Bible places the Christian God on Earth; God's actions are experienced in the specific natural environment. Even the doctrine of 'Natural Revelation' conveys the Earthiness of the Christian God. By destroying nature, we are robbing the Creator of another venue of self-disclosure. From this perspective, the eco-social crisis that confronts the Earth and the global South in particular demands an active missiological response. Here, lines or paragraphs in mission scholarship are not enough. The crisis demands comprehensive attention!

Admittedly, the occurring crisis threatens not only the future of the global South but adversely compromises the lives of millions of peoples and other species. For instance, the fact that the majority of Anglicans reside in the global South and Africa in particular means that the Church cannot engage in the mission of meeting human needs without addressing the environmental security of God's people, Earth and future generations. Because the occurring crisis affects the poor (majority of Christians) in the global South, the church's attempt to meet the needs of the underprivileged is compromised if we fail to address the death of Earth. Currently, the majority of the poor look to Earth for their daily needs. As such, meeting human needs is not possible without addressing Earth's integrity.

Brazilian moral theologian, Leonardo Boff argues that Earth's destruction impacts negatively the lives of over 80% of the world population that live in the poor South. According to Boff, over 1 billion people live in absolute poverty while more than 3 billion do not have enough to eat. Worse still, more than 60 million die from starvation each year; the situation, he argues, illustrates the level of disconnectedness in the world as 'we are pushed back to an ultimate basis for the current ecological impasse: the ongoing disruption of the basis of connectedness with the whole of the universe and with its Creator that the human being has introduced, fueled, and perpetuated.'[52] This disruption, which he calls original sin, or the sin of the world has always dominated and abused Earth.

---

[52] Leonardo Boff, *Cry of the Earth, Cry of the Poor* (Maryknoll, New York: Orbis Books, 1995), 1.

In order to tackle this problem, Boff suggests returning to the spirit of connectedness to Earth, in which we find God in all and all in God. This is expressed in the concept of 'panentheism' – the belief that the Creator Spirit 'is present in the cosmos and the cosmos is present in God.'[53]

Boff's observations have implications for mission theology and ethics. Participants in God's mission should address the growing gap between the rich minority and the poor majority. Working to reform the economic inequalities in the global economy is essential to mission. On the ecological front, however, the missional Church must become an Earth-healer; ensuring Earth's integrity in today's capitalistic world. In our quest to meet human needs, our methods should not compromise the ecological wellbeing of Earth, the poor and future generations. Here any form of economic development that compromises the wellbeing of Earth and the future of coming generations ought to be discouraged. For example, the missionary initiatives of harvesting and exporting of indigenous trees (which usually take hundreds of years to grow) without planting new ones should never be condoned. Likewise, routinely dumping of outlawed or expired chemicals, pharmaceuticals, machinery, and other wastes on African and other Third World countries should raise prophetic rage among Christians.

Living our Faith in the Face of the Ecological Crisis

The theological premise that the Earth is the *locus* of the Creator's mission should propel Christian involvement in Earth-care. No doubt our theological education should be reviewed to address the above premise. Just as liberation theologies have dominated the global south, eco-theology and eco-social ethics deserve a place in mission curricula. In short, Christian educators should aim at aiding the Church to form people with a global eco-conscious spirituality.

Without sidelining the need to meet human needs, the recurring crisis demands immediate attention if we are to ensure the survival of Earth and our own species. The following suggestions are just a few among the many actions in which the Church can enhance the visibility of the fifth mark of mission.

First, the assertion that Earth is the Lord's has moral implications on how Earth's natural goods are shared. The unequal distribution of Earth's goods which favour the Global North over the South should invite prophetic rage from all Christians. In addition, missiological reflections must be centered on God's covenantal relationship with all life. God cares for all life on Earth and participants in mission ought to do the same. Second, Christians should learn from other faith traditions in their application of the mission of God in the face of the recurring crisis. In addition to learning from indigenous wisdom about the interconnectedness

---

[53] Ibid., 152.

of life, the ecumenical tree-planting experiences of African Earthkeepers – groups comprising of Traditionalists and various African Initiated Churches – that saw the planting of millions of trees and conservation of wildlife in Zimbabwe is something that we can learn from.[54]

Like African Earthkeepers, the Church should encourage tree-planting as a missiological obligation. Liturgically, tree planting must be placed in the context of the Holy Communion. In this regard, developing Earth-centered liturgies will enhance ecological awareness in the Church. Imagine the number of trees we would plant if all Christians in the global South planted trees every year.

In addition to safeguarding Earth, tree planting mission can foster cross-cultural mission partnerships. For example, Christ Church in Hyde Park, Massachusetts might not have land to plant trees but its sister congregation, St. Andrews Anglican Church in Zambia's Luapula Diocese does. Christ Church can provide financial support to allow St. Andrew's to purchase seedlings and plant trees. The two congregations can also share Earth-related liturgies to use at specific services as a form of celebrating their interconnectedness to one another and to Earth.

Third, rather than taking pride in numbers of Christians (important as this might be), we should start addressing population growth which is threatening the future of Earth. Regardless of our theological beliefs, Earth's carrying capacity is limited. We ought to realize that it is no longer how many Christians will be in the Global South in 2050 but how many people Earth can sustain. In this scenario, we should start providing theological resources for addressing the population explosion in the Global South and the world as a whole. Here, engaging the Mothers Union and all God's people on the relationship between population growth, responsible parenting and environmental degradation will be an excellent idea.

Consequently, it is not enough to celebrate the simple life of indigenous peoples while the Global North continues with its destructive lifestyles. As long as 20% of the world population continues to consume more than 80% of the Earth's natural goods, our dream for a better world is a fallacy. In short, Global North residents should learn to live by needs rather than wants. Because our excessive materialism impacts negatively on mother Earth, we should attempt to limit our destructive impact (carbon footprint) on planet Earth. Our appetite for meat is not just compromising the livelihoods of millions of indigenous people and encouraging the destructions of rainforests across the world but also robbing animals of their dignity. In addition, rather than having two cars and living in big houses, we can do better with less.

---

[54] Marthinus L. Daneel, *African Earth-keepers: Wholistic Interfaith Mission* (Maryknoll:Orbis, 2001).

[55] Kapya John Kaoma, *Ubuntu, Jesus, and Earth: Integrating African Religion and Christianity in Ecological Ethics*, Th.D Dissertation (Boston University, 2010), 385.

On a theological front, immediate attention should be paid to reforming our theological seminaries into eco-friendly seminaries. Currently, most of our seminaries are yet to start addressing issues of post-modernity. In fact, most seminaries are still using training materials that were developed to meet the needs of modernity mostly by those who gathered in 1910. A typical African syllabus, for example, will focus on evangelism, systematic theology and biblical studies. In cases where ecological and eco-social issues are addressed, they are taught as electives. One wonders how such an education can adequately address modern challenges such as the ecological crisis.

Just as important is the review of the Church or Sunday School materials currently in use in the Church. In most African churches for example, ecological responsibility is not emphasized as a spiritual issue. But as this study has revealed, the integrity of Creation will only be safeguarded once the predicament facing Earth is placed in the religious worldviews of the people. Thus, we need to change our theological paradigms at many levels. Finally, the years 1990-2000 were declared the decade of Evangelism. The Communion and World Council of Churches would do better to consider declaring a 'decade of Environmental Protection.' During this period, Christians can engage in applied acts of safeguarding the integrity of creation and sustaining and renewing the life of the Earth.

Concluding Remarks

The future of Christian mission will be determined by how Christianity confronts the worsening ecological devastation in this century. The worsening air and water pollution, climate change, species extinctions, deforestation, among many other environmental predicaments are threats not just to humanity but to all forms of life. Christian mission as *missio Creator Dei* demands an immediate change in our Earth-Human mission paradigm whereby God's inclusive mission benefits all creation. As this chapter illustrates, to witness to Christ is to participate in the *missio Creator Dei* of safeguarding and sustaining all life on sacramental Earth out of reverence for the Creator and our moral obligation to future generations. Therefore, aside from denouncing growing global poverty, Christian mission should consistently confront excessive materialism in the global North. Because Earth's capacity to sustain life is limited, Christian mission equally addresses population growth, which is negatively impacting Earth's wellbeing. Mindful of the missiological promise of the growing number of Christians in the global South, uncontrolled population growth compromises Earth's integrity and must be theologically and ethically addressed.

On the Christological front, the ecological crisis demands the ecological face of Jesus. Since Christ is the origin and an ecological ancestor of every species, his 'vital force' is inherently active in every creature that exists.

Ignoring the current environmental crisis while species are extincted and Earth dies, means ignoring the ethical sanctions of Christ, who is the origin-ancestor and ecological ancestor of all creation. Finally, Christian mission should promote Earth-healing collaboration between Christians in various parts of the Globe; tree planting, population control and land reclamation are some of Earth healing initiatives that ought to typify Christian partnerships and witness in our time.

Discussion Questions

1. Critics of Christianity argue that Christianity is anti-nature. Reflecting on your faith, how would respond to the critics?
2. This study gives practical steps that Christians can do to help mediate the effects of the ecological crisis. Based on your context, in which others ways can Christians participate in Earth-care and healing?
3. Discuss how the theological conviction that the Earth belongs to God affects human attitudes towards the natural world.
4. What is the relationship between mission as meeting human needs, seeking justice and ensuring the integrity of Creation?
5. How can our understanding of Christ as the origin of Creation inform our understanding of the role of Jesus in Earth-care?
6. How can our understanding of Christian mission as mission of the Creator God (missio Creator Dei) inform the five marks of mission?

OTHER THEMES

GENDER: REPRESENTATION AND PRESENCE AT EDINBURGH 2010

Caitlin Beck

Preface

FEMINISM! It is a word that scares a lot of people. At one point it was a word that scared me and even today, after several years of identifying myself as a feminist, I am still not sure exactly what I or anyone else means by the term. It is probably smart then to explain what is meant by the term 'feminism' in the context of this article.

The people who have taught me about feminism have taught me that being a woman does not mean you are a feminist, or that you offer a feminist perspective on the world. But, being a feminist does mean you are concerned with women's perspectives and experiences of the world along with those of other marginalised groups. Feminism started with women[1] – not all women to be sure – but women who felt that there was something wrong with how being women determined their lives. The history of feminism is often divided into three waves: first wave feminism covers feminist action in the mainly upper class, white, western world in the 19th and early 20th centuries and dealt mainly with education, workers' rights and the right to vote, second wave feminism covers the mid-20th century (1960s) to the 1980s and dealt with continued legal inequality and the social gender roles that supported this inequality; again it was strongly western and upper class, third wave feminism is a product of second wave feminism as well as a reaction to some of its failings. Some of these failings include the lack of diversity amongst feminists who were predominantly upper class, white women from Canada, the United States, Australia, New Zealand and Europe. Many women's groups and associations did not use the label of feminism for this reason and now the women's movement includes an ever-increasing spectrum of voices who question the norms of patriarchal[2] societies in a variety of ways.[3] This

---

[1] This is not to say that the ideas of feminism are uniquely the product of women's minds and actions, simply that they are inspired by women's experience of gender. Many feminists trace the origins of feminist action and association to the Enlightenment and authors such as Mary Wollstonecraft and Jeremy Bentham.

[2] Patriarchy is an entire social, legal, political, economic and theological system of organization whereby power is distributed first to fathers (or father figures in

diversity of experience and perspective is difficult to hold together, but much of the women's movement has developed a strong emphasis on solidarity. This solidarity consists of listening to and standing in support of those whose own experience or struggle may be different from our own. My teachers also told me that feminism is about acknowledging your starting point and the different parts of your identity that affect how you experience and see the world. My framework is one in which nobody has an objective, bird's eye view of the world, we all have some bias, some things that we believe are true or experiences that have shaped our judgement. Since we cannot eliminate our bias we have to own up to it. So here is the first part of my bias – I am a feminist, the kind that is concerned with how the gender and sex of people determines their lives. I believe that together people in a culture decide what biological elements of sex[4] determine a person's gender and that gender becomes a part of an individual's identity; an identity that is formed by both the individual and their relationship to various groups. Besides being a feminist, I am also a person of faith – of multiple-religious belonging. I was raised in both the Bahá'í and Christian (specifically Anglican) faiths and both of these along with other religious affiliations affect how I experience and judge the world.[5] As I look at the Edinburgh 2010 world mission conference, I will be looking at how sex and gender were represented and present both formally and informally and how they were not. I will include examples from our worship, from presentations, from the study process and from informal interactions.

---

organizations) and then to those below on the pyramid. Patriarchs control property, money, ideas, institutions and the people within them. It is dependent upon the subordination of non-patriarchs which includes women, children, the physically weak, the poor, in order to support the privileged places and voices of the patriarchs. Various forms of patriarchy have been the societal norm in most of the world for most of history.

[3] Of note are the voices of Latin American women who identify as *mujeristas* and black women who identify as womanists. There are also notable groups of women from around the world as well as young, elderly, disabled, poor, indigenous and religious women.

[4] Biological elements of sex include chromosomes and how they are affected by the production of certain hormones, the appearance, shape and function of the body especially genitals, and participation in reproduction by bearing children or impregnation. For example, in some cultures being able to bear children is a more significant marker of being a woman than physical appearance or chromosomes.

[5] For those who are truly concerned, I am also white, Canadian, from a bilingual, divorced, upper class family in Ottawa with four brothers and parents who are psychiatrists, and I self-identify with the female gender.

Different from Edinburgh 1910 – Representation and Presence

Representation is when someone or something (an image, word, idea, person etc.) speaks about or on behalf of something bigger. This can include everything from the use of photographs and videos to electoral representation. Presence on the other hand, is a much more immediate, experiential reality. Like the immanence of God, it is perceived and felt, it is missed and longed for or it is completely off the radar. Both representation and presence are important and connected. For instance, our experience of the presence of God or lack thereof is linked to our experience of the representation of God – in images, ideas, institutions, etc. This is also the case with the representation and presence of humanity and gender. In the First Testament, God tells the people to be attentive and cautious with how representations of God and humanity are used lest these representations become idolatrous. Idolatry is the literal identification of an object or symbol with that which it is meant to represent. When Moses comes down from Mount Sinai, the people are worshipping the golden calf itself, but in the wilderness, they look to the serpent of bronze seeking salvation from God, not from the serpent. The first is idolatry; the second is symbol or metaphor. These objects or words or symbols are representations. An idolatrous representation of gender can be found when certain characteristics generally associated with people of one gender or another change from being descriptive to prescriptive. For example, the statement 'Men are physically strong, rational and abstract thinkers' becomes idolatrous when it is held up as necessarily true or more true than the real presence of a man who is physically weak, relational and a practical thinker. It is this kind of gender idolatry of which we must be mindful in our representation of gender.

The first way to explore the representation and presence of gender at Edinburgh 2010 is by looking at the statistics of who attended. This examination of statistics acknowledges that delegates are both present as unique human beings made in the image of God from their own social locations as well as being representatives of others with whom they may share faith tradition, gender, nationality or opinions.

The website for Edinburgh 2010 lists ways in which this past year's mission conference is different from its predecessor. One of these is 'Whereas 1910 was confined to mainline Protestantism, the participants in 2010 are drawn from the whole range of Christian traditions and confessions, including Roman Catholic, Orthodox, Pentecostal, and Independent Churches, *and show a better gender and age balance.*'[6] (Emphasis mine). What does it mean to have a better balance in terms of gender? Is this true?

---

[6] http://edinburgh2010.oikoumene.org/index.php?id=4646 (accessed 27.4.2011).

Figure 1: Edinburgh 1910

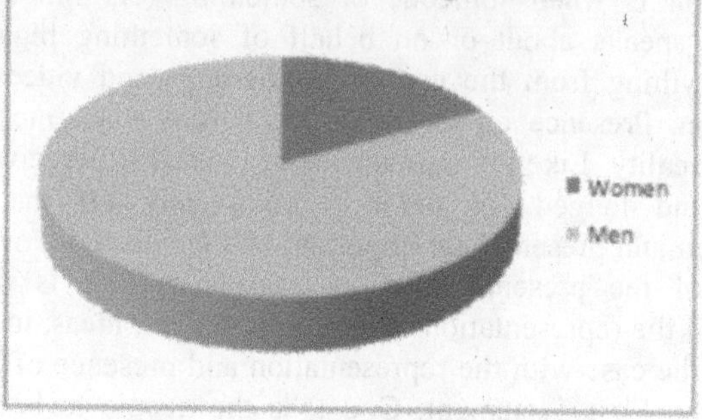

Figure 2: Edinburgh 2010

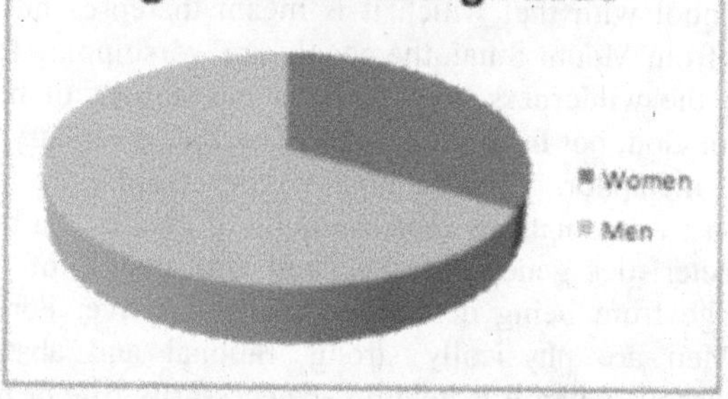

In his historical reflections on the 1910 Edinburgh World Mission Conference, Kenneth R. Ross makes the following comments:

> The participants were overwhelmingly male despite the fact that women were already making a massive contribution to the missionary movement. While the participants were struck by their diversity, from a longer historical perspective it is striking how limited was their range.[7]

In other words, the 1910 conference was not even close to achieving any kind of gender balance among participants, nor did it have any such goal. It is not at all surprising then that women represented a higher percentage of the delegates to the Edinburgh 2010 world mission conference than in 1910. The explicit goal of the organizing committee was for women to be 50% of the delegates at the conference (150 out of 300 delegates). This did not happen. The fact that this did not happen is even more revealing when placed in the broader historical context. In 1910, few of the women present at the conference would have ever been able to vote, hold elected office, consider a vocation to ordained ministry, be legally considered persons (or not minor persons) or have been able to divorce if they were married. In

[7] Kenneth R. Ross, *Edinburgh 2010: Springboard for Mission* (Pasadena: William Carey International University Press, 2009), 6.

1910, the pressure from women's suffrage groups had succeeded in getting some women the vote in New Zealand, Australia, Sweden, Finland and a few other countries. In Canada, for example, some provinces had recognized the right of widows, spinsters and property-holding women to vote, but not all women. It wasn't until 1929 that women were declared persons in Canada. It was in this context that the Edinburgh 1910 conference took place. At the 1910 conference there were 200 women delegates out of 1200 total or 1/6th of the delegates.[8] These women were counted as delegates to this conference in a world where they were not considered persons. At the 2010 conference, despite their goal to have women represent at least 50% of the delegates, organizers placed this figure closer to 32% of the delegates.[9] There were 95 women delegates out of the 290 at Edinburgh 2010. Considering that there were 200 women delegates in 1910 and more than 50% of the world's human population and more than 70% of the membership of Churches worldwide are women and finally that the stakeholders had set themselves the goal of having 50% women delegates, this is a very disappointing result. In addition, today in almost every part of the world, women can vote,[10] be elected to hold office, be legally considered persons and many are able to get divorced or consider a vocation to ordained ministry. Is it true then, that Edinburgh 2010 had a better gender balance than 1910? There were actually fewer women present than in 1910 and only twice the figure in terms of proportion. In terms of women's participation, at 1/6th of the delegates, 1910 was ahead of its time while 2010 continues to lag behind. This points to the longstanding contrast in the Church between women, who have always been more than 50% of the faithful and men, who have always been more than 50% of the power holders and decision makers.[11] It is important to note that despite this disappointing result overall, the delegates from the Anglican Communion did adhere to the guidelines of gender, country of origin and age set by the

---

[8] See Figure 1.

[9] John F. Gorski, *The Edinburgh 2010 World Mission Conference: What Does it Mean to Us? Impressions of a Catholic Delegate to an Ecumenical Conference* http://edinburgh2010.oikoumene.org/en/resources/papersdocuments.html (accessed 27.4.2011), 3. See figure 2.

[10] In Bhutan, it is one vote per household which currently restricts more women than men from voting. Lebanon requires proof of an elementary school education for women to vote (though has no such requirement for men). Brunei is an absolute monarchy where no one can vote. Saudi Arabia has no suffrage for women. The United Arab Emirates currently has limited suffrage for women but this is in the process of being expanded and finally in the Vatican City, only male Cardinals have suffrage.

[11] Fulata L Moyo. '"Who Is Not at the Table?" Women's Perspectives of Holistic Mission as Mutually Inclusive', in Daryl Balia and Kirsteen Kim (eds), *Edinburgh 2010: Witnessing to Christ Today* (Oxford: Regnum International, 2010), 245-252.

organizers of Edinburgh 2010.[12] There are still many Churches where only those ordained to ministry have a voice in making decisions and many of these Churches do not ordain women or anyone else who deviates from the norms of masculine gender. This is true in many parts of the Anglican Communion and it is significant to note that none of the women delegates is from provinces where women's ordination is still impossible. This raises the question of whether other forms of women's leadership in these provinces are being supported by either the local Church or the Communion. Even in Christian Traditions where women are ordained, they are ordained less frequently and rarely to roles with the highest authority – such as superintendant, bishop or primate.

Certainly we must look at more than simply numbers to evaluate how gender was represented and present at Edinburgh 2010. At Edinburgh 2010, the main way in which human gender was represented was with reference to women. This can be seen in the existence of the transversal topic 'Women and mission'. The existence of this transversal theme rightly recognizes the pervasive involvement of women in all fields of mission and its study as was noted by Kenneth Ross. However, the lack of any other transversal theme relating to gender and in particular gender other than female gender leaves a significant gap. There was no significant mention of how masculinity or gender in men affects the Church in mission. Neither was there mention of the broad diversity of how human gender is and has been manifest across time and space. While some human cultures appear to have two fairly rigidly defined sexes and genders, each person lives out their gender differently and there are outliers to every norm which creates a spectrum of gendered behaviour. In other cultures, there are recognized categories for people who do not fit into one of two polarized genders – eunuchs for example as well as celibate monks and nuns defy these gender poles.[13] Edinburgh's identification of women with the idea of gender misses some important issues in mission. For example, there is no exploration of how the celibacy of the Roman Catholic priesthood questions the standards for living out male gender in many cultures, wherein being a man involves impregnating a woman and producing children. This is an issue of gender and of culture important in the mission of the Church which remains unexplored due to the association of gender exclusively with women. The

---

[12] Of the nine official Anglican Communion delegates six were young Anglican leaders (3 of us under 30), five were from the global south, and four were women. On the other hand, six were ordained people and one other is an ordinand. Thus the communion delegation is still underrepresenting lay leaders and practitioners in mission.

[13] Vanessa Baird explores the breadth of human gender and sexual diversity in 'The No-Nonsense Guide to Sexual Diversity' published in the UK by New Internationalist Publications Ltd. She cites many examples of how gender and sexuality are experienced and performed in a wide variety of ways throughout the world.

result of so strongly linking the idea of gender with women is that it overlooks how gender affects every person in a society. Effectively, gender is associated only with those outside a normative masculine identity; much like believing that race is something that Aboriginal, black, and Asian people have and not white people. The representation of humanity then holds male to be the default position, with female as a second option that may be wonderful, unique and important, but is mostly, not male. This issue was raised by Anglican Communion delegate Dr. Kapya John Kaoma with respect to theology when he noted that people were referring to 'third world theologies' and 'African Theology' and wondered 'Isn't it all just 'theology' no matter where it's from?'[14] Some theologies are considered more standard than these other theologies which must be distinguished as abnormal.

Despite these deficiencies, the study process did produce a significant discussion of women's perspectives on mission which was included in the Volume, *Edinburgh 2010 – Witnessing to Christ Today* along with discussions of the core themes. This chapter was entitled 'Who is Not at the Table?' Women's Perspectives of Holistic Mission as Mutually Inclusive" and was compiled and edited by Dr. Fulata L. Moyo from material produced through a series of consultations on women in mission. In this chapter, an ecofeminist theological approach is applied to the work of these consultations.[15] Dr. Moyo identifies that her compilation of this material is necessarily affected by her own personal perspective and social location. While she is representing the work of these consultations, she is also present herself as a person with particular experiences. This contribution offers many important experiences and perspectives absent from the other parts of the study process, but drawn from the praxis of mission as carried out by women in various contexts. Despite the high quality of this particular contribution to the study process, it was not dicussed in any of the plenary sessions or the parallel sessions on themes 2, 3 and 6.[16] In the core theme of 'Mission and Power', however, there was a response included from the perspective of this transversal theme. Dr. Atola Longkumer's response to the group discussion of Mission and Power points bluntly to many of the most significant issues of gender and power that must be discussed in our development of mission theology and praxis.[17] She notes the following:

---

[14] www.anglicancommunion.org/acns/digest/index.cfm/2010/6/8/World-Mission-Conference-a-joy-but-colonial-mindset-still-lingers (accessed 29.4.2011).

[15] Moyo, 245.

[16] I attended the discussions of these particular themes and since they ran parallel to the others, I was unable to attend those.

[17] Atola Longkumer, *Mission and Power: Transversal Women and Mission*, http://edinburgh2010.oikoumene.org/en/resources/papersdocuments.html (accessed 1.5.2011).

> Mission historians inform us that the most vibrant Christian communities are in the global south, the erstwhile 'mission field', ironically this region is the area that poses most challenges for women, be it the raging epidemic of HIV/AIDS, women trafficking, violence against women, cultural practices that are oppressive to women, illiteracy, patriarchal structures, male-centric worldviews.[18]

It is also significant that Dr. Longkumer like Dr. Moyo, in her own introduction, identifies the ideas of representation and presence and in what ways her contributions relate to both:

> While I do represent the team of women from around the world working on the mentioned project I have not bracketed the specific socio-cultural location I belong. I offer my thoughts as an indigenous person from Northeast India, and as a woman.[19]

She identifies in these sentences, both whom she represents and her own unique presence. She is operating within a framework that prioritizes identifying one's own social location, while simultaneously standing in solidarity with those from other social locations. It is in this way that a multitude of different personal experiences can be brought together and shared in an effort to glean from their common threads, certain shared truths and realities.

Representation and Presence of Women in Mission

As previously mentioned, one of the transversal themes of Edinburgh 2010 was 'Women and Mission'. These themes were 'intended to run like a thread across all the main study themes offering complementary and critical perspectives'.[20] This would allow issues of gender (specifically women's issues) to be raised in all of the nine different themes. I would commend the organizers for this recognition of how the effects of gender are pervasive and cannot be easily isolated. However, in the short time span of the conference, the discussion of the transversal themes seems to have been largely lost. This is likely due to the time restrictions of the conference. With nine core themes and seven transversal themes, three days of deliberations was just not enough. While some discussion of women and mission was included in discussions of the core themes, this was not usually the case. It seems that like the 1910 conference, where discussion of women and mission was foregone in order that women might participate in all the discussions thus leading to a lack of women's perspectives being heard, this transversal topic was lost in the shuffle of an overly ambitious schedule.

---

[18] Longkumer.

[19] Longkumer.

[20] http://edinburgh2010.oikoumene.org/en/study-themes/transversal-topics.html, (accessed 1.5.2011).

Speaking of women's perspectives and voices, there were certainly more of these heard in Edinburgh 2010 than in 1910. As was mentioned repeatedly by conference organizers, the keynote speaker, Dr. Dana Robert, is a woman. However, all four of those who were invited to respond to her keynote address were male. In addition, her gender was one of the most often repeated facts about her identity. This created a situation wherein, her ideas were seen to be determined in large part by her gender. Because none of the respondents to her keynote address was female, the diversity of perspectives that women possess was not represented. This perception is also evident in a small, informal exercise in which the participants in discussions of 'Mission and post-modernities' (Theme 3) were asked to participate. At the beginning of a session, delegates were asked to place a star next to the characteristic or value of post-modernity that they believed was most important. What is significant is that men were given blue stars and women red stars. This identified participants primarily by their gender and assumed, in the absence of any other significant information about the person who placed each star, that gender was somehow a significant factor in their assessment of post-modernity. Without a doubt, our perceptions are affected by significant markers of identity such as gender, but is it true that for everyone who participated this was the part of their identity that was most likely to affect their decision? As it turns out, a lack of significant trends as well as the refusal of some delegates to participate in the informal exercise demonstrated that it was not a useful approach.

Besides Dr. Robert, only one other woman, Teresa Francesca Rossi, spoke in the plenary sessions out of a total of nine speakers.[21] This is far from 50% participation. In the parallel sessions on the core study themes, the gender representation among conveners was balanced as was the case with the listening group. In terms of local Church officials and international representatives who welcomed delegates at the opening ceremonies, all but one of these were men. All of these were people who held positions of significant power in the Church i.e. Bishop, Cardinal, General Secretary of the World Council of Churches. Once again we can see that power within the Christian community is still male-dominated. Gender in worship will be examined later on, but it is worth noting that while the music and worship team was balanced in terms of gender, there was only one woman invited to preach. Preaching, in the absence of any celebration of sacraments or ordinances such as baptism and Eucharist, is certainly perceived among many traditions as a highly important role in worship and is reserved for those in positions of authority.

Just as important as the gender of those who spoke is what it is they said. For example, Dana Robert spoke repeatedly, both in her plenary address and in online videos, about the role of women at Edinburgh 1910 as well as in the mission field before and after this historic conference. She brought

[21] It is also worth noting that both of these women were white, western women.

the voices of these delegates, previously unheard, into the discussion. In addition to her own perspective as a woman, she thought it important to bring forth these other women's perspectives. In this way, she participated in the process of representing women as well as being present as a unique individual. She represents them in her writing in a particular way – as historically overlooked, but active and enthusiastic participants in the mission of the Church. Not only her speech, but also her own missionary and academic engagements bear witness to this representation of women. Her contributions point to the fact that women's sphere of activity in a patriarchal culture is controlled by legitimated space.

Legitimated space is space where women are accommodated into certain spheres of activity rather than invited and welcomed. The mission field has historically been a legitimated space for women wherein they transmitted and translated dominant colonial culture and its patriarchal structures to colonized 'recipients' of the Church's mission. So although many women in mission were defying the cultural norms of their own societies wherein they were not normally able to preach or teach or have authority in the Church, their actions in effect helped to spread this patriarchal culture to other people. From an Anglican perspective, this is an especially important part of our mission history as it relates to gender diversity. As a long-standing colonial power, England along with the Anglican Church is responsible for introducing a particular set of patriarchal norms, ideas, systems and laws in countries around the world. In many places, this patriarchy was imposed on an entirely different cultural system replacing the indigenous understanding of gender and how it determines social location. First and especially second wave Feminism, as a reaction to this particular western patriarchal culture can be seen as another extension of imposed colonial definitions (or in this case re-definitions) of 'correct' gender roles. The history of this patriarchal colonial culture continues to be significant as women in various parts of the Communion seek power within the Church. Because of these established patriarchal systems, they seek power by being authorized as power-holders, mostly by seeking the ordination of women into these patriarchal structures, something that remains impossible in many parts of the Anglican Communion. Ordaining women, however, while it recognizes them as potential power holders does not address how power is distributed within the organization of the Church itself which remains an essentially patriarchal institution. In recent years, there has been more work done on a variety of levels within the Anglican Communion to question these patriarchal structures and approaches so that decision-making processes now vary from one province to another and even one congregation to another. Nonetheless, the Anglican Communion must still deal with the legacy of the colonial imposition of social norms for gender.

Another contribution worth holding up is that of Metropolitan Geervarghese Mor Coorilos. In his response to Dana Robert's keynote address, he lifts up particular issues of social injustice which he believes demand our attention in mission and must be named:

> In today's context of neo-colonialism, we are challenged by Jesus Christ to confront systemic demons and satanic forces that express themselves in the guise of economic globalization, casteism, racism, patriarchy, ecocide and so on. Mission in this context is about calling them by name and casting them out.[22]

Here he names patriarchy as a demonic systemic force thereby representing the experience of those oppressed because of their gender identity. It is also significant that his insistence on naming these particular 'demons' ascribes to verbal representation a certain power. This is the power to make visible and validate realities which had before been hidden. Whether these are realities of injustice and oppression or of diversity, it is a process of openness and inclusion as was practised by Christ.

While the diversity of human gender was not represented or present among the official speakers at the conference, there were many who responded with questions and comments whether in the large group or in small group discussions that helped balance this unequal representation. Women were present at the conference and spoke about a variety of issues that concern them. This was an important reminder of the diversity of perspectives that women and men express on the subject of mission.

Gender in Worship

Worship in the Church is defined in many ways and is regarded very differently from one Christian Tradition to another. That being said, communal worship is highly valued in most Christian Traditions.[23] It is for this reason that the worship team for the Edinburgh 2010 world mission conference had a very challenging task set before them in planning worship for such a group of people. As a participant in the liturgy and a liturgical scholar, I believe that the worship was largely successful. It brought delegates together in sharing parts of their own traditions and cultures as well as entering into entirely new experiences as a group thereby creating trust and building relationships. As for how gender was represented and present in this worship there are several areas to explore including: language, leadership, content and participation.

---

[22] Mor Coorilos Geervarghese, *Witnessing to Christ Today: A Perspective*, http://edinburgh2010.oikoumene.org/en/resources/papersdocuments.html (accessed 2.5.2011).

[23] This discussion is also of particular interest from an Anglican perspective. Worship has played an important role in establishing Anglican identity and still remains a source of constant discussion and debate within the Communion as a result. In addition, there are many who would argue that Anglican worship is a principal source for Anglican theology and an occasion for doing theology in community.

The team of people who planned and lead the worship at Edinburgh 2010, used a variety of different languages for the prayers, readings and songs used. The main languages used both formally and informally in worship were, however, English, French and Spanish and these will be the focus of our discussion of gendered language in worship[24]. It is worth noting that these are all colonial languages and thus they resonate differently for colonized and post-colonial people. First of all we will look at English, which was the primary language for informal introductions and instructions in worship. Careful attention was paid by the worship team to use gender inclusive language with reference to humanity and avoid terms such as mankind. In addition, many of the formal prayers avoided gendered language for God. The main exception to this is the use of the term Lord, a word that is not only male-gendered, but also involves a power relationship (Lord-servant). This creates a metaphorical relationship between maleness and Godly authority. In informal prayers as well as homilies, readings and other addresses in worship, God was regularly referred to using male gendered words such as Father, King and Lord as well as male gendered pronouns. It is also significant to note that God was not once referred to using female gendered imagery or pronouns. While this is certainly in keeping with the mainstream use of gendered language in English speaking congregations today, it overlooks both the historical and contemporary breadth of gendered images and metaphors for God drawn from Scripture, tradition and human experience. Sallie McFague addresses the dangers of overusing particular descriptors or metaphors for how we speak about God. The danger is twofold: that these metaphors become idolatrous and irrelevant:

> It becomes *idolatrous* because without a sense of awe, wonder, and mystery, we forget the inevitable distance between our words and the divine reality. It becomes *irrelevant* because without a sense of the immanence of the divine in our lives, we find language about God empty and meaningless.[25]

From an Anglican perspective, within provinces of the Anglican Communion where women's ordination is now common place, the use of gendered language in worship has become a ground for debate, especially in English. While language referring to humanity has followed the trend of much secular public language to be gender inclusive by avoiding terms like mankind, clergyman, etc., language referring to God in feminine terms or even the avoidance of male gendered language for God is still uncommon. In these cases, the presence of these ordained women in positions of power within a religious institution is still in contrast with Godly power which is

---

[24] This is also the case because I happen to speak all three of these languages fluently while having little knowledge of most of the other languages used in worship. In addition, these were the three official languages of the conference.

[25] Sallie McFague, *Metaphorical Theology: Models of God in Religious Language* (Philadelphia: Fortress, 1982), 2.

represented as almost exclusively male. This is certainly the case within my own province of Canada.

When examining the use of gendered language in French and Spanish, it is important to consider that gender functions in a very different way in these languages from in English. In both Spanish and French, all nouns have one of two genders – either masculine or feminine. Adjectives and pronouns are also gendered according to the gender of the nouns to which they refer. This is significant when it comes to discussions of human gender in language. Most of the studies examining gender in liturgical language have been written about English by English speakers, however, there are common practices for the use of gender inclusive language with reference to humanity in both French and Spanish. One such practice was used by a group of indigenous people from different parts of the world who made a presentation to the delegates during the last plenary session. In French and Spanish, language about humanity used gender-neutral terms such as "enfants" (fr. children) or adapted terms using the '@' symbol such as "hij@s" (sp. children). The official translations provided for worship did not make this same effort to be gender inclusive. Certainly this raises the question of how gender is adapted in translation from one language to another.[26] The case of language used to describe God in French and Spanish, however, is more nuanced. While in both languages, God, is a masculine noun as are many of the common images of God such as "Seigneur" (fr. Lord), "Rey" (sp. King), characteristics of God are of both genders. For example the word for mission in both French and Spanish is a feminine noun. This is not to suggest that all feminine nouns are in some way directly linked to human femininity or femaleness. Instead, what it suggests is that in these languages, linguistic gender does not directly connect us with human gender and sex. The implication is that the connection between male gendered language for God and God as male may not be as strong as in English. Nonetheless, the one-sidedness of gendered language for God is still plainly evident in all articles, pronouns and adjectives used in relation to images of God which were male-gendered.

Besides the language used both formally and informally, we must of course look at who is using it. As previously mentioned, the music and worship planning team for Edinburgh 2010 was quite balanced in terms of gender. Different voices were heard doing readings, leading and teaching songs, and offering prayers. When examining those outside the worship team – Church leaders, both delegates and local officials – these were overwhelmingly male and from positions of power and status within the various Christian communities. Those who lead worship are representations of humanity and in particular the worshipping community. From a

[26] This is a question evident in modern translations of the Greek version of the Nicene Constantinopolitan Creed into English which use male gendered pronouns with respect to the Holy Spirit where in Greek they are neuter.

liturgical perspective, priests (and by extension other worship leaders) are those set apart to make offerings and sacrifices on behalf of the whole community. They represent the community by who they are and what they say and do. For example, the music and worship planning team made a clear effort to represent the variety of people present in the music that was taught and sung and by including people from four continents in this leadership. In addition, part way through the conference, the question was raised by a number of participants of the use of a greater variety of languages for prayer and scripture. The worship team decided to make an additional effort to include some of these languages in worship so that it may be even more representative of the gathered community.

The language used in worship has already been discussed, but there is one significant piece of content that relates specifically to questions of gender. In the closing ceremonies, the question of the directions of mission in the future was raised in a short dialogue between delegates filling the roles of several marginalized people and a worship leader calling the gathered congregation to ask questions about how their voices are heard or not in the Church's discussion and praxis of mission. One such voice was that of women in mission. The leader read a lengthy history of many of the women of faith from the First Testament up to today who have been part of the *missio Dei.* This was followed by a delegate asking the following question of the congregation "I am just wondering whether in the next hundred years, men in the Church are going to take the Bible and my gender seriously?"[27] The fact that this question was raised at the closing ceremony in the presence of delegates, guests, and those watching online is a significant representation of this important question of gender and all those who ask it on a regular basis. In addition, the video of the closing ceremonies is one of the few videos of the actual proceedings of the conference. This makes it potentially more significant from the perspective of those reflecting on the conference in the future. Much like the records of speeches from the 1910 conference, this video will provide future generations with a window into the 2010 World Mission Conference. It will serve as a representation of the work and atmosphere of this conference.

Worship and liturgy are more than the work of those who lead them; they are the offering of the whole assembly. The way that participation is invited and how people respond is important to worship. At Edinburgh 2010, the music was led in large part by John Bell, a member of the Iona community and a well-known composer, author and worship leader. His own theology of music in worship encourages the empowerment of the vocally disenfranchised – those whose voices have been silenced and who feel they should not join in the song of the Church. Those who are marginalized by the Church because of their gender, whose voices are

---

[27] 'Closing Ceremony' in Edinburgh 2010, http://edinburgh2010.oikoumene.org/en/resources/videos.html (accessed 4.5.2011). Approximately 92 minutes.

silenced, are once again called to join the song. His leadership invites this kind of participation both through skilled teaching and leadership and through his enthusiasm. That said part of his method of inviting participation may actually serve to marginalize part of the assembly. Often times, the congregation is invited to sing as either 'men' or 'women'. They are given certain musical lines or stanzas of text based on their gender as either male or female. There are several common assumptions built into this way of inviting participation. The first is that the only two expressions of human gender are male and female. This assumption denies the reality of various other expressions of human gender that do not follow this binary division[28]. The second assumption is that those who identify themselves as women will have high voices and those who identify themselves as men will have low voices. In actuality, while the production of certain hormones such as testosterone does affect vocal register and sound production, and has traditionally been used as a marker of gender identity, there are many people who identify themselves as male who sing in a higher soprano or alto range (such as counter tenors, young boys, those singing falsetto and those who do not naturally produce testosterone) and many people who identify themselves as female who sing in a lower tenor or bass range (such as contraltos and some older women). As important as it is to be invited to participate in the song of the Church, the language used in that invitation must be understood as a fair representation of one's identity. Other forms of invitation using language like 'those with higher voices' or 'sopranos and altos' or even examples 'those who have high voices like Adam' can be a more inclusive representation of humanity in all its gender diversity.

What Does this Mean for the Marks of Mission?

This is just a snapshot of how one person saw gender and sex represented and present at Edinburgh 2010, but it echoes how these things are experienced by people in the Church today both on a conscious and subconscious level. This should concern you because all people are affected by how gender works. How we see and participate in all five (or six) marks of mission[29] is affected by how gender works.

In the first Mark of Mission for example, 'To proclaim the Good News of the Kingdom', gender affects who proclaims, what they proclaim and

[28] An example of this can be seen in the lives of many two-spirited people from indigenous groups in North America.

[29] The Anglican Communion presently has five recognized marks of mission, however, in the Anglican Church of Canada, a sixth mark of mission has been proposed. The marks of mission are: to proclaim the Good News of the Kingdom, to teach, baptise and nurture new believers, to respond to human need by loving service, to seek to transform the unjust structures of society, to strive to safeguard the integrity of creation and sustain and renew the life of the earth and to work for peace-making, conflict resolution and reconciliation.

who is able to hear it. Gender is woven into each of the Marks of Mission and those who seek to live them.

The importance of examining how gender affects the life of the Church has been recognized by the Anglican Consultative Council (ACC). The ACC is one of the four instruments of Communion whose role is to bring together the provinces of the Communion in terms of information and action. The ACC at the suggestion of the International Anglican Women's Network passed two resolutions relating to gender within the Communion. The first was ACC resolution 13-31 which received the report of Anglican Communion delegates to the United Nations Commission on the Status of Women in 2005. The resolution upholds the third Millennium Development Goal of promoting gender equality and empowering women and asks that the Standing Committee and member churches seek ways to realize this goal. The resolution also calls for "a study of the place and role of women in the structures of the Anglican Communion"[30] and requests that each province consider establishing a women's desk. This resolution was followed by resolution 14-33 which more specifically called for equal representation of women on all inter-Anglican Standing Commissions, committees and design groups. This resolution also called on the Provinces to participate in events and programmes designed to eliminate various forms of violence against women and girls. Finally, this resolution recommends the implementation of gender budgeting which is budgeting and budget analysis that takes into account how financial resources are distributed across gender lines.[31] Mission programmes would also fall under the scope of both of these resolutions. This suggests that the Communion, or at least the Anglican Consultative Council, is beginning to promote as important an analysis of the relationship between gender and mission. In addition, this analysis has as its explicit goal the equal representation of women – along with men it is assumed – on decision-making bodies and committees.

In these initiatives we can see a few important things that relate to how gender was present and represented at Edinburgh. Firstly, it is apparent that within the Communion, gender is still something that is seen to be the concern of women's organizations and groups. This is very much in keeping with the approach to gender seen at Edinburgh 2010. Gender is seen as concerning the role and place of women. Some broader analysis of gender, however, is going on in the Communion. In certain provinces, instead of developing a women's desk, there is an effort to establish a gender desk that looks at gender more broadly. There is also an expanding understanding of gender diversity beyond the male/female binary.

---

[30] http://iawn.anglicancommunion.org/reports/docs/ResolutionACC13-31.pdf (accessed 12.9.2011).

[31] http://iawn.anglicancommunion.org/reports/docs/ResolutionACC14-33.pdf (accessed 12.9.2011).

A feminist perspective on mission asks these questions about the relationship between gender and mission. Edinburgh 2010 was a gathering pregnant with possibilities for these questions to be asked. Many of them were not raised at all. The representation and presence of those whose gender has served to exclude them from past conversations was more extensive than in 1910, but still out of step with the lived experience of the Church in mission in 2010. Nonetheless, one can only speculate about the overall record of Edinburgh 2010, its future effects and how it will be remembered. Perhaps in the next hundred years, the Church will begin to take mission and gender seriously, but for now, it appears to be a theme that is mostly overlooked.

Discussion Questions

1. Different languages express gender in very different ways. How does gender work in the languages you speak? How does it affect your understanding of God?
2. How is gender a life-widening or life-limiting part of your identity?
3. How does gender affect our understanding of the marks of mission? For example, in what name do we baptize?
4. How is gender represented in the roles filled by different people in your Church context? Who leads worship? Who prepares food? Who repairs the building?

A Visual Gospel: Imagery as Mission

Luiz Coelho

Preface

It is easy to assume that those of us who have been learning about imagery and its related fields might somehow be more in touch with images than the ordinary person. That is not necessarily true. After studying images for the last ten years or so, both in technical and artistic terms, I still find myself perplexed at the intense overload of imagery we receive nowadays. With an incessant barrage of both static (photographs, websites, illustrations) and dynamic (videos, animations) images flooding our eyes on a daily basis, one wonders how the Church should respond to an ever-growing projection of simulated realities that very often deface, alienate and oppress.

This essay intends to suggest the use of imagery as an effective tool for mission in a rather varied context, which has been called 'postmodern'. It starts with a brief description of the characteristics that delineate the manifold postmodernities, and how they are expressed through imagery. In that regard, it draws some insights from French philosopher Jean Baudrillard's work and his negativistic view of imagery. Then, it proposes some possibilities through which the Church might present imagery as both missional and transformational: liturgical statements that can empower the people of God to act more effectively in the liberation, proclamation and reconciliation of all of Creation through Christ.

The author comes from a Latin American background, and prior to studying theology and sacred art, worked for some years with technology – most notably with digital image processing.

The Postmodern Condition

A comparison with the visual arts

Since this article deals with visual imagery, it might be interesting to note that the terms 'modern' and 'postmodern' were first used in the arts. As the vernacular of its time, art regularly reflects the spirit of its age, and not surprisingly, many scholars later borrow these terms used in the art world and apply them to spiritual, social and political matters. For example, while

Modern art might seem to some as rather varied, all of its schools and styles are unified by common principles and motivations. Social and cultural conditions in the late 19th and early 20th centuries had changed so quickly that many expressed high hopes in humanity. Modern artists from several different artistic movements, by referring to progress, science and new ideologies, aimed to create 'new art' that would completely break free from old constraints and inaugurate a new era of aesthetic standards. So, over the course of the decades of the early 20th century, several different movements tried to innovate art in pursuing 'new representations of self, some even finding the essence of humanity in pure abstraction.'[1] This became even more evident in the last offshoots of Modernism, which took art to a brand new world of minimalism and simplicity.

Postmodern art, however, is based on a growing awareness that context changes according to viewers' own experiences and sentiments. To a postmodern artist, there is little possibility of fixing a meaning to his/her work of art. This stems from a lack of hope in absolute truths and technological progress. Not surprisingly, it is also a period of eclecticism. Instead of trying to reconceive materials, methods and techniques in order to create 'new art forms', postmodern art makes references to its predecessors, sometimes in a creative way, with the intent of appealing to the viewer's inner feelings. It marked the reappearance of references to traditional art forms in galleries and museums, albeit not always purely traditional and labeled as art. But it is, above all, an era and not a style. And its work can be so unique that it is much more difficult to explain it in conventional art historical terms. It is, after all, a response to Modernism, and an attempt to fight its rather utopian focus on innovation and functionalism.

In a certain sense, art is everywhere and nowhere, as we find imagery more and more in diverse forms of media, such as computer screens, movie theatres, billboards, magazines, posters, and other venues not historically defined as venues for art or decoration. The boundaries between what is art and what is not have been blurred, as we 'experience' art in contexts and outlets detached from its original context.

Christianity, mission and postmodernities

'Mission and Postmodernities' was one of the themes discussed before, during and after Edinburgh 2010. This theme might sound intriguing to many readers, but it stems from the growing consensus that it is difficult to define specifically what 'Postmodernity' is. Thus, this paradigm shift from modernity to postmodernity cannot fit into one single definition. This, in

[1] Penelope E. Davies, David L. Simon, Walter B. Denny, Ann M. Roberts, Frima Fox Hofrichter and Joseph Jacobs, *Janson's History of Art* (Upper Saddle River, NJ: Pearson Prentice Hall, 2007), 981.

itself, confirms the common perception that, more than ever, the world is more plural and more diverse that it has ever been.

Modernity, in all its expressions, possesses a spirit of optimism and reliance on human reason, which was born with the Enlightenment, and flourished in the late 19th and early 20th Centuries. Its break with tradition relies on the 'grand narrative, a project designed to convince everyone of the truth of a particular vision or theory about historical development.'[2] Typical of modernity are ideologies and strong beliefs which co-opted masses in organized movements.

'Postmodernity', as the name implies, is simply something that comes after 'modernity'. In that regard, it carries a very sterile definition, but symbolizes what all postmodernities have in common: a rejection of the essence of modernity. 'For postmodernity there are no grand, objective narratives which provide a comprehensive explanation of reality.'[3] It has been shown that organized movements with the intent to change the world have been much less fruitful than expected. In some cases, they were catastrophic, causing terror, deaths and wars. In that regard, the postmodern paradigm shift implies a lack of hope about the future. There is no longer optimism that the world is progressing as it quickly changes. 'When hope is defined in terms of public progress, the individual's experience of non-participation in the fulfillment of such hope becomes displaced into a private realm of despair.'[4]

As a natural result of this lack of trust, more and more people turn to their private lives, trying to survive in the midst of chaos. Personal opinions are confined to a plurality of 'cultural, linguistic, political, and religious options'[5] which we have to live with and tolerate as equally valid and, in a certain way, not really transformative to the wider public. Often, this 'cohabitation' is full of suspicion and fear. It does not lead to conversion of attitudes; it only acknowledges that a 'cease-fire' is the best short-term solution. Also, there is an appeal to human feelings and instincts, as opposed to the reign of reason that once was dominant, often depending on subjective emotions and experiences. This stems from the belief that rigid definitions and meanings are not appropriate anymore and constantly change according to contexts. Even contexts such as time, history and evolution are perceived less and less as linear and logical. The danger regarding this appeal to sentiments is that it might eventually take groups of people to tragic escapist solutions. This is also the time of small extremist

[2] Report on Theme 3, Daryl Balia and Kirsteen Kim (eds), *Edinburgh 2010: Witnessing to Christ Today* (Oxford: Regnum Books International, 2010), 65.

[3] Ibid.

[4] David Kettle, 'The Gospel of Hope in a Postmodern Setting' (2009), paper presented to Edinburgh 2010 Study Group 3 and available at www.edinburgh2010.org.

[5] Kenneth Ross, *Edinburgh 2010: New Directions for Church in Mission* (Pasadena, William Carey University Press, 2010), 60.

groups, short-lived idols and tragic exaggerated reactions to even minor, daily events.

Postmodernities are not as evident in some societies as they are in others. However, the trend 'is no marginal phenomenon, not something happening on the fringe of society. Rather, it is penetrating whole cultures, a paradigm shift consciously and subconsciously transforming commonly accepted habits, notions and patterns of thought in its wake.... It is not essentially a western product, it is also relevant to Third World'[6] and can be found 'existing side by side in every corner of society.' In a rapidly interconnecting environment, this trend only tends to grow.

In the light of postmodernities, both ecumenism and mission as we know it are being reexamined and rethought. The 'Golden Era' of Christian mission can be situated in a thoroughly modern setting. Conferences such as Edinburgh 1910 happened under Western expectations that soon the whole world would be evangelized and gained for Christ. A post-Enlightenment growing awareness that mission held hands with Western progress, implicated Christian missionaries as partners with colonialist enterprises who imposed European and North American cultural and linguistic standards upon evangelized peoples are essential parts of the Christian narrative.[7] Modernity also saw the formulation of the *missio Dei*, which is arguably today's leading theological paradigm for Christian mission. The Trinitarian 'sending forth' of the apostles into the world to do God's mission (Jn 20:21) has been thoroughly digested and referenced in the last few decades.[8]

In a world where there is deep distrust in organizations as a whole, and where institutional ecumenism seems to be stalled, are there any prospects of agreement among different churches (with exponentially growing subdivisions)? It is within this very context that Edinburgh 2010 was convened, and in many ways reflected the spirit of postmodernities, with a rather long Common Call[9], which did not present, however, many signs of visible steps towards the increase of Christian unity and common mission. Furthermore, in an age when conversion is increasingly viewed with utmost suspicion, and people have learned to 'cohabit' rather than to engage openly in transformational relationships, how will mission deal with the 'sending forth' command to announce the Gospel to all of Creation? In that regard, perhaps even the concept of *missio Dei* must be reexamined to

---

[6] Jieren Li, 'Multi-identity of the Chinese Christianity in Post-Olympic China: From Pre-modernity towards Postmodernity' (2009), paper presented to Edinburgh 2010 Study Group 3 and available at www.edinburgh2010.org.

[7] David J. Bosch, *Missão Transformadora: Mudanças de Paradigma na Teologia da Missão* (São Leopoldo: Editora Sinodal, 2002), 329.

[8] Report on Theme 1, Balia and Kim (eds), *Edinburgh 2010: Witnessing to Christ Today*, 23.

[9] Edinburgh 2010 Common Call available at www.edinburgh2010.org.

embrace a stronger commitment to a holistic mission of God[10], which brings peace to the entire created order[11] and does not focus on saving souls only. Social injustice can no longer be detached from ecological injustice. Both have their roots in colonialism and ferocious capitalism. More than ever, integral and authentic evangelization is needed.[12]

Similarly, one wonders how much we should also address our mission to God, by trying to contemplate who God really is. It might help us to affirm new 'knowledge forms that come from the so-called margins'[13] without prejudice and to truly witness to Christ by breaking with the 'chaplaincy model'[14] that keeps our churches focused on their own internal issues. It would also help us to foster relational evangelization that draws people together and connects them with all God's creation, bringing liberation and *shalom* to the structures of our society.[15] Experience becomes another foundation for mission.[16]

This article does not intend to provide conclusive answers to all of these questions. However, it aims to start a discussion on how visual imagery can be a tool for mission in a world that is essentially different from our rather recent Modern past. In that regard, it is necessary to briefly examine the dramatic power of images, and their more and more frequent dangerous use as surrogates of new, alienating realities. In order to do that, I propose to draw on some insights from one of the most recent thinkers on both the power of imagery and postmodernities: French philosopher Jean Baudrillard.

---

[10] It must be noticed that the Anglican Marks of Mission already provide a good starting point to a such holistic approach to the *missio Dei*, but are they enough? Do they need an update?

[11] Kapya John Kaoma, 'Missio Dei or Missio Creator Dei: Witnessing to Christ in the Face of the Occurring Ecological Crisis' (2010), paper presented to Edinburgh 2010, available at www.edinburgh2010.org.

[12] Leonardo Boff, *América Latina: da Conquista à Nova Evangelização* (Coleção Fé e Libertação, São Paulo: Editora Ática, 1992), 33.

[13] J. Jayakiran Sebastian, 'Interrogating Missio Dei: From the Mission of God Towards Appreciating Our Mission to God in India Today' (2009), paper presented to Edinburgh 2010 Study Group 3 and available at www.edinburgh2010.org.

[14] Michael McCoy, *O Povo das Boas Novas* (Porto Alegre: Livraria Anglicana, 1991), 61.

[15] Valdir Steuernagel, 'To Seek to Transform the Unjust Structures of Society (i)', in Andrew Walls and Cathy Ross (eds), *Mission in the 21st Century: Exploring the Five Marks of Global Mission* (London, Darton, Longman and Todd, 2008), 68.

[16] Balia and Kim (eds), *Edinburgh 2010: Witnessing to Christ Today – Volume II*, 12.

Simulation and Death-Giving Images

An overdose of multidimensional images

Day after day we get bombarded with an ever growing amount of images (static, moving and interactive) of all sorts and themes: war, misery, religion, joy, technology, just to name a few. This overload of imagery brings serious implications that both feed and relate to the spirit of postmodernities. Baudrillard was one of the first scholars to write extensively on the power of images as substitutes for reality. He argued that images were first used as pointers to the real: abstractions that referenced something that exists. In a certain way, this is basic semiotics: representation stemming from the principle of **equivalence** between the sign and the real. However, gradually, representation lost its place to **simulation**. 'The circulation of information and images in this sign economy has reached a point of saturation'[17] in which signs no longer point to any reality. Rather, they point to a **simulacrum** and inaugurate 'the era of simulacra and of simulation, in which there is no longer a God to recognize his own, no longer a Last Judgment to separate the false from the true, the real from its artificial resurrection, as everything is already dead and resurrected in advance.'[18]

Therefore, it is possible to say that, for Baudrillard, 'proliferation of commodities multiplied the quantity of signs and spectacles, and produced a proliferation of sign-value.'[19] Commodities are increasingly not judged by their real value, but for what they symbolize in a different system of prestige. A simple piece of clothing gains value in this system only by having a designer's brand seal (no matter if it's an original or a fake!). Money transactions are done through cards and online systems as currency floats daily and bank notes are printed without gold standard. Buildings and objects are treated to look 'old', even though materials and construction methods are completely different from what they seem to be. Food items are presented as having flavours that resemble ingredients that were never used to prepare them. This list could go on, with more and more examples, but it is self evident that increasingly the world around us points to no reality whatsoever. Simulacra precede a reality that will never exist.

In a world with no reference to reality, nostalgia takes full place. And people's lack of hope, which is typical of postmodernities, continues to be

---

[17] James Walters, 'Finding a Prophetic Voice in Hyperreal Culture' (2007), paper presented to the 2007 Society for the Study of Theology at Westcott House, Cambridge.

[18] Jean Baudrillard, *Simulacra and Simulation* (Ann Arbor, MI: University of Michigan Press, 1994), 6.

[19] Douglas Kellner, 'Jean Baudrillard', in Edward N. Zalta (ed), *The Stanford Encyclopedia of Philosophy*, available at www.plato.stanford.edu/archives/win2009/entries/baudrillard

fed by nostalgic signs of a dream time which pointed to the 'real'.[20] This historical 'recreation', however, ends up having little relation to an 'historical real.' Traditions, cultures and archaeological finds are extrapolated into hyper-real renditions that feed people's wishes and alienate them at the same time. Disneyworld, for Baudrillard, is one of the fullest examples of such simulation, for it 'is not only interested in erasing the real by turning it into a three-dimensional virtual image with no depth, but it also seeks to erase time by synchronizing all the periods, all the cultures, in a single traveling motion, by juxtaposing them in a single scenario.'[21] According to Baudrillard, there are four successive phases of an image:[22]

1. Image as reflection of a profound reality;
2. Image as a mask that denatures a profound reality;
3. Image as a mask to the absence of a profound reality;
4. Image as simulacrum, which has no relation to any reality whatsoever.

In the first case, he defines image as a 'good appearance' of a sacramental order. [23] In the second case, it is an 'evil appearance.' In the third case, it 'plays at being an appearance' and is 'of the order of sorcery.'The fourth case is pure simulation. Its signs dissimulate that there is nothing. They point to a **hyper-reality**.

And it all starts innocently. Take for example old-fashioned photographs, with their original flaws and lack of colour. Yet, they pointed to something real (the subject matter), represented by an iconographic and still portrait on a wall. As more advanced image processing systems became available, photos came to a level of detail that replaced reality in many ways. There are full 3D image and video capturing systems nowadays. We meet places and people through computer images. Curiously, image manipulation has achieved a level of technology that provides tools capable of entirely creating three-dimensional scenarios and beings. And nothing goes untouched. There is always something that can be enhanced, hid or entirely recreated in digital images. Therefore, our perception of reality has changed in many aspects due to the hyper-reality presented to us in movies, photo ads and in the fashion world. This hyper-reality both addicts us with its breathtaking beauty, and frustrates us, for it cannot be achieved in nature. Consumerism grows as a natural consequence of this simulation. 'Participation in the "real" is projected for ever beyond

---

[20] Baudrillard, *Simulacra and Simulation,* 44.

[21] Jean Baudrillard, 'Disneyworld Company', *Libération* March 4th 2006, 7.

[22] Baudrillard, *Simulacra and Simulation,* 11.

[23] Sacraments can be defined as visible signs of an invisible grace and are an integral part of Roman Catholic, Orthodox, Anglican, Lutheran and some Protestant theologies. Baudrillard curiously uses the term in a non-religious context, by pointing out that images of the first type do possess some deeper link with a higher reality we cannot fathom.

the consumer, being promised through acts of consumption which fulfill a certain self-image but never fulfill this promise.'[24]

Also, images have never been presented at such a fast pace. Digital images have become so ubiquitous that there is not enough time to check what reality they point to (if there is one) – we just take them to be real.[25] In that regard, images become violent. 'This is the typical violence of information, of media, of images, of the spectacular. Connected to a total visibility, a total elimination of secrecy.'[26] Nonstop coverage and surveillance of world events and personalities, always with new headlines depicting 'exclusive images', contributes to the substitution of content for its medium and to the killing of the real, for 'the more exponential the marketing of images is growing the more fantastically grows the indifference towards the real world.'[27] This hyperinformation not only kills the real but also reinforces the silence of the viewers, who get more and more de-sensitized towards the world's pain and suffering and ultimately lose their sense of hope.[28] In such a setting, 'promiscuity' and passiveness in relationships get reinforced and lives are lived apathetically, without 'either responsible personal giving or receiving in any depth.'[29] Ultimately, this process leads to the destruction of the image as a transmitter of meaning. This destruction does not always happen in a literal way, such as during the Protestant Reformation or the Byzantine Iconoclastic controversy. 'Iconoclasts wanted to destroy images in order to abolish meaning and the representation of God. Today we are still iconoclasts, but in an opposite way: we kill the images by an overdose of meaning.'[30] In an era when images are captured, edited and transmitted electronically, the last violence done to them is technological. 'It is the end of the imagination of the image itself… because in the synthetic operation the referent no longer exists, and the real has not even time to take place as it is immediately produced as virtual reality.'[31]

Religious iconographies and simulacra

In terms of religious imagery (and Christian imagery in particular), a parallel can be traced. Images used in worship originally attempted to

---

[24] Kettle, 'The Gospel of Hope in a Postmodern Setting', www.edinburgh2010.org

[25] Jean Baudrillard, *La Pensée radicale* (Morsure: Sens & Tonka, 1994), 14.

[26] Jean Baudrillard, 'The Violence of the Image' (2002), paper presented at the International Symposium attached to 'media_city,' Seoul's 2002 Biennial and available at www.egs.edu/faculty/jean-baudrillard/articles

[27] Baudrillard, 'The Violence of the Image'.

[28] Jean Baudrillard and Marie Maclean, 'The Masses: The Implosion of the Social in the Media', *New Literary History* 16:3 (Spring, 1985), 577-89.

[29] Kettle, 'The Gospel of Hope in a Postmodern Setting'.

[30] Baudrillard, 'The Violence of the Image'.

[31] ibid.

depict God or holy figures in an iconographic and symbolic language, with no intent of concealing that God existed.[32] They were sacramentals. Gradually, as art progressed and Modernity infused a sense of hope in human reason, human models started to be used as references to what God or the saints should look like. Increasing realism in paintings and sculptures often meant that there was little room for symbols and graphic references. Therefore, gestures, colours, fabric folds, proportions and objects that carried a lot of meaning but seemed to be 'unrealistic' were very gradually removed from Christian iconography after the Renaissance.

It was also important to depict scenes as they 'looked like' in reality, and this led, of course, to a succession of attempts to mimic original clothing, characters and environments, based on recent archaeological discoveries (not rarely mixed with extrapolations and artistic license typical of hyper-real nostalgic pieces). The culmination of this process, so far, led to the point films such as the 'Jesus movie' and Mel Gibson's 'The Passion of the Christ' which are perceived as more than just tools for evangelism. They are also increasingly seen as the 'actual truth as it really looked like', leaving little room for an encounter with the spiritual truths that should take a whole lifetime to be properly digested, instead of a couple of hours in a dark room. This example, in a certain way, still relates to the triumphant model of mission defended in the early twentieth century, with its expectations of 'winning souls for Christ' by preaching the Gospel message according to a predetermined formula and cultural setting.[33] Could the visual vernacular of such a model, especially at a time of feel good religion and loose commitment, be a mere simulacrum of a hyper-real Christ? If so, then God and 'religious traditions become consumer commodities', which might explain the constant need many feel to 'update' their church experience to new styles, and even frequently to switch religious affiliation.[34]

But that is not the only Christian iconography we have been seeing lately. Modern art, with its intent of presenting content in new ways that broke with tradition, also led to rather varied iconographies with Christian-

---

[32] Even though Baudrillard was an atheist, he did use the word 'sacrament' to describe imagery of the first order. This essay intends to adapt his thought to Christian theology, which obviously leads to different beliefs on the nature and existence of God. However, it is safe to say that, apart from that, I have tried to keep the flow of ideas throughout the article as close as possible to Baudrillard's own conclusions.

[33] Patrick Stephan, 'Legitimation and Missions: How do we Reach this Eclectic World?', in Kirk Sandvig (ed), *Edinburgh 2010: Youth Perspectives* (Pasadena, William Carey University Press, 2010), 144.

[34] Olga Zaprometova, 'Bitter and Sweet Tears: Exploring the Spirituality of the Eastern Church Fathers in the Light of Post-modern Pentecostalism in Russia' (2009), paper presented to Edinburgh 2010 Study Group 3 and available at www.edinburgh2010.org.

related themes and in different media. Abstract paintings, collage sculptures, computer-edited images and several other media have been used as tools for Christian worship. Themes have also been varied and sometimes conflicting. Christ and the saints have been seen both as feminist protesters and as gay pride demonstrators. Sometimes they joined parades against abortion. In other moments they were depicted fighting as revolutionaries against oppressive right-wing dictators. But they also could be seen arrayed in gold baroque vestments supporting traditional marriage. The danger behind such representations is that, in a very modern way, they project a certain ideology and its agenda, and fail to present the universal Christ, who continues to speak anew to different contexts and realities. In other words, these iconographies appeal to specific groups only, and to nobody else. And sometimes, these kinds of depictions are so polarizing, and regarded as blasphemous by some, that they raise irrational fears among conflicting church groups, and instead of leading to conversion, they maintain the unsatisfactory *status quo* of a cease-fire Christianity that has already given up the grand narrative of ecumenism and real Christian unity.

Moreover, the overload of imagery also presented in Christian worship reinforces the simulation we presently see in other fields. There is a very strong pressure to make Church experience 'relevant' by speaking the language of an interconnected, fast-paced society. But what if the current language is a mere simulacrum? Then the tools used in Christian liturgy are merely reinforcing the simulation. When people are exposed at the same time to an overdose of video, paintings, lights, theatre, projected images, slideshows, installations, interactive pages, electronic messages, tweets and other sources of information, then there is very little to contemplate, almost nothing to be interested in, and a constant longing for the new fashionable liturgical attraction *du jour*. The Christian message is gradually killed by its rose-colored simulacra.

Rescuing Images in Worship as Means of Grace

Image-making and sacramental symbolism

If iconographies are to make reference to a reality that breaks the cycle of alienating simulacra, they must be restored to their original phase of a 'good appearance', full of sacramental nature. In a certain sense, this involves the work of adding symbolic meaning to imagery and referencing it to the knowledge of God, thus turning icons into true theological statements that both tell the viewer about our God, and also draw him/her into knowing more about the Divine. In a certain way, it involves studying and looking at earlier iconographies, where every single detail was full of symbolic meaning. Colours, gestures, positions, proportions, figures and objects were composed in a way that they could tell a story with manifold references. Mere Christ in Glory or Virgin with Child icons were full of details which express profound theological statements way beyond our initial assumptions that they are 'just a painting' of holy figures.

In the spirit of a living tradition, Christian imagery must be infused with symbols that connect us to the sacred experience of our ancestors, and yet relate to our continuous discernment as people of God guided by the Holy Spirit, being sent out by Christ to proclaim the Gospel to the whole of creation. The Church, therefore, must recommit itself to a process of image-making that adds symbolic theological meaning – in both ancient and new ways – to visual imagery.

To some of us, such a process might be a bit difficult, since some Christian traditions and parties have historically been wary of imagery being used as idolatry. However, if used as pointers to God (instead of substitutes of God), such images become much more than decorative objects, but windows through which our people can discover more about God. 'Icons are sometimes a fine art but, in the sense that they have universal meaning, they are also popular art: they are for everyone. Their function is to convey eternal truths and the highest spiritual concepts to all members of society regardless of class or economic circumstances.'[35] This is especially true in so many church contexts where many of the faithful do not have much formal theological education, and might find it important to use visual aids which will help them grasp such concepts more naturally.

Take, for example, the icon of 'St. Paul and the *Huia*' located in front of the main altar at St. Paul's Cathedral in London. The piece was commissioned by the Bishop of London and designed by New Zealand-born priest and iconographer Regan O'Callaghan. In many ways, it keeps the traditional Byzantine vernacular, with its manifold symbols. For example, around St. Paul's head, there is a golden halo – a symbol of sainthood. He raises his right hand in prayer, and with the left hand he holds the Gospel. On top of the Gospel book, stands a miniature version of St. Paul's Cathedral. Body proportions do not try to mimic reality. Nor do lights cast shadows. In fact, the lack of reflections in the saint's retina indicates that (Christ's) light shines through him. It is very evident that the image points to something 'not of this world.' Interestingly, in addition to the traditional Byzantine symbols, other symbols were added by the artist that relate to his own Maori heritage. For example, on St. Paul's shoulder, a *huia* rests peacefully. The *huia*, a bird originally found in New Zealand, was associated with the sacred by the Maori people. Sadly, its well-sought feathers and the introduction of predators by European colonizers led to the species' complete extinction. On top of the saint's head, a tent with flowers suggests the sweet scent of Heaven's indwelling. The folds in St. Paul's

---

[35] Richard Temple, *Icons: Divine Beauty* (London: Saqi Books, 2004), 11.

robe had another layer of meaning added to their traditional abstraction: a *koru.* This fern-inspired spiral symbolizes eternal life.

Figure 1 – Icon of St. Paul and the Huia by Regan O'Callaghan

And how does all of that relate to imagery as sacramental tools for mission? St. Paul, the apostle to the Gentiles, holds the Gospel as a sign of authority and reminds us of mission among all peoples. He raises his hand in prayer for us, and invites us to pray and meditate with him as we discern how to follow the path of sainthood and do mission in our times. This mission draws from the rich tradition of the Church, sharing a common language with Christians around the world, but has layers of meaning that reference it to newer cultural contexts, announcing the all-redeeming power of the universal Christ who brings eternal life. Finally, it is holistic: it speaks to all of creation – not only to humanity – and reminds us of the fragility of nature and of our need to take the good news of Christ to all of the created order. 'The *Huia* that sits on Saint Paul's shoulder reminds us that even though its song has been silenced, we are all still called to listen for the inspired beauty of God's song found in creation and Holy Scripture.'[36] In that context, Saint Paul's Cathedral is upheld and dedicated as a house of prayer and mission itself.

Several other considerations could be added to this list, which does not intend to limit the depth of fruitful discoveries that arise from meditating upon an icon. In fact, when such images point to God, they should take a whole lifetime to be fully digested. As noticed, an image-making process that is full of symbols refers to God without trying to simulate the Divine. In an era of lost references and hopes, it draws elements from the rich iconographic tradition of the Church, thus providing a common language with which the people of God can talk to one another, and not merely

[36] Regan O'Callaghan, 'Icons as religious artefacts…', in Michelle P. Brown (ed), *The Lion Companion to Christian Art* (London, Lion Books, 2008).

coexist without dialogue. As in postmodern art, it puts tradition and art historical references in conversation with issues of our times and cultures, reinserting themes people are just too afraid or disillusioned to talk about. The same line of thought can be applied to video, banners, installations and other media, which may also convey this conversation and use meaningful symbols drawn from both tradition and the life of the Church.

Consequently, it is imperative that we resist any attempts of over-simplification or total disconnection from our received tradition, under the excuse that 'our people' will not capture the depth of symbols in sacred art. Image literalism limits context-based interpretation (and reinterpretation), reduces symbols to a minimum, or completely kills them. Sacred art that is devoid of symbols and made to be easily readable merely forces upon viewers whatever message the original author proposed, without making room for an encounter with the Living God to which symbols are supposed to point. In some cases, it is a predetermined agenda or just a chimeric dream of portraying religious figures 'as they really looked'. Nonetheless, they limit the Holy One to a point of view and turn the Sacred into a decorative hyper-reality, which is not transformational and does not bear witness to the power of God in a broken society.

Liturgy as moving imagery

At this point, it is important to remember that imagery should not only be created, but used in the life of the Church. Very often, we find beautiful sanctuaries full of meaningful iconographies which stand as mere decorative elements just like paintings in walls of hotel rooms. And this takes us to liturgy as a proper venue for unlocking the power of sacred iconography. However, it can be also understood as multidimensional 'moving imagery' with plenty of meaning and symbols – some of which go beyond the visual, and relate to other senses (words, music, smells, gestures, touch and tastes). One can then easily conclude that liturgy must also be restored to its nature of a sacramental: a 'good appearance' that does not try to conceal God or limit divine power, but a reflection of a profound reality. For that to happen, it must be enriched with symbols that give proper meaning to it, instead of being a mere replication of a tasteless lecture which makes little space for personal encounters with God and forces worshippers to accept passively the hyper-real god that is presented by a specific line of thought or agenda. In a certain way, it involves restoring doing worship as equal to doing theology, with the emphasis 'on the experiential versus the rational way of doing theology'[37] – a principle upheld by the early Fathers. Anglican theology, in a similar way, also emphasizes that it is shaped by how we pray. 'As our praying joins God's

[37] Zaprometova, 'Bitter and Sweet Tears: Exploring the Spirituality of the Eastern Church Fathers in the Light of Post-modern Pentecostalism in Russia'.

initiative in mission, we become more committed to mission, and the rule of praying becomes the rule not only for believing but for acting as well.'[38] In that regard, *lex orandi, lex credendi* could be taken to non-verbal symbols as well.

Multi-sensorial worship that is fully participatory and presents people with symbols that are full of meaning possesses the iconic nature that engages people with God and with each other and breaks down the disconnected, consumer driven and hopeless spirit of this age. Worship ceases to be a stage where people merely stand and watch the altar party do a ritual far away. As with iconographies, it should be filled with references taken from a living tradition (such as, but not limited to vestments, prayers, readings, gestures, aromas, etc.), yet replenished with new symbols that relate to new contexts and situations. Most importantly, as a reflection of the nature of God who is a communion of persons, it needs to make room for all people to feel welcome and invited to take part in the liturgy-making process, so that the people of God can fully join the whole of creation through acts of worship. There should be no need for simplification or fear that they won't be fully understood. Not all will be understood at a first glance. It doesn't need to be. A thoroughly engaging process of participatory worship, where 'God draws nearest to the world' will always provide time for learning more and growing in grace towards God.[39]

And how can visual imagery be used in its full potential as conveyors of meaning in the midst of liturgies? One common example is the set of paintings called 'Stations of the Cross' which are associated with well established sets of liturgies (some of which ended up in our Prayer Books and supplementary materials). A fascinating set of Stations of the Cross is located at Lodwar Roman Catholic Cathedral in Kenya. There, a group of young local artists 'was asked to paint a set of stations that would reflect the life and environment of the people of Turkana.'[40] The iconography both reinforces the symbols contained in centuries old depictions of the *Via Crucis* and adds layers of new symbols that put them in context with local culture and draws people to worship Christ in their own visual language.

On the other hand, I was able to present some very different Stations of the Cross at Edinburgh 2010. Fourteen still lifes, which depict products easily available in our shelves for increasingly cheap prices. Within the production networks which grant this easy access to goods, there are often many cases of human enslavement, which happen in poor countries and far

[38] Titus Presler, *Horizons of Mission* (Boston: Cowley Publications, 2001), 11.

[39] Ken Cristoph Miyamoto, 'Worship is Nothing But Mission: a Reflection on Some Japanese Experiences', in Andrew Walls and Cathy Ross (eds), *Mission in the 21st Century: Exploring the Five Marks of Global Mission* (London, Darton Longman Todd, 2008), 161.

[40] Seamus O'Neill, 'Through Nomadic Eyes: Stations of the Cross in Lodwar Cathedral, Kenya', *Australian e-Journal of Theology* 7 (Pentecost, 2006), available at www.dlibrary.acu.edu.au/research/theology/ejournal/aejt_7/lodwar.htm.

away from our view. The artwork is accompanied by a liturgical booklet, which both informs about diabolic exploitation networks and invites worshipers to consider ethical buying and church-based activism to open people's eyes and help promote change and equality.

Figure 2 – 4th Station:
Jesus meets his Mother at Lodwar Roman Catholic Cathedral

Figure 3 – 11th Station: Jesus is nailed to the cross
(Stations of the Cross of Globalization) by Luiz Coelho

But are Stations of the Cross the only possibility of liturgical use of imagery? What if all of the iconography that fills our churches were liturgically appropriated likewise? What if, in different seasons of the

Christian year, other images were actively used in worship, with liturgies that bring everybody's attention to them and invite viewers to meditate upon the symbols they carry? And what if imagery found in Nature – which surrounds us indistinctly – could also be appropriated in this liturgy-making process?

In that context, images are no longer forced to a decorative background. They are lived, examined, witnessed, prayed for, prayed with and connected with gestures, acts, sounds, colours, and full participation in multisensorial worship which draws the people of God towards the Most Holy One. Most importantly, God is *felt*, and no longer presented as one of the (many) modern ideologies or parties that intended to change the world through the use of reason. That's when true conversion can happen, and when true change can take place in our world. 'In a society where space and time are compressed in the immediacy of visual, liturgy presents itself as a kind of therapeutic arena in which human agency, even humanity itself, can be rehabilitated.'[41] In this scenario, sacraments take their full nature as the epitome of symbolic efficacy, and are enshrined by liturgies that are sacramentals themselves. The Church can, consequently, be empowered to have a 'prophetic role… as a school of humanity',[42] and worship as mission takes a central role in that task. It might be a good idea, then, to update our Anglican Communion marks of mission[43] and add 'worship full of imagery symbolism' as a sixth, integrating mark that empowers the people of God to promote 'peace, conflict transformation and reconciliation.'[44]

Turning image-creating sacred again

It might be interesting to remember the original meaning of the word 'sacred' before we proceed with this discussion. This word refers to Latin word, *sacrum* (pertaining to God), but also takes the meaning of the Latin word *sanctum* (set apart). In the latter case it is better translated in English as 'holy', which shares common roots with 'whole' and adds to it a sense of completeness. It is not surprising that these terms are all interconnected. The same word in Hebrew (kedushah) carried the connotation of קדושה separateness. In a certain sense, much of early Christian and Eastern iconography held this notion of setting apart and consecrating icons for liturgical and devotional use. According to this understanding, the whole of God's creation is inherently good, even if we degrade and cover it (and

41 Walters, 'Finding a Prophetic Voice in Hyperreal Culture.'

42 Gianni Colzani, 'Presentation of Postmodernity' (2010), paper presented to Edinburgh 2010 Parallel Session 3 and available at www.edinburgh2010.org.

43 Miyamoto, 'Worship is Nothing But Mission: a Reflection on Some Japanese Experiences', 158.

44 ACC 14 – Resolution 14.05, available at www.aco.org/communion/acc/meetings/acc14/resolutions.cfm#s5.

ourselves) with layers of sin. Therefore, in creating and setting apart sacred art for Christian worship, we are consecrating matter that is part of God's creation to be used in God's worship. 'If we believe in a creative God, then we who are ourselves formed by Divine hands and given breath by the Holy Spirit and who are made in God's likeness must contain within ourselves the gift of creativity.'[45] It is a missionary act and a response to God through which we join the Godhead in the process of constant creation.

So, how could this process be reappropriated in the life of the Church? First of all, Christians must resist the temptation of acquiring 'ready to go' art for their liturgical space. If we are to collaborate with God in the process of setting apart holy imagery, then all of this image-creation process should be done in the life of the local Christian community. Holistic image-making must reflect holistic mission and be concerned about mission before, during and after their creation process. Some questions that might arise during the process itself could be:

- What materials are being used? Are they obtained through supply channels that take into account basic human rights and environmental concerns?
- Was the local community asked about themes and iconographies that relate to issues related to their experience of God?
- Are there local artists and theologians whose work could be used in the process of adding symbolism to the final piece, or guiding a commissioned artist into doing it?
- How will such imagery be used? Is it possible to engage the local community as liturgy-makers who will plan how to bless and pray with the final artwork?
- How will the piece be used as a means of spreading the Good News? Are there ways of involving parishioners into widening the circle of possible viewers by inviting friends and neighbours to contemplate artwork full of symbols that tell about the Good News of God in Christ?

Such considerations do not need to be done only during major artistic interventions, nor do they require impressive funding sources. Even simple projects such as flower arrangements or banner-making can be done prayerfully in the life of the community and gradually be taken to new levels of artistic interventions. For example, St. James' Scottish Episcopal Church in Leith, Edinburgh, has been exploring participatory image-making in its fullness for over ten years. Led by artist Carol Marples, the church community has been working 'exploring each liturgical season by changing the environment' in a way that allows parishioners of all ages to 'take part in helping to create the symbols and overall effects of the space.'

---

[45] O'Callaghan, 'Icons as religious artefacts…'.

The whole liturgical space is adapted to easily become a participatory seasonal installation.

> On three of the four walls, large panels have been mounted that are painted and then re-painted as liturgical seasons change. Small shelves are attached to the wall for the display of three-dimensional objects. In addition, spotlights are mounted that illuminate the work, creating a gallery effect in the space. The intentional decisions that have been made in modification of the space in addition to the decision to meet in the round point to a high value for participation and the use of arts in the church.[46]

Figure 4 – St. James' Easter Celebration

The process often involves a day of work where people are invited to paint, draw, cut, weave and participate in many other art-making activities. 'Imagine the impact of moving from the stark, barren colours and textures of Lent to a space bathed in bright yellow for Easter Day, with the huge crown of thorns centrepiece which had previously been rough and cruel now transformed by flowers.'[47] This successful experiment at St. James' Church led the artist to found Soul Marks, a charity in Edinburgh that promotes community art as a means of inspiring faith in God. Throughout the Edinburgh 2010 Conference, Soul Marks sponsored an installation of artificial trees with leaves made out of pieces of fabric from around the

---

[46] Sara Schumacher, 'From Artist to Participant to Artist: An Assessment of Participatory Art in the Life of the Church' (MLitt dissertation, University of St. Andrews School of Divinity, 2010).

[47] Carol Marples, 'Soul Marks', *Coracle: The Magazine of the Iona Community* June 2004, 12.

world, which enhance the multicultural aspect of mission and remind us of our interconnectedness in Christ.

Local communities could try to explore image-making processes similar to St. James' Church's experience. Recycling often presents a low-cost alternative to expensive materials. Also, nature offers us plenty of materials which can be easily used as liturgical aids and imagery itself. Even in deprived environments, it is possible to appropriate local crafts and traditions in order to retell the Gospel story in a way that is full of symbols which relate to the local people's daily experience.

Conclusion

And how should the Church respond to the plethora of images that both kill meaning and kill themselves, overdosing humankind with over-signification, over-information and over-reference and causing indifference towards the real world? Baudrillard indicates that it is imperative that we must restore the original power of the image by resisting 'this automatic overflow of images and their perpetual succession.'[48] The image should be, once again, put in suspense. It must be contemplated in all of its details. Its process of creation should be emphasized, as opposed to the visual flux of actuality, which 'does not know anything but change, it does not know the concept of becoming, which is radically different from change.'[49]

Therefore, sacred imagery and liturgy must resist both the oversimplification of sterile worship services and literal images and the flux of multitasking information that kills the Christian message by producing constant noise and visual pollution. There must be contemplation and **stillness**, with deep gazing of icons that gaze back at you. There must be **time** to 'live' the liturgy. There must be 'space' for each gesture, each song, each image. There must be room for everyone, and there must be a clear sense that worship is not 'just one more task' like the ones we do in this world full of simulations and simulacra.

At first, exploring such contemplation might not feel natural – especially to young people, which is why we ought to resist the appropriation in our liturgical space of the 'languages' of over-information: the language of broadcasting, the language of networking, the language of multitasking and the language of virtual communication. In essence, our church experience should be 'not of this world.' It must be different from what we are used to. It should point to a reality which is not of constant change, but of *becoming*, which is something the flux of sterilizing information cannot provide. In that context, real transformational encounters are allowed to happen. We are finally able to *meet* each other face-to-face, *feel* the pain and suffering of our brothers and sisters and stand in solidarity with them,

---

[48] Baudrillard, 'The Violence of the Image'.

[49] Baudrillard, 'The Violence of the Image'.

learn about God's Kingdom and *experience* the Divine Presence that surrounds us. In that context, images can be restored to their original power. They can be read and interpreted in their fullness, convincing us to strive for justice and liberation of the oppressed. They can motivate us about the future Kingdom of God that we proclaim – not as a distant dream, but as a coming reality whose impacts can be demonstrated.[50] Indifference towards the world's suffering is reverted and we are able to find real hope and motivation one more time, as we grow in grace towards being one with God. This is especially true in the heart of the Eucharist, in which, as put by St. Isaac of Nineveh, 'the true love of God is revealed to a human being.'[51] The Mass 'subverts market logic by gathering all people around a table at which all are equal and all enter into a communion of interdependence with one another.'[52] Truly empowering worship of God where all are given an equal share teaches us how to be prophetic in the world, 'crossing boundaries and making inclusion possible' and overcoming social and cultural boundaries.[53] And then, we can finally *become*. We stop merely changing and finally become more like Christ. We become more like the *image of Christ* and truly able to affirm in our conscience the identity of Jesus.[54] We ultimately become *sacramentals* ourselves: *images* of a good appearance and full of *symbols* that reflect God. And then, we can be fully prophetic in doing the mission of 'rescuing and liberating our historical decadence'[55] and restoring the world to what God meant it to be.

Discussion Questions

1. Does your parish have any sort of community art project? How do you think this could be integrated with the liturgical and missiological life of your church community?
2. Many of our church buildings possess a reasonable amount of imagery, such as stained glass, fabric, paintings, posters, sculptural elements and other media. How does this imagery reflect mission and prompt you to engage in it?

---

[50] Ken Gnanakan, 'To Proclaim the Good News of the Kingdom (i)', in Andrew Walls and Cathy Ross (eds), *Mission in the 21st Century: Exploring the Five Marks of Global Mission* (London, Darton Longman Todd, 2008), 5.

[51] Zaprometova, 'Bitter and Sweet Tears' (2009).

[52] Walters, 'Finding a Prophetic Voice in Hyperreal Culture'.

[53] Michael Herbst, 'Plural Mission and Missionary Plural in a Post-Socialist Context: Using the Example of a Post-Volkskirche, East German Region' (2009), paper presented to Edinburgh 2010 Study Group 3 and available at www.edinburgh2010.org.

[54] Achylle Alexio Rubin, *A Novidade da Novidade: Novo Milênio, Nova Evangelização* (Santa Maria: Palotti, 2001), 39.

[55] Boff, *América Latina: da Conquista à Nova Evangelização*, 44.

3. Visual statements are often used as a tool to communicate the Gospel to groups of people who do not feel comfortable with reading texts (for example: children, people with little schooling, immigrants who do not have full domain of the local language, cultures based on oral traditions, etc.). How could you implement a specific ministry for them in your church involving visual arts as a tool for inclusion?
4. We also see many visual elements that relate to God outside churches. Sometimes they are found in our houses, sometimes in public places and all the time in nature. How does your community express this beauty and devotion in worship?
5. Every piece of art intends to transmit a message, just like a speech or written commentary. How would you see art-making and interpreting in comparison to preaching? Could a work of art replace a sermon?

Conclusion

RECEIVING A NEW DAY OF MISSION

Mark McDonald

Though convened as a commemoration, the emphasis of the Edinburgh 2010 Conference was not on the past. A critical remembering of the Edinburgh 1910 Conference was placed in the context of a contemporary reflection on God's Mission in Creation and history. It was hoped that the gathering could make a substantial contribution to the way that the Church, particularly in the West, perceives this Mission. To make this possible, organizers did their best to present a comprehensive cross-section of the multiform reality of Christian faith around the world today. They are to be commended for the overall quality of their work, given the constraints of time, money, and geography. Conference attendees who had little experience of the rapid and widespread changes to Christian faith in the past few decades went away with a solid introduction to a very interesting new world.

But any attempt at describing God's mission should come with a reminder that the logic and horizon of God's mission is always beyond precise human description. An accurate picture of the scope of missional change in the past few decades has been especially illusory. The rate and extent of missional change is as great as or greater than any time since the apostolic era. But this is far from fully appreciated by the churches of the West. They have shown a surprising lack of appreciation or understanding of a reality that is seen to exist outside the course of their history and culture. When change is noticed, its significance is almost always evaluated within the framework of the Western churches' own struggles and priorities. Though there have been some attempts at exploitation in the midst of Western intramural conflict, there is virtually no discernible interest in absorbing or adapting to these changes as a part of the worldwide Christian community.[1] This is true even when the change and growth are happening in churches that are a part of their global community, as we have seen in the Anglican Communion.

It should not be surprising then, that, although the reality of a worldwide awakening of Christian faith was present at Edinburgh 2010, the full and multiform dimensions of this awakening were not accessible. Some attendees mentioned that the conference was constrained in its ability to

[1] A theme that often appears in Lamin Sanneh's *Whose Religion is Christianity? The Gospel Beyond the West* (Grand Rapids: Eerdmans, 2003).

perceive the range of faith and experience present in the gathering.[2] This was, in part, due to the use of academic and cultural protocols of the Western churches that dominated the 1910 Conference. But the real problems are deeper.

Some of the basic dimensions of the missional phenomena outside of the Western cultural framework have been reported in the West but, since they are not well understood in their own context, they are often crudely interpreted. Much of the reporting presents caricatures based on Western religious categories. A little bit of exposure to Christian communities outside of the West makes it clear that terms that may mean a lot in a Euro-American context – like liberal or conservative, ecumenical or evangelical – don't fit very well. The lack of coherence across these cultural divides will not be solved by more reporting or documentation. At present, the churches of the West seem to lack the spiritual and theological tools to receive what is happening elsewhere.

Ethnocentrism

Ethnocentrism is a part of this, a reality that has been oddly strengthened by the process we now call globalization. Globalization has given us the appearance of cultural exchange, while strengthening stubborn and persistent cultural prejudice. For the churches of a Western cultural framework, the perception of cultural and religious development around the world has been complicated by the transition from a somewhat limited presence of overt hard power to the almost universal and inescapable soft power of economic and cultural dominance. When the West looks at phenomena outside its sphere, the ubiquity of its culture – through economics, technology, and entertainment – means that it is often unable to see anything but a reflection of its own image or hear anything but its own pre-developed narrative of events and peoples. Sadly, the churches of the West also display this inclination in their analysis of religious phenomena outside their cultural competence or experience.

There is an additional problem for the churches of the West, something much more challenging. Seemingly unaware of alternative possibilities, they have viewed their own trajectory of faith as singular, divinely privileged, and spiritually necessary. Replicating the path of the Western churches' development has been seen as an essential precondition to the growth of orthodox Christian faith. The patterns of inculturation in the Western churches have been considered so privileged that learning and mimicking them has been considered a prerequisite for ordained Christian

---

[2] A concern of Pentecostal and Indigenous participants at Edinburgh 2010 – see 'A Statement of the Pentecostal Participants' and 'Statement by Indigenous Participants', in Kirsteen Kim and Andrew Anderson (eds) *Edinburgh 2010: Mission Today and Tomorrow* (Oxford: Regnum, 2011), 343-350.

ministry – with a special force that is increased when applied outside of Western contexts. Non-Western candidates for ministry in the Western churches have had a special and strict mandate to fulfill the protocols of Western cultural styles of ministry. This limited capacity to see beyond its own story, its own well-developed system of meaning, seems to be the key factor in the inability of the Western churches to receive the fullness of what is happening elsewhere.[3]

Whether this spiritual myopia is a product of idolatry, a lack of imagination or, more likely, both, its consequences are damaging to the missiological capacity of the churches and the quality of Christian witness and community around the world. In the West, the churches are cut off from the well-spring of incarnational life, as it is now developing in other contexts; in those other contexts, Christian communities must interact with powerful global church systems that imagine churches outside of a Western cultural framework are lesser versions of themselves. The churches outside of the West are often seen as being in a stage of development somewhere on the path to cultural and ecclesiastical maturity, a maturity that is defined entirely in Western terms. The Western churches pay a high cost in terms of missional horizon. Beyond the West, there is the pain and spiritual distortion that is the cost of being a battlefield for competing church interests from the West.

As formidable as this situation might sound, its remedy is not far away. If the problems of receiving the worldwide arc of contemporary mission, of being a worldwide community of faith, were present at the Conference, the basic elements of new possibilities, a new reality, were also near at hand. The trajectory of faith we see in the development of multiple forms of indigenous faith throughout our world has an echo in a contemporary trajectory of faith and renewal in the churches of the West. We are speaking here of an expanding movement of missional renewal among Western churches, as evidenced at the Conference by the widespread use of the concept of *missio Dei* and a generally held missiology that assumes God's presence in all cultures and contexts. Both of these are a contrast to many of the missiological assumptions of Edinburgh 1910. When placed in the context of a widespread reappraisal of Christendom, these ideas provide a conceptual framework that will enhance the worldwide community of Christian faith.

[3] It should be noted that the Orthodox churches present a more complex and nuanced relation to these issues. This should receive much more attention but, in this short treatment, must be referenced by footnote. The significant missiological reflection of Michael Oleksa in *Orthodox Alaska: A Theology of Mission* (St. Vladimir's Press, 1992) is a good place to begin this discussion.

Missional Renewal: *Missio Dei* and an Emerging Missiology of Presence

Missio Dei was a pivotal idea at Edinburgh 2010. Assumed by virtually every presentation, there appeared to be general agreement about the concept's meaning: Mission is God's work in Creation and history. This theocentric understanding of mission, a Trinitarian vision, is offered in sharp contrast to the late Christendom project of missionizing, especially in the context of the West's colonial expansion. Christian community, viewing Creation through the lens of *missio Dei*, understands that God's work is the animating principle for all ministry.

Related conceptually to *missio Dei*, a missiology of presence was also assumed throughout much of the Conference. Without controversy, it could be announced that "what is called for in our time is a mission spirituality that recognises that God is already working, has been working within all cultures, revealing Godself."[4] As an example of this, the Conference heard that the traditional spirituality of Koreans and the primal religions of Indigenous Peoples play a critical role in the spread of the Gospel in those contexts.[5] This is a sharp distinction from the missiology of an earlier generation. Clerics of my generation can clearly recall that these traditional and indigenous religions were once considered obstacles to Christian faith. They were never imagined to be a preparation for it.

There has been a major change in the perception of God's presence in creation, culture, and history. We have gone from a missiology premised on the idea of absence – in the past, God's presence was presumed to come with the Christian message and its messengers – to a missiology premised on the idea of presence – God's presence, the Living Word of God in Creation, anticipates the message; the message itself unveils the presence. It would be hard to overstate the significance of this idea. Held together with *missio Dei*, an emerging missiology of presence is part of a missiological revolution.

It may be said that both *missio Dei* and a missiology of presence are a part, perhaps an inaugural part, of a Western expression of the missional change that is seen elsewhere around the world. These concepts are formed and animated by the same forces that have produced the explosion of indigenous expressions of Christian faith around the world. We may mention the collapse of colonial missions and the end of Christendom as among these forces. But there is certainly more involved. Without doubt the changing and saving power of the Gospel is clearly the most pervasive element of all. In our day, as in ages past, God is doing great things among the nations. The vibrancy and diversity of the Word made flesh in this new day of Mission reveals, once again, the life giving vitality of the Gospel.

---

[4] Daryl Balia and Kirsteen Kim (eds), *Edinburgh 2010: Witnessing to Christ Today* (Oxford: Regnum, 2010), 241.

[5] See, for instance, Balia and Kim (eds), *Edinburgh 2010,* 52-54 and 238.

We see this, not only in the churches outside of the Western cultural framework, but also in the power of the Gospel to renew a missional imagination in the churches of the West. It appears that God has given birth to a dynamic diversity of faith outside of the West's cultural framework. With this development, there is also an opening door of understanding and renewal within the churches of the West.

The Path Ahead

Edinburgh 2010 framed a number of complex challenges for Christian faith communities around the world, both in its direct presentations but, more to the point, in demonstrating the difficulties faced as Christian communities try to understand and receive the scope of missional change around the world. The Global Christian organizations that began as Western institutions, like my own Anglican Communion, are confronted by a world that was and, in many respects, still is unimaginable within the theological and cultural structures that have been predominant. Although the Edinburgh 1910 Conference had an expansive, some would say arrogant, ambition for the missions of the West, the arc of Mission today makes many of the hopes of the past seem both misdirected and meagre. Today, the churches of 1910 must place the consideration of this new missiological horizon very high on their agenda.

This new day engages us at a fundamental level. This moment in God's mission reveals the depth, breadth, and mystery of God's work in Creation in a way that confronts the narrowness of institutional imagination. We should feel a growing sense of awe as we witness the multiform diversity of God's active love towards humankind and Creation. With awe comes a new sense of vocation, a calling to a level of corporate and individual discipleship that has not been common in the period of late Christendom. This is a discipleship of the Word made flesh, the living embodiment of God's eternal Word in the many diverse cultures of the world. It is a discipleship in which the whole church develops a capacity for humble and constant spiritual discernment – the prayerful discipline of listening for God's Word in Scripture, creation, and in one other.

For the Anglican Communion, and other church bodies like it, we should be able to re-frame the difficult and divisive discussions of our recent past in the expansive missional horizon that calls us to a new level of Christian partnership and communion. This will certainly require a new type of theological clarity – clear, yet open; certain of essentials, but ever more aware of the unfolding variety of God's revelation in Creation. Scripture must be foundational in this, as the centre of an on-going process of mutual consultation and discovery. This will include, at a primary level, a re-reading of Scripture in the context of a frank and earnest appraisal of the legacy of Christendom. This would not be to demonize the past, but to identify the distortions that may obscure the future. The goal is not to be anti-Western, but to recognize the power of God in an uncountable number of contexts. In all these things, the clarity sought is not primarily doctrinal – doctrine defined here as a product of human intellect, conversation, and agreement. On the contrary, the clarity that we may say is now seeking us will be found in a Biblical question: Who do you say that Jesus is? This type of clarity is found in witness, commitment, and spirit and, it must be admitted, it can only subsist in human doctrinal formulations.

The pattern of consultation that is suggested by the Anglican Communion's participation in Edinburgh 2010, as it is also employed in this book, may be a model for future missiological conversation. It will, however, have to be sharpened by the urgency and theological import of our present worldwide missiological context. This context is not only defined by the enormous diversity and opportunity of this moment in time. There is also, in the revelation that God is working in Creation, an unveiling of another reality: the principalities and powers that act in opposition to the Word of life in Creation. We are, both in our opportunity and challenge, on the precipice of one of the great defining moments of Christian faith, a moment unlike any other. If we did not see this clearly at Edinburgh 2010, it was not too far off in the distance.

APPENDIX

THE FIVE MARKS OF MISSION AND THE ANGLICAN COMMUNION

John Kafwanka

Introduction

The Anglican Communion is a family of churches which are self governed in thirty-eight regions known as Provinces. Some of these provinces are nationally based, like the Anglican Province in Canada, while others constitute a number of countries such as the Province of Southern Cone, (Iglesia Anglicana del Cono Sur de America) which includes Argentina, Bolivia, Chile, Paraguay, Peru, and Uruguay. Some of the churches in the Anglican Communion family are known as Episcopal, such as the Scottish Episcopal Church, the Episcopal Church of the Sudan, and The Episcopal Church in USA, just to mention a few. While others are known as United Churches, and these include the Church of Bangladesh, the Church of North India, the Church of Pakistan, and the Church of South India.

As a global family of some 80 million Christians, the Anglican Communion member Churches have over the years developed many and vibrant ways of relating to and enriching one another. However, there are also formal global structures that exist, known as Instruments of Communion, and they include the Anglican Consultative Council, the Lambeth Conference (which meets every ten years), and the Primates Meeting. Meanwhile, the Archbishop of Canterbury, who is the President of the Anglican Consultative Council, and Chair of the Lambeth Conference and the Primates Meeting, is referred to as the 'focus of unity' in the Communion. The Instruments of Communion and indeed the Anglican Communion at large are served by a permanent secretariat based in London, United Kingdom, known as the Anglican Communion Office. The current Secretary General of the Anglican Communion is Revd Canon Kenneth Kearon from Ireland.[1]

Why Young Anglican Leaders?

As a follow up on the 14th Anglican Consultative Council (ACC-14) meeting in Jamaica, where the importance of growing and investing in

---

[1] www.anglicancommunion.org/ministry/secretariat/index.cfm.

young leaders was discussed at length, the Mission Department developed a programme that aimed at investing in, encouraging and developing young Anglican/Episcopal leaders; particularly those involved in 'cutting edge' or pioneering mission/ministry around the Communion. This initiative aims at giving potential young Anglican leaders an opportunity to experience, contribute to and participate in international mission events. The centenary Edinburgh 2010 ecumenical mission conference, in June 2010, provided such an opportunity. So, in 2009, each Province in the Communion was invited to send two or three names of promising young mission leaders to participate in this initiative.[2] Six were chosen to participate in the Edinburgh 2010 centenary conference.

Besides participating in the Edinburgh 2010 Centenary Conference (2-6 June), the group also participated in the pre and post-conference programmes. The pre-conference programme was a hospitality initiative generously offered by the Scottish Episcopal dioceses from 28th May to 1st June. This provided an opportunity for the delegates not only to experience the life and ministry in the Scottish Episcopal Church, but also to share with their hosts about the life and ministry of their churches of origin; as well as relaxing and acclimatising before the conference. The hospitality initiative programme also included time for delegates to get together and know one another, and reflect on the Scottish experience so far. There was an opportunity to look at the Conference programme and expectations. The Anglican delegates also talked about how to capture and share conference experiences with the Communion. The programme also included a meeting with Bishop David Chillingworth, the Primus of the Scottish Episcopal Church, who shared about the history and ministry of his Province. This programme concluded with an invitation to dinner from Bishop Brian Smith of Edinburgh Diocese at his residence. This time together successfully enabled the delegates to gel as a group ahead of the conference which took place at the Pollock Halls of the University of Edinburgh.

Meanwhile, the post-conference programme was aimed at giving the delegates an opportunity to experience and visit some Church of England mission initiatives around the London area, meet with Anglican Communion Office staff, and also to visit Lambeth Palace and meet the Archbishop of Canterbury, Dr Rowan Williams, whose humility and leadership they described as an 'example of what Christian leadership should be.'

There was a session for debriefing, to share experiences and insights of the Edinburgh Conference and the whole programme in general, and explore ways to share the experience and the conference outcomes with their Church and the rest of the Anglican Communion. It was here the idea

---

[2] There were many other Anglicans/Episcopalian delegates at the Edinburgh 2010 Conference but only nine were the ones officially sent as representatives of the Anglican Communion.

to write a book that would reflect on the Edinburgh 2010 and the whole UK experience emerged. Most of the young Anglican delegates were exposed to the Five Marks of Mission for the first time during this trip, and they lamented how unknown in the Anglican Communion these Marks of mission and the Instruments of Communion were. So, they decided to focus the book on the Edinburgh 2010 experience but in the context of the Five Marks of Mission.

Some of the mission initiatives the Young Anglican leaders visited included the Greater London Presence and Engagement Initiative, an initiative which promotes programmes that foster Christian-Muslim relations and equips 'Christians for ministry and mission in a multi faith society'[3]; taking part in an Alpha workshop on integrating Alpha into the Church led by the Vicar of Holy Trinity Church Brompton, Nicky Gumbel, during The Alpha Conference; and a visit to Southwark Cathedral where the group met the former Dean of Southwark Cathedral, Colin Slee, who shared with the group an example of how cathedrals can position themselves as places for visitors to experience hospitality and renew their faith.

It is important to mention that the Anglican Communion participated in the planning of the Edinburgh 2010 conference as one of the twenty Church bodies and mission organisations that made up the General Council with an overall oversight of the Conference planning process. The Anglican Communion's Director for Mission, John Kafwanka, represented the General Secretary of the Anglican Communion, Canon Kenneth Kearon, on the Edinburgh 2010 General Council.

The Anglican Communion was allocated nine places at the Edinburgh 2010 conference. As well as the six young Anglican leaders aged between 25 and 35 years, there were three other delegates who had participated in the Edinburgh 2010 planning process. Out of the nine delegates, four were women, five men, three lay and six clergy. They came from seven Provinces of the Anglican Communion: Brazil, Canada, Central Africa, England, Hong Kong, Kenya and Southern Africa. While at the Conference, the delegates interacted with, among others, a number of Anglican delegates who had come to the Conference as representatives of other Church mission bodies around the world. One of these delegates (Andrew Thompson from The Episcopal Church – USA) was a young Anglican who had participated in the Edinburgh 2010 Youth writing contest. The aim of the contest was to encourage young people to participate in the Edinburgh 2010 study process as well as the whole Edinburgh 2010 celebration. The prize for this contest, which Andrew won, was to attend the Edinburgh 2010 Conference. So, while at the Conference, Andrew became part of the Young Anglican leaders group, and thus one of

---

[3] http://londonpen.org; www.presenceandengagement.org.uk.

the contributors to this Book project.[4] It must be mentioned here that the presence and participation of the Young Anglican delegates at the Edinburgh 2010 conference was widely acknowledged by many people. Their ability to engage with the conference sessions and interaction with other delegates as well as their sense of collegiality as a group while representing a global diversity of Anglicanism were very impressive. The group stood out in a special way and was described by some as 'a gift to Edinburgh 2010'. The Anglican contribution to the Edinburgh 2010 conference was described as more significant than would have been expected from 9 delegates.[5]

Five Marks of Mission and the Anglican Communion

The Five Marks of Mission are a significant expression of a common Anglican Communion statement about mission and they also form an important basis of the Communion's holistic understanding of God's Mission. The Five Marks of Mission are:

1. To proclaim the Good News of the Kingdom
2. To teach, baptise and nurture new believers
3. To respond to human need by loving service
4. To seek to transform unjust structures of society
5. To strive to safeguard the integrity of creation and sustain and renew the life of the earth

The Bishops at the 1998 Lambeth Conference defined mission as "God's way of loving and saving the world"[6], which manifested and found fulfilment in the life and ministry of Jesus Christ through the power of the Holy Spirit. Meanwhile, the Bishops at the 2008 Lambeth Conference stated that 'The Church as an instrument for mission' has been called to participate in 'the movement of God's love toward people [and the rest of creation]'.[7] Therefore, God's Mission is at the heart of the life and existence of the Church and Christian ministry.

---

[4] It is possible that there were other young Anglicans among the many Anglican delegates in the conference but apart from Andrew, I only managed to meet one other young Anglican from Trinity College in Melbourne, Australia.

[5] Many people commented to me privately and openly of how impressed they were by the Anglican delegates, with specific reference the Young Anglicans. There were several other ways the Young Anglican delegates stood out during the Edinburgh 2010 conference, both as a group and individually. For example, one of them (Luiz Coelho) had an Arts' exhibition throughout the conference period, which was greatly appreciated by many. During the closing worship in the Conference Hall at the Mound, the young Anglicans played a prominent role in reciting key messages.

[6] The Official Report of the Lambeth Conference 1998 (Morehouse: Pennsylvania, 1999), 121.

[7] 'Lambeth Indaba – Equipping Bishops for Mission and Strengthening Anglican Identity', Lambeth Conference 2008, 8.

By definition, the mission of the Triune God is fundamentally and biblically holistic in that, 1) it takes seriously the totality of God's creation, that is, it is concerned for the transformation of human and non-human creation; and, 2) it takes seriously the totality of the human person, that is, body mind and spirit as both its object and subject. Therefore, mission is both proclamation and social action. This holistic understanding of God's mission is adequately, although not exclusively, expressed in the Five Marks of Mission.

The first four of the Five Marks of Mission were first considered and adopted in 1984 at the sixth Anglican Consultative Council meeting in Nigeria and were set out in its report, Bonds of Affection.[8] The Marks of Mission were then later refined and another one (the fifth Mark) was added to form the Five Marks of Mission in 1990 at the eighth Anglican Consultative Council meeting in Wales.[9] Since then, mission in general and indeed the Five Marks of Mission in particular have been highly recommended and are constantly reflected upon and feature highly at meetings of the official structures of the Communion – the Anglican Consultative Council (and the Standing Committee), Primates Meeting and Lambeth Conference. The 2008 Lambeth Conference, whose main theme was 'Equipping Bishops for Mission and Strengthening Anglican Identity' had prominently featured topics from the Five Marks of Mission.[10]

It is very important to emphasise here that all the Five Marks of Mission are biblical and reflect the ministry and work of Jesus Christ, in whom God's mission has complete manifestation in the world. The life and ministry of Christ, in the power of the Holy Spirit, was to bring about healing, wholeness and reconciliation of God's creation, and the Five Marks of Mission express both the reconciling and the holistic nature of God's mission. As Cathy Ross puts it the Five Marks of mission 'form a good working basis for a holistic approach to mission.'[11] Therefore, the Five Marks of Mission can be described as a DNA of holistic or integral mission, in that while each mark is complete in itself, it is nevertheless an important part of the whole and contributes to the whole, and is a potential 'doorway' to faith.

It must be acknowledged from the outset that the Five Marks of Mission are neither a perfect nor a complete statement about mission, and certainly not a final statement on mission or indeed an articulation of every aspect of mission. However, the Five Marks of Mission reveal the fact that God's mission is much bigger and wider than we sometimes reckon, while at the same time showing that they can be integral, contextual, personal, local,

---

[8] *Bonds of Affection*, Proceedings of ACC-6, Badagry, Nigeria – 1984, 49.

[9] *Mission in a Broken World*, Report of ACC-8: Wales 1990, 101.

[10] See 'Lambeth Indaba' report for the various topics covered at 2008 Lambeth Conference.

[11] Andrew Walls & Cathy Ross, *Mission in the Twenty-First Century* (London: DLT, 2008), xiv.

national and global – an essential reality about mission being local-global. In another sense the Five Marks of Mission prevent a 'mono focused' ministry and narrow approach to mission, whereby one defines mission by one or a set of activities, while at the same time the Five Marks of Mission can sharpen the Church's response to God's mission, avoiding the worry that everything is mission and mission is everything and therefore nothing is mission!

The Anglican Communion has always encouraged the adaptation and revision of the Five Marks of Mission to suit the context of each local Church as it seeks to be a sign and foretaste of the Kingdom. Some churches, such as the Anglican Church in Australia, have revised the Five Marks of Mission and included news ones that are relevant to their context.

Recently, at the fourteenth Anglican Consultative Council meeting in Jamaica, a resolution was passed to develop a sixth Mark of Mission around peace and reconciliation following a proposal from the Anglican Church of Canada and the 2009 Mutual Responsibility and Mission Consultation in Costa Rica. The full resolution reads:

The Anglican Consultative Council

1. Endorses the request from the Anglican Church of Canada and the 2009 Mutual Responsibility and Mission Consultation in Costa Rica to add a sixth 'Mark of Mission' that relates to peace, conflict transformation and reconciliation to the current list of five,
2. Requests the Mission Department of the Anglican Communion Office to take this process forward and report to ACC-15.

The proposed additional Mark of Mission is expected to be approved by the ACC-15 and may not necessarily appear in the sixth place of the current list!

Although the Five Marks of Mission have been in existence for more than twenty years now, and are even recognised by churches outside of the Anglican Communion, it is nevertheless sadly true that these Marks of Mission are not as widely known, used or promoted in the Communion as they deserve and should be.

In some parts of the Communion where Christianity is a minority faith, the Five Marks of Mission, especially the first and second are seen as potential problems and therefore cautiously 'embraced' due to the sensitivities around issues of conversion and proselytisation. Terms such as 'proclamation' can be quite touchy, but when understood in the broader sense of holistic mission, the Marks of Mission can provide creative ways of engaging people of other faiths.[12] It is also true that there are some

---

[12] Standing Committee, Minutes of a meeting held at St Andrew's House, London, 26 to 30 March 2011, 21; www.anglicancommunion.org/communion/acc/scac/resources/docs/standing_committee_minutes_march_2011.pdf; Standing Comm. Draft minutes of the meeting held at St Andrew's House, London, 23 to 27 July 2010, 17. www.anglicancommunion.org/communion/acc/scac/resources/docs/standing_committee_minutes_july_2010.pdf

provinces that have taken them seriously as a resource to inspire the Church's participation in God's mission; and therefore used them in a variety of ways. It is quite possible too that some in the Communion simply do not know quite how best to use the Marks of Mission.

Now I intend to explore some of the possible ways they are being or can be used as a resource for mission in the life and ministry of the Church at community (congregation) or/and individual level.

Prayer and Worship

Worship is central to the life of Anglican Christians, and public worship or shared worship is especially important for a community of faith 'as the gathered people of God.' The gathered community brings with it the 'the joys and sorrows of our varied everyday lives. When we open ourselves to God in worship, our eyes are opened to God's ways with the world and we are empowered for service and mission.'[13]

Public worship is one important opportunity during which the Marks of Mission can come alive and form part of the liturgy. For instance, a sermon or a series of (thematic) sermons on any of the Marks of Mission can be preached, and that way help Church members 'discovering the mission work being done by local churches, affirming what is in place, spotting the gaps, [and] deciding the best ways of moving forward.'[14] Sermons can also be preached on the Marks of Mission when celebrating or marking liturgical seasons, festivals and commemorations such as Mark of Mission one and two on St Andrew's Day (30th November), three and four during Lent, three on HIV & AIDS International Day (1st December), and five during harvest season and Environment Day (5 June). There are many other relevant Church events during which the Marks of Mission can be promoted and also serve as a resource, and on all these occasions relevant sermons can be preached, or a drama acted out.

The Five Marks of Mission can and do also form a basis for intercession prayers during worship, either when marking a liturgical season or on an ordinary Sunday or day. Equally there are hymns and songs that are relevant to the various Marks of Mission which can be used on appropriate liturgical, national or international festivals or commemorations, such as the following from the 'Mission Praise': 'Go tell it on the Mountain', 'Take my Life' (Mark of Mission 1); 'All to Jesus I surrender', 'Just as I am', 'When we walk with the Lord' (Mark of Mission 2); 'Make me a channel of your peace' (Mark of Mission 3); 'O Jesus I have promised' (Mark of Mission 4); 'For the fruits of His creation' (Mark of Mission 5), etc.

---

[13] Stephen Pickard, with Duleep de Chickera, *The Anglican Way: Signposts on a Common Journey*, Signposts Series No. 1, (The Anglican Communion Office: London, July 2008), 9.

[14] www.methodist.org.uk/index.cfm?fuseaction=opentogod.content&cmid=2346

There are also great opportunities to design lessons for the Junior Church (or Sunday school) around the Marks of Mission. Introducing the significance of the Marks of Mission, in appropriate ways, to young people would be a wonderful way of sowing the seed of a holistic sense of God's mission to the present and future Church. Drama and art would be just two of the ways children and young people can explore and use the Marks of Mission.

It is worth mentioning that there are many appropriate scriptural readings in both the Old and New Testaments that would be relevant in exploring the Marks of Mission. Here are some of the examples:

- Mark One – Exodus 3, Isaiah 61: 1-3, Mark 1: 1-8, Luke 9: 1-6, John 13: 1-17, Acts 8: 25-40
- Mark Two – Deuteronomy 6: 1-9, Nehemiah 8: 1-18, Luke 24: 13-35, John 3: 1-15, Acts 19: 1-10, Titus 2.
- Mark Three – 2 Kings 5: 1-14, Job 2: 11-13, Matthew 22: 34-40, Matthew 25: 31-46, Luke 3: 10-14, Luke 10: 24-37, John 4: 1-30, Hebrews 13: 1-6, 1 Peter 5: 1-7.
- Mark Four – Exodus 23: 1-13, Isaiah 61, Amos 2: 4-16, Micah 6: 8, Matthew 23: 23-36, Mark 10: 13-27, Luke 19: 1-10.
- Mark Five – Genesis 1 & 2, Genesis 6-7, Psalm 65, Leviticus 25: 1-24, Deuteronomy 26, Romans 8: 18-25, Matthew 6: 25-31, Mark 6: 30-52, Revelation 22: 1-5.

Worship is a time when Christians deepen their personal and corporate relationship with God and are energised for God's mission in their day-to-day lives. In fact the word 'Mass', which many Anglicans use for Eucharist is a Latin word which means dismissal or sending forth. It is therefore a fitting common practice in many Anglican Church liturgies around the Communion to send forth worshippers at the end of a Church service to 'go in peace to love and serve the Lord' – to live out God's mission from Monday through to Sunday! What a great way to end and send forth Christians to embody and participate in the holistic nature of God's mission as expressed through the Marks of Mission!

Workshops and Meetings

Parishes, congregations and dioceses from time to time set up meetings and workshops to explore and develop strategies on mission priorities. Such workshops can be designed to explore the various ways the Marks of Mission can be lived out and reflected in the life of the church. It might also be that a workshop could produce banners or/and cards that express the meaning of the Marks of Mission in the life of that congregation, parish or Diocese, and explore the best and appropriate ways they can be lived out and promoted at individual or/and community level.

Bible Study

Anglicans often understand themselves as a community of faith that is 'formed by Scripture'; and that Scripture plays a very important role in their life and faith. One of the the Anglican Communion signposts has this to say, 'the Bible is meant to form us as a holy people, ready, willing and able to do God's will and offer our lives in worship and service.'[15] Therefore it is not surprising or uncommon for Anglicans to sit around the Bible for personal and group reflection on the Scripture.

The Five Marks of Mission provide an opportunity to gather around the Bible and explore the Scriptures in an intentional way that encourages us to identify appropriate ways of responding to God's mission in our own context.[16] As such the Five Marks of Mission form an important Bible study resource appropriate for use in a congregation or parish.[17] They can be used either in their current form or indeed creatively expounded and packaged to meet the requirement in a given context. The resource can be designed for use by either mixed or age or gender specific group(s) such as the Youth, Women, Men, Mothers Union, Boys Brigade, Girls' Brigade, Choir, etc.

Social Media and Communication

In this era of social media and remote communication, it is absolutely vital that the Five Marks of Mission are shared and promoted as a valuable mission resource through all the available means in the Church. Some Churches and institutions have publicised the Five Marks of Mission on their websites, and some have even produced web based resources and other ideas on websites, electronic and print newsletters/magazines, youtube and facebook.

The Five Marks of Mission can also be promoted through writing competitions among young people who can bring out creative ways of highlighting how the local church articulates the Marks of Mission in its ministry vision and strategies. Although there are endless ways the marks of mission can be utilised and promoted it is important is to recognise the value they can bring to our mission thinking and practice as we participate in the mission of the Triune God.

---

[15] Stephen Pickard, with Duleep de Chickera, *The Anglican Way*, 3.

[16] A contextual Bible study course on the fourth mark of mission: www.aco.org/ministry/theological/bible/docs/pdf/case_study2.pdf.

[17] See here 'A Case Study of Biblical Engagement with the Fifth Mark of Mission', www.aco.org/ministry/theological/bible/docs/pdf/case_study1.pdf.

Conclusion

Let me conclude with this wonderful quotation from the Methodist Church in Britain, which articulates well my understanding of the Five Marks of Mission:

> These 'Five Marks' can be used as a tool for discovering the mission work being done by local churches, affirming what is in place, spotting the gaps, deciding the best ways of moving forward. In this way 'The Five Marks' can promote a sense of Churches Together engaging in Mission Together.[18]

---

[18] www.methodist.org.uk/index.cfm?fuseaction=opentogod.content&cmid=2346; www.anglican.ca/help/faq/marks-of-mission.

BIBLIOGRAPHY

Allen, Roland, *Missionary Methods: St. Paul's or Ours?(* Grand Rapids: Eerdmans, 1962)

Anglican Consultative Council and Pontifical Council, *Growing Together in Unity and Mission* (Great Britain: SPCK, 2007)

Avis, P., *A Ministry Shaped by Mission* (London: T&T Clark Ltd, 2005)

Balia, Daryl and Kirsteen Kim, (eds), *Edinburgh 2010: Witnessing to Christ* (Oxford: Regnum Books International, 2010)

Baudrillard, Jean, *La Pensée radicale. (*Morsure: Sens & Tonka, 1994.)

———, *Simulacra and Simulation.* (Ann Arbor, MI: University of Michigan Press, 1994.)

———, 'The Violence of the Image'. Paper presented at the International Symposium attached to 'media_city,' Seoul, 2002.

———, 'Disneyworld Company', *Libération* March 4th 2006,

Baudrillard, Jean and Maclean, Marie, 'The Masses: The Implosion of the Social in the Media', *New Literary History* 16:3 (Spring, 1985),

Bellingham, Robert George, 'A Biblical Approach to Social Transformation', DMin, Eastern Baptist Theological Seminary, 1987

Benhabib, Seyla, *Situating the Self: Gender, Community, and Postmodernism in Contemporary Ethics* (Cambridge: Polity Press, 1992)

Boff, Leonardo, *América Latina: da Conquista à Nova Evangelização* (São Paulo: Editora Ática, 1992)

———, *Cry of the Earth, Cry of the Poor* (Maryknoll, New York: Orbis Books, 1995)

———, *Ecology and Liberation: A New Paradigm* (Maryknoll, New York: Orbis Books, 1995)

Boff, Leonardo and Virgil, Elizondo (eds), *Ecology and Poverty* (Maryknoll: Orbis Books, Concillium, 1995)

Borgman, D, *When Kumbaya is Not Enough: A Practical Theology for Youth Ministry* (Massachusetts: Hendrickson Publishers, 1997)

Borthwick, P, *Organizing Your Youth Ministry* (Michigan: Zondervan Publishing House 1988)

Bosch, David J., *Transforming Mission: Paradigm Shifts in Theology of Mission* (Maryknoll, NY: Orbis Books (fourteenth printing), 1999)

———, *Missão Transformadora: Mudanças de Paradigma na Teologia da Missão* (São Leopoldo: Editora Sinodal, 2002)

Bragg, Wayne G., 'From Development to Transformation', in Samuel, Vinay and Sugden, Chris (eds) *The Church in Response to Human Need* (Grand Rapids: Eerdmans, 1987),

Brueggemann, Walter, 'Old Testament Theology and the Problem of Justice', in *Theology of the Old Testament: Testimony, Dispute and Advocacy* (Minneapolis: Fortress Press, 1997),

Cheeseman, Nic, 'The Kenyan Elections of 2007: An Introduction', *Journal of Eastern African Studies* 2, no. 2 (2008),

Closing Ceremony - Edinburgh 2010. http://edinburgh2010.oikoumene.org/en/resources/videos.html

Comblin, José, *Retrieving the Human: A Christian Anthropology* (Maryknoll, N.Y: Orbis Books, 1990)

'Communion in Mission & Travelling Together in God's Mission', Report of the Inter Anglican Standing Commission and Evangelism 2001 – 2005 (London: The Anglican Communion Office, 2006)

Coorilos, Geervarghese Mor, *Witnessing to Christ Today: A Perspective* in http://edinburgh2010.oikoumene.org/en/resources/papersdocuments.html

Corrie, J., 'Transforming Anglicanism: Elements of an Emerging Anglican Mission Paradigm', paper presented at OCMS, November, 2008

Daneel, Marthinus L., *African Earthkeepers: Wholistic Interfaith Mission* (Maryknoll, NY: Orbis Books, 2001)

Davies, Penelope E., David L. Simon, Walter B. Denny, Ann M. Roberts, Frima Fox Hofrichter and Joseph Jacobs (eds), *Janson's History of Art* (Upper Saddle River, NJ: Pearson Prentice Hall, 2007)

Edinburgh 2010, 'Key Terms for Mission and Christian Unity in 2010', http://www.edinburgh2010.org/en/news/en/article/4645/key-terms-for-mission-and.html

Everist, N.C., *The Difficult but Indispensable Church* (Minneapolis Fortress Press, 2002)

Forrester, Duncan B., *Christian Justice and Public Policy* (Cambridge: Cambridge University Press, 1997)

———, *Just Sharing: A Christian Approach to the Distribution of Wealth, Income and Benefits*. (Augsburg: Fortress, 1987)

Fung, Raymond, *The Isaiah Vision: An Ecumenical Strategy for Congregational Evangelism* (Geneva: WCC, 1992)

Gnanakan, Ken., 'To Proclaim the Good News of the Kingdom (i)', in Walls, Andrew, and Cathy Ross, (eds), *Mission in the 21st Century: Exploring the Five Marks of Global Mission* (London: Darton Longman Todd, 2008)

Gollieher, Jeffrey M., 'This Fragile earth Our Island Home: Environmental Crisis'," in Douglas, Ian T. and Kwok Pui-Lan, (eds), *Beyond Colonial Anglicanism: The Anglican Communion in the Twenty-First Century* (New York: Church Publishing, 2000),

Gorski, John F., *The Edinburgh 2010 World Mission Conference: What Does it Mean to Us? Impressions of a Catholic Delegate to an Ecumenical Conference* in http://edinburgh2010.oikoumene.org/en/resources/papersdocuments.html

Gossai, Hemchand., *Justice, Righteousness and the Social Critique of the Eighth-Century Prophets*, Vol. 141, American University Studies Series Vii, Theology and Religion (New York: Peter Lang, 1993)

Gregory, Eric, *Politics and the Order of Love: An Augustinian Ethic of Democratic Citizenship* (Chicago: University of Chicago Press, 2008)

Gustafson, James M., *The Church as Moral Decision-Maker* (Philadelphia: Pilgrim Press, 1970)

———, *Treasure in Earthen Vessels: The Church as Human Community* (Louisville: Westminster John Knox Press, 2009)

Hart, John, *Sacramental Commons: Christian Ecological Ethics* (Lanham: Maryland, Rowman and Littlefield, 2006)

Hauerwas, Stanley, *After Christendom? How the Church is to Behave if Freedom, Justice and a Christian Nation are Bad Ideas* (Nashville: Abingdon Press, 1991)

Herbst, Michael, 'Plural Mission and Missionary Plural in a Post-Socialist Context: Using the Example of a Post-Volkskirche, East German Region', Paper presented to Edinburgh 2010 Study Group 3, Prague, 2009

Houston, Walter J., *Contending for Justice: The Ideology and Theology of Social Justice in the Old Testament*, Library of Hebrew Bible/Old Testament Studies (London: Continuum, 2006)

Hughes, Michael E., *Young Hearts Be Free: Christian Youth Ministry and a Theology of Liberation* (Auckland: Churches Youth Ministry Association, 2004)

IASCOME, *Communion in Mission and Travelling Together in God's Mission* (Anglican Communion, London: AC, 2006).

Johnson, Elizabeth, 'Heaven and Earth are Filled with Your Glory: Atheism and Ecological Spirituality', in Himes, Michael J. and Stephen J Pope,. (eds) *Finding God in all Things* (New York: The Crossroad Publishing Company, 1996),

Johnson, E., and J. Clark (eds), *Anglicans in Mission: A Transforming Journey* (London: SPCK 2000)

Kaoma, John, 'God, Humanity and Nature', *Listening: Journal of Religion and Culture* 35, no. 3 (Fall, 2000),

Kaoma, John, 'Earthkeeping as a Dimension of Christian Mission: David Livingstone's attitude Towards Life: A Challenge to Earthkeeping Missions', in Petersen, Rodney L. and Simion, Marian Gh. (eds), *Tracing Contours: Reflecting on World Mission and Christianity* (Newton Center, BTI, 2010), 74-76

Kaoma, Kapya J., 'Missio Dei or missio Creator Dei: Witnessing to Christ in the Face of Occurring Ecological Crisis', in Kim, Kirsteen and Andrew Anderson, (eds), *Edinburgh 2010: Mission Today and Tomorrow* (Oxford: Regnum Books, 2011)

Kaoma, Kapya John, 'Missio Dei or Missio Creator Dei: Witnessing to Christ in the Face of the Occurring Ecological Crisis', paper presented to Edinburgh 2010.

———, *Ubuntu, Jesus, and Earth: Integrating African Religion and Christianity in Ecological Ethics* (Th.D Dissertation, Boston University, 2010)

Kettle, David, 'The Gospel of Hope in a Postmodern Setting', paper presented to Edinburgh 2010 Study Group 3, Prague, 2009

Kim, Kirsteen and Andrew Anderson, (eds), *Edinburgh 2010: Mission Today and Tomorrow* (Oxford: Regnum Books, 2011)

Kirk, Andrew J., *What is Mission? Theological Explorations* (Augsburg: Fortress Press, 2000)

Kobia, Samuel, *The Courage to Hope: The Roots for a New Vision and the Calling of the Church in Africa* (Risk Books, Geneva:, 2003)

Labi, Kwame, 'Transforming Ecumenism in Africa in the 21st Century', *Ecumenical Review* 53, no. 8 (2001), 366

Lebacqz, Karen, *Justice in an Unjust World: Foundations for a Christian Approach to Justice* (Minneapolis: Augsburg, 1987)

Li, Jieren, 'Multi-identity of the Chinese Christianity in Post-Olympic China: From Pre-modernity towards Postmodernity', paper presented to Edinburgh 2010 Study Group 3, Prague, 2009

Longkumer, Atola, *Mission and Power – Transversal Women and Mission*, http://edinburgh2010.oikoumene.org/en/resources/papersdocuments.html

Malphurs, A., *A New Kind of Church* (Michigan: Baker Publishing Group, 2007)

Marshall, Christopher D., *The Little Book of Biblical Justice: A Fresh Approach to the Bible's Teachings on Justice* (Intercourse, PA: Good Books, 2005)

Martinson, R. D., *Effective Youth Ministry: A Congregation Approach* (Minneapolis: Augsburg Publishing House, 1988)

Mbiti, John S., *African Religion and Philosophy* (New York: Preager,1990)

McCoy, Michael, *O Povo das Boas Novas* (Porto Alegre: Livraria Anglicana, 1991)

McFague, Sallie, *Life Abundant:* ***Rethinking Theology and Economy for a Planet in Peril*** (Minneapolis: Fortress Press, 2000)

McFague, Sallie, *Metaphorical Theology: Models of God in Religious Language* (Philadelphia: Fortress, 1982)

Moltmann, Jürgen, *The Church in the Power of the Spirit: A Contribution to Messianic Ecclesiology* (New York: Harper & Row, 1977)

Morris, W. (ed), *The Heritage Illustrated Dictionary of the English Language* (New York: American Heritage Publishing Co, 1973)

Moynagh, M., *A Changing World: Changing Church* (London: Monarch Books, 2001)

Moyo, Dambisa, *Dead Aid: Why Aid is Not Working and How There Is Another Way for Africa* (London: Penguin, 2009)

Moyo, Fulata L., '"Who Is Not at the Table?" Women's Perspectives of Holistic Mission as Mutually Inclusive', in Balia, Daryl and Kirsteen Kim, (eds), *Edinburgh 2010: Witnessing to Christ* (Oxford: Regnum Books International, 2010)

Miyamoto, Ken Cristoph, 'Worship is Nothing But Mission: A Reflection on Some Japanese Experiences'. in Walls, Andrew and Cathy Ross, (eds), *Mission in the Twenty-First Century: Exploring the Five Marks of Global Mission* (London: Darton Longman Todd, 2008)

Mundine, Graemme, 'Mission and Power', a paper presented at Edinburgh 2010.

Mwaura, Philomena Njeri, 'Christian Identity and Ethnicity in Africa: Reflections on the Gospel of Reconciliation', in Stinton, Diane B. (ed), *African Theology on the Way: Current Conversations*, (London: SPCK, 2010)

Nash, James, *Loving Nature: Ecological Integrity and Christian Responsibility* (Nashville: Abingdon Press, 1991)

Nel, M., *Youth Ministry: An Inclusive Congregational Approach* (Pretoria: Jeugbediening Publishers, 2000)

O'Callaghan, Regan, 'Icons as Religious Artefacts', in Brown, Michelle P. (ed), *The Lion Companion to Christian Art* (London, Lion Books, 2008)

O'Neill, Seamus, 'Through Nomadic Eyes: Stations of the Cross in Lodwar Cathedral, Kenya', *Australian e-Journal of Theology* 7 (Pentecost, 2006)

Olupona, Jacob, 'Comments on the Encyclopedia of Religion and Nature', *Journal of the American Academy of Religion* 77, 1, (2009), 60-65

Presler, Titus, *Horizons of Mission* (Boston: Cowley Publications, 2001)

Robert, Dana L., 'Historical Trends in Mission and Earth Care', *International Bulletin of Missionary Research* 35, 3, (July 2011),

Ross, Kenneth, *Edinburgh 2010: New Directions for Church in Mission* (Pasadena, William Carey University Press, 2010)

Ross, Kenneth, *Edinburgh 2010: Springboard for Mission* (Pasadena: William Carey International University Press, 2009)

Rubin, Achylle Alexio, *A Novidade da Novidade: Novo Milênio, Nova Evangelização* (Santa Maria: Palotti, 2001)

Saayman, Willem, 'David Bosch – Some Personal Reflections', in *Mission Studies: Journal of the International Association for Mission Studies* 26, no. 2 (2009),

Sagovsky, Nicholas, *Christian Tradition and the Practice of Justice* (London: SPCK, 2008)

Santmire, Paul, *The Travail of Nature: The Ambiguous Ecological Promise of Christian Theology* (Philadelphia: Fortress Press, 1985)

Schumacher, Sara, 'From Artist to Participant to Artist: An Assessment of Participatory Art in the Life of the Church', MLitt dissertation, University of St. Andrews School of Divinity, 2010

Schweitzer, Albert, 'The Ethics of Reverence for Life', originally published in *Christendom* 1. 1936, http://www1.chapman.edu/scheitzer/sch/reading4/html

Sebastian, Jayakiran, 'Interrogating Missio Dei: From the Mission of God Towards Appreciating Our Mission to God in India Today', paper presented to Edinburgh 2010 Study Group 3, Prague, 2009

Sider, Ronald J., and Stott, John R.W., *Evangelism, Salvation and Social Justice* (Bramcote: Grove Books, 1977)

Stephan, Patrick, 'Legitimation and Missions: How Do We Reach this Eclectic World?' in Kirk Sandvig (ed), *Edinburgh 2010: Youth Perspectives* (Pasadena: William Carey University Press, 2010)

Steuernagel, Valdir, 'To Seek to Transform the Unjust Structures of Society (i)' in Walls, Andrew and Cathy Ross, (eds), *Mission in the Twenty-First Century: Exploring the Five Marks of Global Mission* (London: Darton Longman Todd, 2008)

Stott, John R.W., *Christian Mission in the Modern World* (Downers Grove: IVP, 1975)

Temple, Richard, *Icons: Divine Beauty* (London: Saqi Books, 2004)

Trudell, Barbara, 'Introduction: Vulnerability and Opportunity among Africa's Youth', in Trudell, Barbara, King, Kenneth, McGrath, Simon and Nugent, Paul (eds) *Africa's Young Majority* (Edinburgh: Centre of African Studies, University of Edinburgh, 2002) 1-16

United Nations, *The Earth Charter*, www.earthcharterinaction.org/content/pages/The-Earth-Charter.html

United Nations, 'World Youth Report 2005', 2005

Volf, Miroslav, *Exclusion and Embrace: A Theological Exploration of Identity, Otherness, and Reconciliation* (Nashville: Abingdon Press, 1996)

Volf, Miroslav, 'Soft Difference: Theological Reflections on the Relation Between Church and Culture in 1 Peter', *Ex auditu* 10 (January 1, 1994),

Walker, D., 'Marks of Mission and Ways of Belonging: Shaping the Anglican Agenda for Occasional Churchgoers in Countryside', *Journal of Anglican Studies* Vol 9, 101

Walters, James, 'Finding a Prophetic Voice in Hyperreal Culture', paper presented to the Society for the Study of Theology, Cambridge, 2007.

Ward, P., *Youth Culture and the Gospel* (Grand Rapids: Zondervan, 1992)

Ward, P., *Youth Work and the Mission of God* (London: SPCK, 1997)

White Jr, Lynn, 'The Historical Roots of Our Ecologic Crisis', www.uvm.edu/~gflomenh/ENV-NGO-PA395/articles/Lynn-White.pdf

Young, Iris Marion, *Justice and the Politics of Difference* (Princeton, N.J: Princeton University Press, 1990)

Zaprometova, Olga, 'Bitter and Sweet Tears: Exploring the Spirituality of the Eastern Church Fathers in the Light of Post-Modern Pentecostalism in Russia', paper presented to Edinburgh 2010 Study Group 3, Prague, 2009

List of Contributors

Irene Akinyi Ayallo was born in Kenya and is a priest and social worker in the Anglican Diocese of Bondo in Kenya. She has spent the last several years in New Zealand completing an MTh and is finishing her doctoral thesis on the role of the Anglican Church in Kenya in facilitating socially-inclusive public policy-making in Kenya. Her ministry and academic interests are in the areas of interpreting the bible for social transformation and holistic empowerment of people from all walks of life, social justice and a critical articulation of the church's authentic public relevance.

Caitlin Reilley Beck has degrees in mission studies and interreligious dialogue, and liturgical studies from Saint Paul University, and the Institute of Sacred Music at Yale Divinity School respectively. As a liturgist, her interests centre on gender in worship, congregational song, world music and the music of the Eastern Churches. Caitlin continues to respond to her call to lay ministry by consulting with parishes and dioceses on topics as diverse as ecumenical and interreligious relations, music in worship, ecclesiology and church architecture. She is currently Coordinator of Christian Education and Lay Pastoral Associate at the Church of St John the Evangelist in downtown Ottawa, Ontario, Canada.

Kwok Keung Chan was Diocesan Youth Officer of the Diocese of Eastern Kowloon and now serves as a curate in Holy Carpenter Church working with educational and social service professionals as a team of mission. He graduated from United College, Chinese University of Hong Kong in 1996 and after serving as a teacher of English as a second language for eight years, Revd Chan graduated with a Master of Divinity in 2007 from SKH Ming Hua Theological College. His rich experience in the education field is closely related to his ideas and practices in mission. He was also elected as a member of the Diocesan Pastoral and Nurturing Committee in 2008 and 2010 respectively.

Luiz Coelho was born in Rio de Janeiro, Brazil, and is an Engineer, Visual Artist and Candidate for Holy Orders in the Anglican Diocese of Rio de Janeiro. Luiz holds a BEng from the Military Institute of Engineering (Rio de Janeiro, Brazil), a MSc in Image Processing from the Federal University of Amazonas (Manaus, Brazil), and a Bachelor in Theology through Egmont Machado Krischke Seminary (Porto Alegre, Brazil), with an emphasis in Sacred Art. His main area of interest is the study of the post-modern condition, especially Visual Semiotics, the power of imagery and its multidisciplinary implications in the fields of Technology, Art, Liturgy and Theology.

John Kafwanka is an ordained priest in the Anglican Church in Zambia, with parish ministry experience in Zambia and Australia. John taught at the national Anglican theological seminary of St John's where he was also its Principal before working with Church Mission Society (CMS Britain) as Regional Manager for Southern Africa. In this role John related to churches and organisations in Angola, Madagascar, Malawi, Mozambique, South Africa, and Zambia. After six years in Southern Africa, John was seconded to the Anglican Communion Office where he now works as Director for Mission. Recently, John represented the Anglican Communion on the Edinburgh 2010 General Council, and served on its Executive Council as well as being a member of the Study Process Monitoring Group (SPMG). John serves as a member of the Board of Trustees of Northrise University (Zambia).

Kapya John Kaoma teaches at St. John's Anglican Seminary in Zambia and is a visiting researcher at Boston University Center for Global Christianity. He is also Rector of Christ Church, Hyde Park, and Political Research Associates Project Director in Massachusetts, USA.

Vicentia Kgabe is an Anglican priest in the diocese of Johannesburg. She has just completed a PhD in Practical Theology at the University of Pretoria. She is Rector of St Peter's, Auckland Park and an archdeacon for the Diocese of Johannesburg. She has experience in community involvement as a Training Facilitator for Theology and Development in the Anglican Church of Southern Africa.

In addition to serving many years as a priest in indigenous communities across North America, **Mark MacDonald** has served as the Bishop of Alaska and the pastoral bishop of Navajoland, both in the USA. In 2007 he became the first National Indigenous Anglican Bishop for Canada. His pastoral relationships include over 200 indigenous churches in rural Canada, as well as many urban ministries across the land.

Janice Price is World Mission Policy Adviser and Co-ordinator of Partnership for World Mission of the Church of England Archbishops' Council. Previously she was Director of the Churches' Mission Network of Churches Together in Britain and Ireland and Director of Development for the Diocese of Worcester. Publications include *Telling Our Faith Story* (Grove Books, 2009) and joint author of *Foundations for Mission: A Study in Language, Theology and Praxis* (CTBI 2010). She was joint convenor for the Foundations for Mission Study Theme at the Edinburgh 2010 World Mission Conference. Janice has been a Lay Reader/Minister in the Church of England for 23 years and has worked in parishes in urban, suburban and rural contexts.

Andrew R. H. Thompson is a doctoral candidate in Christian ethics at Yale University, where his research focuses on the ethics of the church and its relationship to different cultural contexts. His dissertation will reflect on this relationship with respect to a particular ethical problem, mountaintop removal mining in his home state of West Virginia. As a member of the Episcopal Young Adult Service Corps, Andy served as a missionary and community development worker in the Episcopal Church of El Salvador, where he and his wife, the Reverend Leigh Preston, established a primary school. In 2011 he was named a fellow of the Episcopal Church Foundation. Andy lives in Hartford, Connecticut with Leigh and their son, Cabell.

REGNUM EDINBURGH CENTENARY SERIES
Series Listing

David A. Kerr, Kenneth R. Ross (Eds)
Mission Then and Now
2009 / 978-1-870345-73-6 / 343pp (paperback)
2009 / 978-1-870345-76-7 / 343pp (hardback)

No one can hope to fully understand the modern Christian missionary movement without engaging substantially with the World Missionary Conference, held at Edinburgh in 1910. This book is the first to systematically examine the eight Commissions which reported to Edinburgh 1910 and gave the conference much of its substance and enduring value. It will deepen and extend the reflection being stimulated by the upcoming centenary and will kindle the missionary imagination for 2010 and beyond.

Daryl M. Balia, Kirsteen Kim (Eds)
Witnessing to Christ Today
2010 / 978-1-870345-77-4 / 301pp

This volume, the second in the Edinburgh 2010 series, includes reports of the nine main study groups working on different themes for the celebration of the centenary of the World Missionary Conference, Edinburgh 1910. Their collaborative work brings together perspectives that are as inclusive as possible of contemporary world Christianity and helps readers to grasp what it means in different contexts to be 'witnessing to Christ today'.

Claudia Währisch-Oblau, Fidon Mwombeki (Eds)
Mission Continues
Global Impulses for the 21st Century
2010 / 978-1-870345-82-8 / 271pp

In May 2009, 35 theologians from Asia, Africa and Europe met in Wuppertal, Germany, for a consultation on mission theology organized by the United Evangelical Mission: Communion of 35 Churches in Three Continents. The aim was to participate in the 100th anniversary of the Edinburgh conference through a study process and reflect on the challenges for mission in the 21st century. This book brings together these papers written by experienced practitioners from around the world.

Brian Woolnough and Wonsuk Ma (Eds)
Holistic Mission
God's plan for God's people
2010 / 978-1-870345-85-9 / 277pp

Holistic mission, or integral mission, implies God is concerned with the whole person, the whole community, body, mind and spirit. This book discusses the meaning of the holistic gospel, how it has developed, and implications for the church. It takes a global, eclectic approach, with 19 writers, all of whom have much experience in, and commitment to, holistic mission. It addresses critically and honestly one of the most exciting, and challenging, issues facing the church today. To be part of God's plan for God's people, the church must take holistic mission to the world.

Kirsteen Kim and Andrew Anderson (Eds)
Mission Today and Tomorrow
2010 / 978-1-870345-91-0 / 450pp

There are moments in our lives when we come to realise that we are participating in the triune God's mission. If we believe the church to be as sign and symbol of the reign of God in the world, then we are called to witness to Christ today by sharing in God's mission of love through the transforming power of the Holy Spirit. We can all participate in God's transforming and reconciling mission of love to the whole creation.

Tormod Engelsviken, Erling Lundeby and Dagfinn Solheim (Eds)
The Church Going Glocal
Mission and Globalisation 2011 / 978-1-870345-93-4 / 262pp

The New Testament church is… universal and local at the same time. The universal, one and holy apostolic church appears in local manifestations. Missiologically speaking… the church can take courage as she faces the increasing impact of globalisation on local communities today. Being universal and concrete, the church is geared for the simultaneous challenges of the glocal and local.

Marina Ngurusangzeli Behera (Ed)
Interfaith Relations after One Hundred Years
Christian Mission among Other Faiths 2011 / 978-1-870345-96-5 / 334 pp

The essays of this book reflect not only the acceptance and celebration of pluralism within India but also by extension an acceptance as well as a need for unity among Indian Christians of different denominations. The essays were presented and studied at a preparatory consultation on Study Theme II: Christian Mission Among Other Faiths at the United Theological College, India July 2009.

Lalsangkima Pachuau and Knud Jørgensen (Eds)
Witnessing to Christ in a Pluralistic Age
Christian Mission among Other Faiths 2011 / 978-1-870345-95-8 / 277 pp

In a world where plurality of faiths is increasingly becoming a norm of life, insights on the theology of religious plurality are needed to strengthen our understanding of our own faith and the faith of others. Even though religious diversity is not new, we are seeing an upsurge in interest on the theologies of religion among all Christian confessional traditions. It can be claimed that no other issue in Christian mission is more important and more difficult than the theologies of religions.

Beth Snodderly and A Scott Moreau (Eds)
Evangelical Frontier Mission
Perspectives on the Global Progress of the Gospel
2011 / 978-1-870345-98-9 / 312pp

This important volume demonstrates that 100 years after the World Missionary Conference in Edinburgh, Evangelism has become truly global. Twenty-first-century Evangelism continues to focus on frontier mission, but significantly, and in the spirit of Edinburgh 1910, it also has re-engaged social action.

Rolv Olsen (Ed)

Mission and Postmodernities

2011 / 978-1-870345-97-2 / 279pp

This volume takes on meaning because its authors honestly struggle with and debate how we should relate to postmodernities. Should our response be accommodation, relativizing or counter-culture? How do we strike a balance between listening and understanding, and at the same time exploring how postmodernities influence the interpretation and application of the Bible as the normative story of God's mission in the world?

REGNUM STUDIES IN GLOBAL CHRISTIANITY

(Previously GLOBAL THEOLOGICAL VOICES series)

Series Listing

David Emmanuel Singh (Ed)
Jesus and the Cross
Reflections of Christians from Islamic Contexts
2008 / 978-1-870345-65-1 / 226pp

The Cross reminds us that the sins of the world are not borne through the exercise of power but through Jesus Christ's submission to the will of the Father. The papers in this volume are organised in three parts: scriptural, contextual and theological. The central question being addressed is: how do Christians living in contexts, where Islam is a majority or minority religion, experience, express or think of the Cross?

Sung-wook Hong
Naming God in Korea
The Case of Protestant Christianity
2008 / 978-1-870345-66-8 / 170pp

Since Christianity was introduced to Korea more than a century ago, one of the most controversial issues has been the Korean term for the Christian 'God'. This issue is not merely about naming the Christian God in Korean language, but it relates to the question of theological contextualization - the relationship between the gospel and culture - and the question of Korean Christian identity. This book demonstrates the nature of the gospel in relation to cultures, i.e., the universality of the gospel expressed in all human cultures.

Hubert van Beek (Ed)
Revisioning Christian Unity
The Global Christian Forum
2009 / 978-1-870345-74-3 / 288pp

This book contains the records of the Global Christian Forum gathering held in Limuru near Nairobi, Kenya, on 6 – 9 November 2007 as well as the papers presented at that historic event. Also included are a summary of the Global Christian Forum process from its inception until the 2007 gathering and the reports of the evaluation of the process that was carried out in 2008.

Young-hoon Lee
The Holy Spirit Movement in Korea
Its Historical and Theological Development
2009 / 978-1-870345-67-5 / 174pp

This book traces the historical and theological development of the Holy Spirit Movement in Korea through six successive periods (from 1900 to the present time). These periods are characterized by repentance and revival (1900-20), persecution and suffering under Japanese occupation (1920-40), confusion and division (1940-60), explosive revival in which the Pentecostal movement played a major role in the rapid growth of Korean churches (1960-80), the movement reaching out to all denominations (1980-2000), and the new context demanding the Holy Spirit movement to open new horizons in its mission engagement (2000-).

Paul Hang-Sik Cho
Eschatology and Ecology
Experiences of the Korean Church
2010 / 978-1-870345-75-0 / 260pp

This book raises the question of why Korean people, and Korean Protestant Christians in particular, pay so little attention to ecological issues. The author argues that there is an important connection (or elective affinity) between this lack of attention and the other-worldly eschatology that is so dominant within Korean Protestant Christianity.

Dietrich Werner, David Esterline, Namsoon Kang, Joshva Raja (Eds)
The Handbook of Theological Education in World Christianity
2010 / 978-1-870345-80-4 / 759pp

This major reference work is the first ever comprehensive study of Theological Education in Christianity of its kind. With contributions from over 90 international scholars and church leaders, it aims to be easily accessible across denominational, cultural, educational, and geographic boundaries. The Handbook will aid international dialogue and networking among theological educators, institutions, and agencies

David Emmanuel Singh & Bernard C Farr (Eds)
Christianity and Education
Shaping of Christian Context in Thinking
2010 / 978-1-870345-81-1 / 374pp

Christianity and Education is a collection of papers published in *Transformation: An International Journal of Holistic Mission Studies* over a period of 15 years. The articles represent a spectrum of Christian thinking addressing issues of institutional development for theological education, theological studies in the context of global mission, contextually aware/informed education, and academies which deliver such education, methodologies and personal reflections.

J.Andrew Kirk
Civilisations in Conflict?
Islam, the West and Christian Faith
2011 / 978-1-870345-87-3 / 205pp

Samuel Huntington's thesis, which argues that there appear to be aspects of Islam that could be on a collision course with the politics and values of Western societies, has provoked much controversy. This study is offers a particular response to Huntington's thesis by making a comparison between the origins of Islam and Christianity.

David Emmanuel Singh (Ed)
Jesus and the Incarnation
Reflections of Christians from Islamic Contexts
2011 / 978-1-870345-90-3 / 250pp

In the dialogues of Christians with Muslims nothing is more fundamental than the Cross, the Incarnation and the Resurrection of Jesus. Building on the *Jesus and the Cross*, this book contains voices of Christians living in various 'Islamic contexts' and reflecting on the Incarnation of Jesus. The aim and hope of these reflections is that the papers weaved around the notion of 'the Word' will not only promote dialogue among Christians on the roles of the Person and the Book but, also, create a positive environment for their conversations with Muslim neighbours.

REGNUM STUDIES IN MISSION
Series Listing

Kwame Bediako
Theology and Identity
The Impact of Culture upon Christian Thought in the Second Century and in Modern Africa
1992 / 978-1870345-80-2 / 508pp

The author examines the question of Christian identity in the context of the Graeco–Roman culture of the early Roman Empire. He then addresses the modern African predicament of quests for identity and integration.

Christopher Sugden
Seeking the Asian Face of Jesus
The Practice and Theology of Christian Social Witness in Indonesia and India 1974–1996
1997 / 1-870345-26-6 / 496pp

This study focuses on contemporary holistic mission with the poor in India and Indonesia combined with the call to transformation of all life in Christ with micro-credit enterprise schemes. 'The literature on contextual theology now has a new standard to rise to' – Lamin Sanneh (Yale University, USA).

Hwa Yung
Mangoes or Bananas?
The Quest for an Authentic Asian Christian Theology
1997 / 1-870345-25-5 / 274pp

Asian Christian thought remains largely captive to Greek dualism and Enlightenment rationalism because of the overwhelming dominance of Western culture. Authentic contextual Christian theologies will emerge within Asian Christianity with a dual recovery of confidence in culture and the gospel.

Keith E. Eitel
Paradigm Wars
The Southern Baptist International Mission Board Faces the Third Millennium
1999 / 1-870345-12-6 / 140pp

The International Mission Board of the Southern Baptist Convention is the largest denominational mission agency in North America. This volume chronicles the historic and contemporary forces that led to the IMB's recent extensive reorganization, providing the most comprehensive case study to date of a historic mission agency restructuring to continue its mission purpose into the twenty-first century more effectively.

Samuel Jayakumar

Dalit Consciousness and Christian Conversion

Historical Resources for a Contemporary Debate 1999 / 81-7214-497-0 / 434pp

(Published jointly with ISPCK)

The main focus of this historical study is social change and transformation among the Dalit Christian communities in India. Historiography tests the evidence in the light of the conclusions of the modern Dalit liberation theologians.

Vinay Samuel and Christopher Sugden (Eds)

Mission as Transformation

A Theology of the Whole Gospel

1999 / 978-18703455-13-2/ 522pp

This book brings together in one volume twenty five years of biblical reflection on mission practice with the poor from around the world. This volume helps anyone understand how evangelicals, struggling to unite evangelism and social action, found their way in the last twenty five years to the biblical view of mission in which God calls all human beings to love God and their neighbour; never creating a separation between the two.

Christopher Sugden

Gospel, Culture and Transformation

2000 / 1-870345-32-0 /152pp

A Reprint, with a New Introduction, of Part Two of Seeking the Asian Face of Jesus

Gospel, Culture and Transformation explores the practice of mission especially in relation to transforming cultures and communities. - 'Transformation is to enable God's vision of society to be actualised in all relationships: social, economic and spiritual, so that God's will may be reflected in human society and his love experienced by all communities, especially the poor.'

Bernhard Ott

Beyond Fragmentation: Integrating Mission and Theological Education

A Critical Assessment of some Recent Developments in Evangelical Theological Education

2001 / 1-870345-14-2 / 382pp

Beyond Fragmentation is an enquiry into the development of Mission Studies in evangelical theological education in Germany and German-speaking Switzerland between 1960 and 1995. The author undertakes a detailed examination of the paradigm shifts which have taken place in recent years in both the theology of mission and the understanding of theological education.

Gideon Githiga

The Church as the Bulwark against Authoritarianism

Development of Church and State Relations in Kenya, with Particular Reference to the Years after Political Independence 1963-1992

2002 / 1-870345-38-x / 218pp

'All who care for love, peace and unity in Kenyan society will want to read this careful history by Bishop Githiga of how Kenyan Christians, drawing on the Bible, have sought to share the love of God, bring his peace and build up the unity of the nation, often in the face of great difficulties and opposition.' Canon Dr Chris Sugden, Oxford Centre for Mission Studies.

Myung Sung-Hoon, Hong Young-Gi (eds.)

Charis and Charisma

David Yonggi Cho and the Growth of Yoido Full Gospel Church

2003 / 978-1870345-45-3 / 218pp

This book discusses the factors responsible for the growth of the world's largest church. It expounds the role of the Holy Spirit, the leadership, prayer, preaching, cell groups and creativity in promoting church growth. It focuses on God's grace (charis) and inspiring leadership (charisma) as the two essential factors and the book's purpose is to present a model for church growth worldwide.

Samuel Jayakumar

Mission Reader

Historical Models for Wholistic Mission in the Indian Context

2003 / 1-870345-42-8 / 250pp

(Published jointly with ISPCK)

This book is written from an evangelical point of view revalidating and reaffirming the Christian commitment to wholistic mission. The roots of the 'wholistic mission' combining 'evangelism and social concerns' are to be located in the history and tradition of Christian evangelism in the past; and the civilizing purpose of evangelism is compatible with modernity as an instrument in nation building.

Bob Robinson

Christians Meeting Hindus

An Analysis and Theological Critique of the Hindu-Christian Encounter in India

2004 / 987-1870345-39-2 / 392pp

This book focuses on the Hindu-Christian encounter, especially the intentional meeting called dialogue, mainly during the last four decades of the twentieth century, and specifically in India itself.

Gene Early

Leadership Expectations

How Executive Expectations are Created and Used in a Non-Profit Setting

2005 / 1-870345-30-4 / 276pp

The author creates an Expectation Enactment Analysis to study the role of the Chancellor of the University of the Nations-Kona, Hawaii. This study is grounded in the field of managerial work, jobs, and behaviour and draws on symbolic interactionism, role theory, role identity theory and enactment theory. The result is a conceptual framework for developing an understanding of managerial roles.

Tharcisse Gatwa

The Churches and Ethnic Ideology in the Rwandan Crises 1900-1994

2005 / 978-1870345-24-8 / 300pp

(Reprinted 2011)

Since the early years of the twentieth century Christianity has become a new factor in Rwandan society. This book investigates the role Christian churches played in the formulation and development of the racial ideology that culminated in the 1994 genocide.

Julie Ma

Mission Possible

Biblical Strategies for Reaching the Lost

2005 / 978-1870345-37-1 / 142pp

This is a missiology book for the church which liberates missiology from the specialists for the benefit of every believer. It also serves as a textbook that is simple and friendly, and yet solid in biblical interpretation. This book links the biblical teaching to the actual and contemporary missiological settings with examples, making the Bible come alive to the reader.

Allan Anderson, Edmond Tang (Eds)

Asian and Pentecostal

The Charismatic Face of Christianity in Asia

2005 / 1-870345-43-9 / 596pp

(Reprinted 2011)

(Published jointly with APTS Press)

This book provides a thematic discussion and pioneering case studies on the history and development of Pentecostal and Charismatic churches in the countries of South Asia, South East Asia and East Asia.

I. Mark Beaumont

Christology in Dialogue with Muslims

A Critical Analysis of Christian Presentations of Christ for Muslims from the Ninth and Twentieth Centuries

2005 / 1978-1870345-46-0 / 228pp

This book analyses Christian presentations of Christ for Muslims in the most creative periods of Christian-Muslim dialogue, the first half of the ninth century and the second half of the twentieth century. In these two periods, Christians made serious attempts to present their faith in Christ in terms that take into account Muslim perceptions of him, with a view to bridging the gap between Muslim and Christian convictions.

Thomas Czövek,

Three Seasons of Charismatic Leadership

A Literary-Critical and Theological Interpretation of the Narrative of Saul, David and Solomon

2006 / 978-1870345-48-4 / 272pp

This book investigates the charismatic leadership of Saul, David and Solomon. It suggests that charismatic leaders emerge in crisis situations in order to resolve the crisis by the charisma granted by God. Czovek argues that Saul proved himself as a charismatic leader as long as he acted resolutely and independently from his mentor Samuel. In the author's eyes, Saul's failure to establish himself as a charismatic leader is caused by his inability to step out from Samuel's shadow.

Jemima Atieno Oluoch

The Christian Political Theology of Dr. John Henry Okullu

2006 / 1-870345-51-4 / 137pp

This book reconstructs the Christian political theology of Bishop John Henry Okullu, DD, through establishing what motivated him and the biblical basis for his socio-political activities. It also attempts to reconstruct the socio-political environment that nurtured Dr Okullu's prophetic ministry.

Richard Burgess

Nigeria's Christian Revolution

The Civil War Revival and Its Pentecostal Progeny (1967-2006)

2008 / 978-1-870345-63-7 / 347pp

This book describes the revival that occurred among the Igbo people of Eastern Nigeria and the new Pentecostal churches it generated, and documents the changes that have occurred as the movement has responded to global flows and local demands. As such, it explores the nature of revivalist and Pentecostal experience, but does so against the backdrop of local socio-political and economic developments, such as decolonisation and civil war, as well as broader processes, such as modernisation and globalisation.

David Emmanuel Singh & Bernard C Farr (Eds)

Christianity and Cultures

Shaping Christian Thinking in Context

2008 / 978-1-870345-69-9 / 260pp

This volume marks an important milestone, the 25th anniversary of the Oxford Centre for Mission Studies (OCMS). The papers here have been exclusively sourced from Transformation, a quarterly journal of OCMS, and seek to provide a tripartite view of Christianity's engagement with cultures by focusing on the question: how is Christian thinking being formed or reformed through its interaction with the varied contexts it encounters? The subject matters include different strands of theological-missiological thinking, socio-political engagements and forms of family relationships in interaction with the host cultures.

Tormod Engelsviken, Ernst Harbakk, Rolv Olsen, Thor Strandenæs (Eds)

Mission to the World

Communicating the Gospel in the 21st Century: Essays in Honour of Knud Jørgensen

2008 / 978-1-870345-64-4 / 472pp

Knud Jørgensen is Director of Areopagos and Associate Professor of Missiology at MF Norwegian School of Theology. This book reflects on the main areas of Jørgensen's commitment to mission. At the same time it focuses on the main frontier of mission, the world, the content of mission, the Gospel, the fact that the Gospel has to be communicated, and the context of contemporary mission in the 21st century.

Al Tizon

Transformation after Lausanne

Radical Evangelical Mission in Global-Local Perspective

2008 / 978-1-870345-68-2 / 281pp

After Lausanne '74, a worldwide network of radical evangelical mission theologians and practitioners use the notion of "Mission as Transformation" to integrate evangelism and social concern together, thus lifting theological voices from the Two Thirds World to places of prominence. This book documents the definitive gatherings, theological tensions, and social forces within and without evangelicalism that led up to Mission as Transformation. And it does so through a global-local grid that points the way toward greater holistic mission in the 21st century.

Bambang Budijanto

Values and Participation

Development in Rural Indonesia

2009 / 978-1-870345-70-4 / 237pp

Socio-religious values and socio-economic development are inter-dependant, inter-related and are constantly changing in the context of macro political structures, economic policy, religious organizations and globalization; and micro influences such as local affinities, identity, politics, leadership and beliefs. The book argues that the comprehensive approach in understanding the socio-religious values of each of the three local Lopait communities in Central Java is essential to accurately describing their respective identity.

Alan R. Johnson

Leadership in a Slum

A Bangkok Case Study

2009 / 978-1-870345-71-2 / 238pp

This book looks at leadership in the social context of a slum in Bangkok from a different perspective than traditional studies which measure well educated Thais on leadership scales derived in the West. Using both systematic data collection and participant observation, it develops a culturally preferred model as well as a set of models based in Thai concepts that reflect on-the-ground realities. It concludes by looking at the implications of the anthropological approach for those who are involved in leadership training in Thai settings and beyond.

Titre Ande

Leadership and Authority

Bula Matari and Life - Community Ecclesiology in Congo

2010 / 978-1-870345-72-9 / 189pp

Christian theology in Africa can make significant development if a critical understanding of the socio-political context in contemporary Africa is taken seriously, particularly as Africa's post-colonial Christian leadership based its understanding and use of authority on the Bula Matari model. This has caused many problems and Titre proposes a Life-Community ecclesiology for liberating authority, here leadership is a function, not a status, and 'apostolic succession' belongs to all people of God.

Frank Kwesi Adams

Odwira and the Gospel

A Study of the Asante Odwira Festival and its Significance for Christianity in Ghana

2010 /978-1-870345-59-0 / 232pp

The study of the Odwira festival is the key to the understanding of Asante religious and political life in Ghana. The book explores the nature of the Odwira festival longitudinally - in pre-colonial, colonial and post-independence Ghana - and examines the Odwira ideology and its implications for understanding the Asante self-identity. Also discussed is how some elements of faith portrayed in the Odwira festival can provide a framework for Christianity to engage with Asante culture at a greater depth.

Bruce Carlton

Strategy Coordinator

Changing the Course of Southern Baptist Missions

2010 / 978-1-870345-78-1 / 268pp

This is an outstanding, one-of-a-kind work addressing the influence of the non-residential missionary/strategy coordinator's role in Southern Baptist missions. This scholarly text examines the twentieth century global missiological currents that influenced the leadership of the International Mission Board, resulting in a new paradigm to assist in taking the gospel to the nations.

Julie Ma & Wonsuk Ma

Mission in the Spirit:

Towards a Pentecostal/Charismatic Missiology

2010 / 978-1-870345-84-2 / 312pp

The book explores the unique contribution of Pentecostal/Charismatic mission from the beginning of the twentieth century. The first part considers the theological basis of Pentecostal/Charismatic mission thinking and practice. Special attention is paid to the Old Testament, which has been regularly overlooked by the modern Pentecostal/Charismatic movements. The second part discusses major mission topics with contributions and challenges unique to Pentecostal/Charismatic mission. The book concludes with a reflection on the future of this powerful missionary movement. As the authors served as Korean missionaries in Asia, often their missionary experiences in Asia are reflected in their discussions.

S. Hun Kim & Wonsuk Ma (eds.)
Korean Diaspora and Christian Mission
2011-978-1-870345-91-0 / 301pp

As a 'divine conspiracy' for Missio Dei, the global phenomenon of people on the move has shown itself to be invaluable. In 2004 two significant documents concerning Diaspora were introduced, one by the Filipino International Network and the other by the Lausanne Committee for World Evangelization. These have created awareness of the importance of people on the move for Christian mission. Since then, Korean Diaspora has conducted similar research among Korean missions, resulting in this book

Jin Huat Tan
Planting an Indigenous Church
The Case of the Borneo Evangelical Mission
2011 / 978-1-870345-99-6 / 343pp

Dr Jin Huat Tan has written a pioneering study of the origins and development of Malaysia's most significant indigenous church. This is an amazing story of revival, renewal and transformation of the entire region chronicling the powerful effect of it evident to date! What can we learn from this extensive and careful study of the Borneo Revival, so the global Christianity will become ever more dynamic.

GENERAL REGNUM TITLES

Vinay Samuel, Chris Sugden (eds.)
The Church in Response to Human Need
1987 / 1870345045 / xii+268pp

Philip Sampson, Vinay Samuel, Chris Sugden (eds.)
Faith and Modernity
Essays in modernity and post-modernity
1994 / 1870345177 / 352pp

Klaus Fiedler
The Story of Faith Missions
1994 / 0745926878 / 428pp

Douglas Peterson
Not by Might nor by Power
A Pentecostal Theology of Social Concern in Latin America
1996 / 1870345207 / xvi+260pp

David Gitari
In Season and Out of Season
Sermons to a Nation
1996 / 1870345118 / 155pp

David. W. Virtue
A Vision of Hope
The Story of Samuel Habib
1996 / 1870345169 / xiv+137pp

Everett A Wilson
Strategy of the Spirit
J.Philip Hogan and the Growth of the Assemblies of God Worldwide, 1960 - 1990
1997 /1870345231/214

Murray Dempster, Byron Klaus, Douglas Petersen (Eds)
The Globalization of Pentecostalism
A Religion Made to Travel
1999 / 1870345290 / xvii+406pp

Peter Johnson, Chris Sugden (eds.)
Markets, Fair Trade and the Kingdom of God
Essays to Celebrate Traidcraft's 21st Birthday
2001 / 1870345193 / xii+155pp

Robert Hillman, Coral Chamberlain, Linda Harding
Healing & Wholeness
Reflections on the Healing Ministry
2002 / 978-1- 870345-35- 4 / xvii+283pp

David Bussau, Russell Mask
Christian Microenterprise Development
An Introduction
2003 / 1870345282 / xiii+142pp

David Singh
Sainthood and Revelatory Discourse
An Examination of the Basis for the Authority of Bayan in Mahdawi Islam
2003 / 8172147285 / xxiv+485pp

For the up-to-date listing of the Regnum books see www.ocms.ac.uk/regnum

regnum

Regnum Books International

Regnum is an Imprint of The Oxford Centre for Mission Studies
St. Philip and St. James Church
Woodstock Road
Oxford, OX2 6HR
Web: www.ocms.ac.uk/regnum